BUSINESS ORGANISATION
IN GREAT BRITAIN
1856-1914

BUSINESS ORGANISATION IN GREAT BRITAIN 1856-1914

James B. Jefferys

ARNO PRESS

A New York Times Company

New York / 1977

Editorial Supervision: ANDREA HICKS

————◆————

First publication 1977 by Arno Press, Inc.

Copyright © 1977 by James B. Jefferys

DISSERTATIONS IN EUROPEAN ECONOMIC HISTORY
ISBN for complete set: 0-405-10773-0
See last pages of this volume for titles.

Manufactured in the United States of America

————◆————

Library of Congress Cataloging in Publication Data

Jefferys, James Bavington.
  Business organisation in Great Britain, 1856-1914.

  (Dissertations in European economic history)
  Originally presented as the author's thesis, Univer-
sity of London, 1938.
  Bibliography: p.
  1. Corporations--Great Britain--Finance--History.
I. Title. II. Series.
HG4135.J43 1977   658.1'52'0941   77-77176
ISBN 0-405-10789-7

BUSINESS ORGANISATION IN GREAT BRITAIN,
1856-1914

A study of trends, with special reference
to the financial structure of companies, the
mechanism of investment and the relations
between the shareholders and the company.

JAMES B. JEFFERYS

(Doctoral dissertation, University of London,
1938)

CONTENTS

INTRODUCTION.

This thesis is concerned with the changes in the
methods of organisation of business units in Great Britain
in the period 1856 to 1914. By the term "methods of
organisation of business units" we mean the methods by which
the entrepreneur raised capital for the undertaking and the
methods of control and direction of the unit that were
adopted. We are not directly concerned with the size of
the unit or the recruitment of labour power.

The most conspicuous form of business organisation that
was developed in this period was that of the limited liability
company, and it is with the introduction of this form of
business organisation, its use, and the changes that took
place in its form and character that we have to deal.

Three observations on method must be made. In the
first place this is not a chronological study but a study
of trends. We have, therefore, analysed long term
developments and made comparisons and contrasts rather than
studied the year by year developments in the limited liability
company. In the second place, both the trends in the
general economic history of the period and the method of
analysing long term developments make it convenient to treat

the middle of the 'eighties as a watershed. In the third
place, after a general survey of the reasons that led to
the introduction of the limited company and the extent to
which this form was adopted in business units in Great Britain
during this period, we concentrate on particular aspects of
the developments that took place within the company. The
changes fall under two headings - firstly, technical, i.e.
changes in the denomination of shares and in the types of
stocks and shares issued; secondly, the wider changes in the
methods of promotion, in the composition and outlook of the
investors, and in the methods of control and direction of
the company.

We are not concerned with the developments within the
joint stock companies that were established by Charter or
Special Act of Parliament, such as railway, gas, dock or
water companies, except in as far as such developments
influenced the course taken by limited liability companies.
Also, as implied in the title, we are concerned only with the
use of the company in industrial and commercial units which
carried on business within Great Britain.

PART I.

THE INTRODUCTION AND DEVELOPMENT OF THE
LIMITED LIABILITY JOINT STOCK COMPANY
AS A FORM OF BUSINESS ORGANISATION
IN GREAT BRITAIN, 1856 to 1914.

In this part we do not wish to deal in great detail
with either the changes in the law relating to joint
stock companies or the course of adoption of the limited
liability joint stock form in each and every industry.
Some of this detailed study has already been done.[1] These
details are taken as given and we concentrate attention
on two questions.   The first is "what were the motive
forces behind the introduction and the use of limited
liability?"   The second is "what were the changes in the
spirit and content of its adoption?"

The first is a two-fold question of why was the
limited liability system introduced into the law of this
country and what determined its use, at first very uneven,
later becoming general, in individual industries.   The

---

1) The legal changes, besides innumerable legal books, are
well analysed in M. Rix, unpublished M.Sc. thesis, 1936,
"An Economic Analysis of existing Legislation concerning
the Limited Liability Company." For details of the use
of the company form, vide J. H. Clapham, "An Economic
History of Modern Britain", Vols. II (1932) and III (1938).
For the early period B. C. Hunt, "The Development of
the Business Corporation in England, 1800-1867", 1936,
and various articles by H. A. Shannon (see bibliography).
Little has been done specifically on the spread of
company organisation after 1885. The volumes of "The
Statist" and "The Economist" are the sources for the
year by year development.

second is a study of the differentiation in form and
spirit of its adoption in different industries and, with
the adoption becoming almost universal, the almost complete
transformation of the idea of limited liability.

A study of these factors will, it is suggested, make
easier the interpretation of the details of the spread of
the limited liability company form of business organisation
in terms of the number of companies, total and average
capital, percentage of failures, etc., and will also
provide the necessary background for the study of the
changes in the financial structure of companies, in the
mechanism of investment, and in the methods of promotion
and management.

We have divided this part into three chapters.
The first sketches the general organisation of business in
the middle of the nineteenth century in Great Britain, and
in this context analyses the discussion around the
introduction of limited liability.   The second deals
with the uneven adoption of the system in different
industries between 1856 and 1885, the reasons for this,
and the spirit and character of the company.   The third

deals with the years 1885 to 1914, the period of greatest
advance of the company system and at the same time leading
to the greatest differentiation in the spirit and form of
its use.

CHAPTER I

The Organisation of Industry in Great Britain in the Middle
of the Nineteenth Century and the Discussions concerning
the General Legalisation of the Joint Stock Company
with Limited Liability.

Business units in the middle of the nineteenth
century were organised on roughly two distinct bases: first,
the individual or partnership organisation involving direct
participation of the partners; second, the joint stock
grouping of a number of capitalists with the actual control
delegated to a board of directors. These methods of
organisation secured the capital and the direction of the
undertaking; for the day to day working of the unit,
additional credit was supplied by banks, discount houses,
other intermediary organisations, and by private loans. We
intend to discuss briefly the sphere of these two methods
at this date and to elaborate further the role played by
the banks.

The Industrial Revolution had been carried through in
the main by the partnership form of business organisation;
the joint stock form was insignificant until early in the

nineteenth century.   The reasons for this were two-fold.
The first and foremost factor was the small amount of
fixed capital (compared with the present day) which was
needed to establish a business unit, together with the
fairly slow progress of any individual unit, thus allowing
the individual entrepreneur or partnership themselves to
accumulate the capital necessary for the start or the
extension of an enterprise.   [1]   The second reason was the
geographical "accident" that the leading centres of the
industrial Revolution were away from the leading
financial centre, London.

The smallness of the fixed capital required in
industrial units in the period of the industrial Revolution
and the power of the "captains of industry" to supply this
capital themselves are too well known to need elaboration
here.   The effects of the isolation from London have not,
however, been fully dealt with.   One effect, we suggest,
was the use of the partnership rather than the joint stock
form in industrial units.

---

1) The capital for the extension was found just as locally
as the original capital.   "When the larger venture was
made, any neighbour who had unemployed capital was
welcome to take a share in the joint venture .... You
see all the trade was carried on by men on their own
capital", A. Crump, "A New Departure in the Domain of
Political Economy" 1878, p.3.   Crump is quoting from an
acquaintance who is describing the methods of financing
in the 'forties.   Banks, of course, were important in
these extensions.   We deal with them later.

Outside London capital was accumulated by the slow
process of capitalising agricultural rents and later, at
a slightly faster rate, by the profits of manu- and machino-
facture.   In London and the other commercial centres
capital had been accumulating at a good rate for centuries
through the profits from trade and commerce.   As the
world was rapidly opened up to trade in the nineteenth
century and with the establishment of colonies and colonial
markets, so the accumulations in these centres increased.
But there was little or no connection, except through the
developing banking and discount house system, between the
commercial sources of accumulation and the industrial uses
of capital during the period of the Industrial Revolution.
This connection developed very slowly indeed even in the
era of the limited liability company, which had removed
some of the dangers of a London merchant putting capital
in a Cleveland blast furnace of whose running he knew
nothing.

This geographical factor of the separation of London
from the chief areas of the Industrial Revolution cannot be
claimed to have hindered industrial development.   The
capital necessary in those areas was adequately supplied
by the partnership form of accumulation and re-accumulation,

but this separation was a factor in the maintenance of
the partnership form.   Had the chief areas of the
Industrial Revolution been Middlesex, Surrey, and Kent,
instead of Lancashire, Northumberland, and Durham, then
inevitably a much greater amount of capital would have
flowed into industry in the first stages of the "revolution"
and with a greater number of capitalists taking part, the
joint stock form, Bubble Act or no, would have been
established much earlier.

    This, however, was not the case.   Consequently, the
partnership form - the local individual method of
financing industry - was dominant in all enterprises where
the fixed capital was not too large to be supplied by a
small number of capitalists, and where there was no
pressure on the part of the London and commercial type of
capitalist to join in and share the profits.   But contrary
tendencies can be noted to some degree by the 'fifties.
On the one hand the scale of industrial enterprise was
reaching a point where the possibility of the individual
entrepreneur starting from nothing and accumulating
sufficient capital within his working life to possess
factories, mines and furnaces had decreased.   The "new"

capitalists of the 'forties were often men who inherited
(1)
rather than accumulated a fortune.   This difficulty of

obtaining sufficient individual capital is further

illustrated by the extent to which these partnerships

were now using the banks for loans and over-drafts.   On

the other hand the success of the industrial and commercial

revolutions had resulted in London and other commercial

centres in the growth of a body of capitalists not directly

engaged in trade, who were now seeking an outlet, with

profit, for their accumulations.   The National Debt,

savings banks, the practice of joint stock banks in

allowing interest on deposits, the canal and railway

investments, had increased their numbers and had whetted

their appetite for investments at a profit.   They resented

the division between the profitable industries of the North
(2)
and themselves.   They were willing to take the first

opportunity which the necessities of northern industrialists

might give them for investing their capital.   That this

---

1) e.g. H. W. Bolckow, who started iron works in the new
   area of Middlesborough in the late 'forties, had
   inherited a fortune of £40,000 to £50,000. (J. S. Jeans,
   "Pioneers of the Cleveland Iron Trade", 1875, p.50.)
2) Examples of this resentment occur time and time again in
   the discussions around limited liability. e.g. E. Moss,
   "Remarks on the Act of Parliament 1856", 1856, p.9,
   compares with indignation the £3-8-0 return on Consols
   and the 30% to 40% profit made in business.

class were the chief instigators of the limited liability
legislation and that their great eagerness to give their
savings outran the demand for them by the industrialists,
which fact coloured the first twenty years of limited
liability development, we shall discuss later.   Here it
is only necessary to note that although the partnership
form was for the most part, with the assistance of the
banks, a perfectly adequate form of business organisation
in Great Britain in the middle of the nineteenth century,
there were at the same time signs of a coming weakness in,
and pressure against the "pure" partnership system.

The scope of the joint stock undertakings[1] had been
defined, and for a long period satisfactorily defined, by
Adam Smith in the eighteenth century.[2]   This system applied
to all those undertakings which could or would not be

---

1) In this brief outline of the extent of the joint stock
   system of business organisation we do not distinguish
   between the joint stock company with limited liability
   and that without. For our purposes here this
   distinction is not vital. In general, it can be said
   the public utility companies, which were either
   incorporated by Act of Parliament or received a Charter
   from the Board of Trade, usually possessed Limited
   Liability. The banking, insurance, and finance companies,
   on the other hand, were usually unlimited.
2) Adam Smith, "Wealth of Nations", (Cannan edition), Book V,
   Chapter I, Part III, p.246 ff. "... two criteria, first
   if the undertaking is of greater general utility than
   the greater part of common trades. Second, if it requires
   a greater capital than can easily be collected into a
   private partnery".

undertaken by private enterprise. In the first part of
the Industrial Revolution this type of undertaking was in
the background. Banking, transport and risky types of
foreign trade, did in part use this method and possibly
would have adopted it on a more extensive scale if the
capital had been available. But most of the spare capital
of the country was directed, with the help of prohibitions
on joint stock enterprise, towards the Government loan
market. Success in the Napoleonic wars was considered
more important than allowing investors to fritter away
their·capital on untried joint stock schemes. As a result
joint stock schemes were kept down to a minimum.

In the nineteenth century, however, both the demand
for this type of organisation increased and the requirements
of the Government in the loan market diminished. The
organisation of an effective transport system became an
absolute necessity for the development of capitalism and
the capital outlay required for canals, railways, harbours,
docks, and some great shipping lines, was so immense that
it was far beyond the means of any individual or group of
individual capitalists. The joint stock system in one
form or another was the only method, and this was adopted.
These enterprises had two characteristics distinguishing

them from the later types of industry adopting the joint
stock form.   First, they were for the most part entirely
new enterprises, very little effective development having
been accomplished in their particular fields by private
enterprise.   Secondly, they were not so much the core of
capitalism in the sense of producing goods for the market,
but necessary adjuncts to the development and spread of
the capitalist method of production.

A second group of enterprises which were forced to
adopt the joint stock system had somewhat similar
characteristics.   These were the enterprises which, owing
to the urbanising tendency of capitalism and owing to the
non-existence of both state and local enterprise, sought
to deal with the problems of gas, water, housing, and
public halls, in the rapidly growing towns.   Again the
scope of these undertakings was far beyond the powers of
the individual capitalist or small competing units.   Closely
allied to this group was the development of the joint
stock system in banking.   Here private enterprise was
already in the field, but the problem of an effective
banking system which would have a national rather than a
local outlook, was becoming a necessity for the integration
of capitalism, and such a system was beyond the powers of
the private competing banks.   However, up to the 'fifties

it should be noted, the profits being made by private banks, the large capitals required, and the high risk attaching to banking, were probably more important factors in bringing joint stock banking into the field than the demand for a national system of banking. Similarly, this need for large capitals and the risk factor led to a quite important development of the joint stock system in insurance. Of the 910 companies fully registering under the Companies Act of 1844, the largest single group were insurance companies, ranking above water and gas enterprises. [1]

Outside these spheres there was but little attempt to develop the joint stock system up to the middle of the nineteenth century. Small, and technically illegal, joint enterprises existed in some tin, copper, lead and coal mines, and a few in cotton and in the Y orkshire woollen industry. [2] Their existence was influenced by both the high risk factor attaching to some of these undertakings and the spirit of co-operation of the many small men against the few big capitalists already in the

1) B. C. Hunt, op.cit., p.114.
2) For details of those in minerals, A. H. Dodd, "The Industrial Revolution in North Wales", 1933, Chapter IX, and for those in Yorkshire, B.C. Hunt, op.cit., p.78.

field.   Their importance in the country's economic life
as a whole, however, was small.   The lack of interest of
the larger industrialists in the joint stock method of
raising capital for their enterprises is shown in some
degree by the extremely few applications that were made by
them for a Charter of Incorporation from the Board of
Trade. (1)

Joint stock enterprise had developed only in those
spheres suggested by Adam Smith.   Outside the enterprises
he defined there was little adoption of joint stock, partly,
of course, owing to the legal position (2) and partly owing
to lack of necessity.   But while this was the position in
practice, in theory, as we shall show later, his
definition was being hotly challenged on innumerable
grounds.   And the "hair-splitting" of the 'forties and

---

1) There were only 161 applications noted in "Return of all
   Applications for Charters with Limited Liability under
   1 Vict. c.73", 1854, and less than 50 of these could be
   described as manufacturing or industrial.   Of 910
   unlimited companies completely registered under the 1844
   Act (1844-1856) there were only 16 for coal and iron
   mines and 13 for cotton manufacturing. (B. C. Hunt,
   op.cit., p.114)
2) There had been changes in the legal position in the first
   half of the nineteenth century slowly widening the scope
   of joint stock enterprise but the refusal to admit
   general limited liability had slowed down its use in
   industry. cf. B. C. Hunt, op.cit., Chapters lV and V.

and 'fifties was to be followed by action in the 'sixties.

The role of banks in business organisation at this date was the two-fold task of providing working capital for industry and in a growing number of cases providing part of the fixed capital. With the developing industrialism in the early nineteenth century there grew at the same time a demand for a more satisfactory means of credit,to pay for materials and to pay wages,than the too local token payments and the too distant Bills of Exchange. [1] This was supplied by the country bankers who sprang up in every town with their own note circulation and their own system of credit. But further demands were made for credit as the scale of industrial enterprise increased and the private banks were supplemented rapidly by joint stock banks, which were able and willing through their inability to make profit from note circulation to lend to industry both short and long term.

For the extension of an enterprise,when the resources of the partners had been exhausted,the bank was frequently the source of the capital. Richard Tangye of the Cornwall Works in Birmingham describes his visit to "The

---

1) A. H. Dodd, op.cit., p.312 ff.

Bankers' Sweating Room" when his young enterprise was in
this position.[1] Another industrialist, James Platt, a
Yorkshire woollen manufacturer, generalised his experience
with bankers and wrote, "I say that any honest solvent man
can borrow of his bankers more willingly, more pleasantly
and at a lower rate of interest than he can of father,
brother or friend".[2] Although the degree of "pleasantness"
as well as the rate of interest depended on the reputation
of the firm, a visit to the bank and the local bank
manager, who knew the firm and the partners well, was the
usual course taken when the partnership needed additional
capital. In the North particularly the industrialists
were dependent on the banks.[3] As an example of long term
lending there is the well known instance of the Derwent

---

1) Richard Tangye, "One and All, the Growth of a Great
Industry", 1889, p.95.
2) James Platt, "Essays", Vol. 1, p.388, 1863.
3) Cf. J. E. Wadsworth and W. F. Crick, "A Hundred Years
of Joint Stock Banking", 1936, pp. 225-226.
"Manchester Man" (Edmund Potter, sometime chairman of
the Manchester Chamber of Commerce) is quite definite on
this active part to be played by banks. "... it is
impossible to stop them trading: they will do so directly
or indirectly; they will speculate in or become possessed
of shares and scrips of mills and manufactures of all
kinds, which it would be folly to prevent them holding or
even working temporarily - they are traders from
necessity". ("Practical Opinions against Limited Liability"
1856, p.38) This is not altogether true of the London
banks at the time and a far cry from Bagehot's "timidity."

Iron company which had to be sold to the shareholders of
the Northumberland and Durham District Bank in 1857, because
on the stoppage of the bank in that year it was found that
the company owed the bank almost one million pounds.[1]

Arising partly out of this extensive credit which
banks were giving to industry, was the very high rate of
failure among banks.   Between 1846 and 1857 about 100
banks, private and joint stock, failed with liabilities
totalling almost £50,000,000.[2]   A twentieth century
observer looking back on this high rate of mortality remarks,
in view of later experience, that the mid-Victorian banks
were "too closely linked with local industry" or "too
closely linked with one firm in their district", with the
result that "when local industries expanded the banks
tended to over-lend".[3]   But at this date there was little
alternative.   Industry was expanding as a whole throughout
the country and even if some of the additional fixed costs
could still be met by the local partnership method, their
increasing working costs had more and more to be met by

---

1) "Description of Consetts Iron Works", 1893.
2) "The Law of Limited Liability and its Application to
   Joint Stock Banking Advocated", 1863, p.20.
3) T. E. Gregory, "T he Westminster Bank", 1936, Vol.I,
   p.182.

loans and overdrafts from the bank.   Not until the
general adoption by industrial undertakings of the limited
liability system and the development at the same time of
relatively smaller working costs to fixed costs, did this
interdependance of banking and industry cease.   The
banking failures in 1875 and those in 1878 showed that
this interdependance was still to some degree prevalent.[1]
But the shock of these failures, and the resulting turn
towards timidity and amalgamation in banking, and the
adoption of limited liability by industry, which lessened
the demand for long term loans, brought to an end in the
'eighties this "formative period of British banking".[2]

This was in outline the organisation of business in
Great Britain in the middle of the nineteenth century.
Manufacture, trade and commerce were carried on for the
most part by the individual "captain of industry", or the
small partnership; the larger undertakings of transport
and other public utilities were conducted on a joint stock
basis; and credit and loans for the working capital of
these organisations were obtainable from the banks and

---

1) Cf. C. W. von Wieser, "Die Financielle Aufbau der
   Englishe Industrie", Jena, 1919, p.136 ff.
2) T. E. Gregory, op.cit., p.215.

other financial institutions.   But this is a static
picture.   We have glanced only in passing at the active
factors that were leading to a change in this system. We
now go on to consider these forces and analyse through the
writings and speeches of contemporaries the reasons
advanced for and against the general legalisation of the
limited liability joint stock company and the facts that
lay behind these arguments.   In doing this we discover
both the forces that brought about the change of law and
the forces that determined for some period in the future
the course and character of the limited liability system.

The legalisation of the limited liability joint
stock company, although rushed through Parliament in 1855
with what one contemporary called "extreme and indecent
haste," [1] was certainly not unheralded. From "Blackwood's
Magazine" and Chambers' Journal" to "Household Hints" and
the Law Society, the question had been argued and discussed.
Between 1844 and 1854 there were three Select Committees

---

1) E. W. Cox, "Practice of Joint Stock Companies with
   Limited Liability", 1855, preface, p.i, and for an
   explanation of the suddenness, cf. H. A. Shannon,
   "Economic History Review", November 1937.

and one Royal Commission set up to deal with this and
kindred subjects. "Innumerable pamphlets"[1] were
published, at least sixteen between the years 1853 and 1856
alone.[2] Opinions were sought and published not only from
the commercial classes at home and abroad, the Chambers of
Commerce, the legalists, and the political economists, but
also from men like "the Lucasian Professor of Mathematics
at Cambridge" and a lecturer to the Philosophical Society
of Liverpool.[3] Everyone seemed to have something to say
and a right to say it.

Second only to the number of witnesses called,was the
diversity of opinions expressed. The very groups of
people who had found themselves agreeing on the repeal of
restrictions on trade, on opposition to the Factory Acts,
on opposition to Chartism, on this problem were split
from top to bottom. Anti-Corn Law Leaguer found himself
opposed to "brother Leaguers".[4] Theoreticians of

---

1) "Bankers' Magazine", 1854, p.424.
2) See bibliography. This number does not include
   pamphlets by lawyers explaining the Acts, though
   opinions were usually expressed forcibly in the prefaces.
3) Altogether 85 witnesses were called by the Royal
   Commission on Mercantile Law, 1854.
4) Cf. E. W. Field's attack on W. A. Brown, M.P., in his
   "Observations of a Solicitor on the Right of the
   Public to form Limited Liability Partnerships", p.51.

"laisser faire" came to diametrically opposite conclusions.
Richard Cobden and John Bright were in some measure of
disagreement on the importance of the question. [1] Both
sides tried the hitherto omnipotent slogans of "Freedom of
Contract" and "Down with Monopoly", both with equal ease
and ability quoted Adam Smith, invoked Providence and
pointed to past experience, but reason alone was not
successful - the gap remained. Twenty years of discussion
had not narrowed it.

This puzzled contemporaries. Palmerston said, "I must
confess I am quite surprised" that there should be this
difference.   John Lalor regarded it as "an unfortunate
coincidence". [2]   Some of the pamphleteers, however, found
more direct and personal reasons.   The active support
given by lawyers to the changing of the law [3], was said to
be a result of their wish for more fees through setting up
companies.   George Sweet described the Act as the "result

---

1) Cf. W. S. Lindsay & R. Cobden, "Remarks on the Law of
   Partnership and Limited Liability", 1856, and John
   Bright's speech at the Manchester Chamber of Commerce
   quoted in A. Redford, "Manchester Merchants and Foreign
   Trade", p.216.
2) John Lalor, "Money and Morals", 1852, p.199.
3) 20 of the 23 lawyers answering the questionnaire sent
   out by the 1854 Commission were in favour of limited
   liability. ("First Report, Mercantile Law Commission", 1854)

of a well-organised agitation by some capitalists and
speculators who had been unable to obtain Charters from
the Board of Trade". [1]   The big manufacturers opposing
the change were accused of stifling free competition. And
so it went on.

The Mercantile Law Commission summed up this
confusion quite well in their report.

> "Your Majesty's Commissioners have been much
> embarrassed by the great contrariety of opinion
> entertained by those who favoured them with
> answers to their questions. Gentlemen of great
> experience and talent have arrived at conclusions
> diametrically opposite, and in supporting those
> conclusions have displayed reasoning power of
> the highest order." [2]

This "high reasoning power" is particularly striking
to the present day observer.   It tends, together with
the "a priori" methods of thinking used, to give an air
of unreality to three parts of the discussion.   Debating
points seemed to be more important than facts and
actualities. [3]

However, in order to understand the later lines of
development of the principle and practice of limited

---

1) George Sweet, "Limited Liability Act", 1855 edition,
   preface, p.v.
2) 1854 Commission's Report, p.5.
3) Cf. E. W. Field's criticism of the 1854 Commission
   evidence, op.cit., p.54.

liability some attempt must be made to discover what lay
behind this mass of confusing opinion, to discover around
what points the disagreement took place, why there were
disagreements, why the principle passed into law, and what
was the spirit of the Act.

The outstanding feature of the discussions is that they
were not confined to limited liability – they were enlarged
into a general debate on the history and development of
British capitalism.   Half a century's conscious advance
of capitalism made it impossible for Chambers of Commerce,
the House of Commons or pamphleteers to discuss any subject
without weaving into it their regrets and pleasures, hopes
and fears of the past and future.   The problem of limited
liability in industry was a particularly apt subject for
such a general debate, partly because it dealt directly
with industrial development and partly because of the time
at which it took place.

By the middle of the century capitalism was triumphantly
established in England.   The Great Exhibition was on the
stocks, a network of railways and factories covered the
countryside, hymns were being sung of eternal advance and
prosperity to the tune of laisser faire.   "Come into the
garden, Maud, for the black, bat night has flown". At the

same time the less pleasant and more incomprehensible
sides of capitalist development had faded sufficiently to
make their objective discussion a possibility. Chartism
had officially died in 1848, though everybody well
realised that the "condition of England question" had not
been finally solved by a peaceful dispersion on Kennington
Common. And the next recurring speculative mania and
crisis were not yet due, which gave the political economists
and business men a chance to discuss how they could rid
England forever of this curse.[1]

It was with this background of successes and failures
that the principle of limited liability was discussed and
tested to see whether it was in accordance with the
successes of capitalism and whether it could remedy in
the future any of the failures of the past.[2] An
expression is given to this feeling by Edwin Field when he

---

1) In addition to these factors there was a general spirit
   of criticism in the air. Benthamism had been partly
   stilled during the most serious periods of Chartist
   agitation, but now through organisations like the
   "Financial Reform Association" it was coming to life
   again with criticism of the Crimean War, of wasteful
   Government expenditure, etc.
2) An interesting comparison arises here between this
   discussion and that centering around the Royal Commission
   on the Depression in Trade in 1886. The range of
   topics covered, crises, foreign competition, strikes,
   investment, all are almost identical though more
   consciously and thoroughly treated in the second case.

wrote, "I am solemnly convinced,that (except education) there is no public legislative question so all-important to the future of England, as the one on which I am treating".[1]

There were roughly four focal points of the discussion. First, what was the relationship of the principle of limited liability to the doctrines of laisser faire? Second, would it intensify or eliminate the periodical crises? Third, could it be used to bind together the two classes in society, capitalists and working class, and render strikes and Chartist organisations unnecessary and impossible? Fourth, and this was the real core of the narrower question of limited liability or no, was there sufficient capital coming forward for industry and trade, and were there sufficient investments coming forward for capital?

It is proposed to deal briefly with the first three questions in order to get a general idea of the spirit of the discussions and to deal in detail with the fourth.[2]

---

1) E. W. Field, op.cit., p.1. He was a London solicitor who had gained much publicity over his advocacy of Chancery Reform. His opinions on limited liability should possibly be judged in the light of the estimate of his character given in the National Dictionary of Biography, "All his ideals were high."
2) This limitation is necessary, for, as "The Economist" wrote in 1854, p.700, "We would never get to an end were we to notice all the fears of evil and all the hopes of good that are expected to ensue from this alteration of the law."

The doctrines of Utilitarianism which had served admirably the purposes of the capitalists who wished to break down mercantilist restrictions on industry and commerce,were based on two formulas: freedom of the individual and the greatest good of the greatest number. These were assumed to be coincidental, but as capitalism developed the coincidence of the two grew less and less frequent. Limited liability was a case where they were rather askew.

The chief protagonists for limited liability based their arguments on the individual. It was pointed out that individuals can make any contract they wish, that this was not a new principle but a very old one. "It does not make possible that which was formerly impossible, but renders easy what was difficult." [1]   Why should the law interfere "if one man chooses to lend at a steady rate and another at a fluctuating rate?" [2]   The Usury Laws had been repealed affecting the steady rate, the next logical step was to remove beyond all doubt the position of lending at

---

1) David Gibbons, "Limited Liability Act", 1855, p.iv.
2) W. S. Lindsay and R. Cobden, op.cit., p.4; cf. also the speech by the Rt. Hon. E. P. Bouverie, "Hansard", 1855, CXXXIX, Ser.3, p.318.

a fluctuating rate.   Robert Lowe in his famous speech on
the 1856 Bill declares, "It is not a question of privilege;
if anything, it is a right."[1]

The opposers of limited liability based their
theoretical objections on the argument of the "greatest
good of the greatest number", the effect on the nation as
a whole.   "There is a moral obligation, which it is the
duty of the laws of a civilised and Christian nation to
enforce, to pay debts, perform contracts and make
reparations for wrongs. Limited liability is formed on
the opposite principles."[2]   To men who had accumulated all
the capital they needed by saving and re-investment, "by
the sweat of our brows, inside and out,"[3]   and, more
important still, could see no possibility in the future
when they would need more capital than was within the
powers of their own accumulation, such a principle seemed
"degrading"[4] and "immoral".[5]   The nation would suffer, the

1) Robert Lowe, "Speech of the Rt. Hon. Robert Lowe on the
   Amendment of the Law of Partnership and Joint Stock
   Companies, February 1, 1856", 1856, p.32.
2) E. W. Cox, op.cit., 5th edition, 1862, p.1.
3) Brownlow, Pearson & Co., shipowners, Hull, quoted by
   E. W. Field, op.cit., p.91.
4) "A Manchester Man", op.cit., p.13.   This "Manchester
   Man", whom we note all through as a very outspoken
   opponent of limited liability, was Edmund Potter, whom
   Marx described as "sometime chairman of the Manchester
   Chamber of Commerce and mouthpiece of the cotton lords".
5) E. W. Cox, op.cit., 3rd edition, 1856, preface.

greatest good would not be served, McCulloch thunders "in the scheme laid down by Providence for the government of the world, there is no shifting or narrowing of responsibilities". [1] Countries that had adopted such a principle [2] were run on doubtful moral principles and any way were not successful. If companies were formed on this basis, the promoters were "either fools or knaves". [3] Both theory and practice showed to them that limited liability would ruin the commercial organisation and spirit of the country.

Robert Lowe attempted to answer this argument of the "greatest good", but he tended to be abstract and theoretical rather than practical. [4] The real answer to this question was in proving apart from hypothetical moral considerations that the principle was both helpful and necessary to capitalism.

---

1) J. R. McCulloch, "Dictionary", 1882 edition, "Partnership", p.1012.
2) Almost every country in Europe had adopted the principle except Sweden. It was also adopted in the U.S.A., cf. Woodforde Ffooks, "Law of Partnership an Obstacle to Social Progress", 1854, p.15.
3) J. R. McCulloch, "Considerations on Partnership with Limited Liability", 1856, p.20.
4) "The Joint Stock Companies Journal", February 9th, 1856, which supported limited liability described Lowe's speech as "sweeping away his opponents with a few mystic words." John Howell, a London business man, though a supporter regretted that Lowe's mind "Had a tendency to be unduly governed by arguments purely abstract". ("Partnership Law Legislation", 1868, p.9). This certainly seems to be true of the last section of his speech on "the wonders of the science of political economy."

The recurring crises of the first half of the nineteenth century were discussed mainly in terms of speculation, overborrowing and over-lending. There was little attempt made to analyse deeper. With the "railway mania" vivid in the memories of all, the discussions on this subject in connection with limited liability displayed the same tendency to concentrate on the causes of the spectacular manifestations of the crisis rather than on the cause of the periodicity of the cycle, and this may account in some degree for the indefinite conclusions reached.

Those supporting limited liability took the fight into the enemy's camp by suggesting that if anything had caused over-lending it was the unlimited system itself. "The parties from whom the money was borrowed did not trouble themselves before they lent to inquire into the state and prospects of the company; they see on the list of shareholders perhaps a hundred men whom they thought perfectly competent to repay them, and they lent the money in the full security that, if the directors did not pay, they could pounce on the shareholders." [1]   Unlimited

---

1) Speech by the Rt. Hon. E. P. Bouverie, op.cit., p.339, and cf. M. B. Begbie, "Partnership en Commandite", 1852, p.4.

liability has led to a system of "reckless credit" and, attacking the "pro-creditor" attitude taken up by the opponents of the change, the Westminster Reviewer quotes E. W. Field and urges all to remember "there are such things as dishonest creditors as well as dishonest debtors."[1] It would have been as well if some of the Commissions on the Companies Acts later on in the century had borne this in mind.

The suggestion that the "railway mania" was due to the limited responsibility of the shareholders was countered by the argument that it was lack of adequate outlet that made "the middle class fly into speculation."[2] There "had been an unnatural diversion of capital into the channel of chartered and incorporated companies."[3] By allowing all companies to become limited, if they so wished, the law would "take away from railways their special seductive features."[4]

The limited system, it was urged, if generally adopted

1) "Partnership with Limited Liability", reprinted with additions from "The Westminster Review", 1854, p.13.
2) "Partnership en Commandite", 1848, p.xlii, and cf. Lord Hobart, "Remarks on the Law of Partnership Liability", 1853, p.20.
3) Speech by Mr. Collier, "Hansard", 1854, CXXXIV, p.750.
4) W. R. Greg, "Edinburgh Review", April, 1852, p.447.

would lessen the amount of credit granted. "The capital of a limited Company would be easier to raise and therefore the temptation to borrowing less."[1] E. W. Field expressed this dramatically - "... to lessen the liability of a company is to lessen its brute force of credit; but then that is to lessen its awful powers of mischief and ruin; to make its existence depend on deserving credit."[2] And if it did borrow, the publication of the capital of the company and the word "Limited" after its name would give all the security to a creditor that he could possibly want.

The opponents were impressed chiefly with the fact that such companies could try anything and everything, and would have all to win and only a limited amount to lose. Edmund Phillips in 1856, just after the Bill had been passed, wrote, "This Limited Liability Bill ought therefore to be called 'An Act for the better enabling Adventurers to interfere with and ruin Established Traders, without risk to themselves!'"[3] But like so many of the arguments put forward on both sides, while they are undoubtedly true

---

1) Robert Lowe, op.cit., p.34.
2) E. W. Field, op.cit., p.30.
3) Edmund Phillips, "Bank of England Charter, Currency, Limited Liability and Free Trade", 1856, p.36.

in the abstract, they have little, if any, relevance to
the demands of industry and investors at the time and are
proved hopelessly false as a prophecy of the future.   "The
Economist", with more practical sense, suggested that this
whole question of fraud and speculation should be removed
from the discussion around limited liability as all could
"be assured that no more fraud will ensue from the law
sanctioning limited liability than from its enforcing
unlimited liability." [1]

The highest hopes were held out for the principle of
limited liability in the sphere of relations between
capital and labour; and these hopes have been more
thoroughly dashed by subsequent history than the others.
That society had been split "into two hostile camps" by the
development of capitalism was recognised by everyone from
Marx to Disraeli.   But now the cause and the remedy of
this split had been found.   The cause, the "barbaric Law
of Partnership", "by preventing the union of the richer
and the poorer orders in the prosecution of enterprises for
a common object, the law has operated powerfully to keep
these classes separated from each other, and ignorant of
each others' good qualities." [2]   John Stuart Mill agreed,

---

1) "The Economist", 1854, p.699.
2) "Partnership with Limited Liability", p.61.

"The law of partnership opposes obstacles of various
kinds to the improvement of the working classes."[1]   And
the remedy was apparently equally clear - limited liability.
"To some such plan, we look with hope ... as the only mode
of eradicating the hostile feeling between capital and
labour", wrote "The Economist" in 1850.[2]   They were joined
in this hope by a motley of Christian Socialists, social
reformers, economists and a few businessmen. The only
satisfactory solution was ... by combining the two
contraversialists in one actual experiment together,"[3]   and
once this happened England was to be a most idyllic and
happy land.

The Westminster Reviewer, who hitherto had shown
greater contact with realities in his arguments than most
of the other writers, led the way in painting this happy
England and outdid the Christian Socialists at their own
game. "Friendships without number would flourish on a
soil now virgin or overspread with weeds."[4]   "Improvement
in knowledge, in manners and in habits of thought would

---

1) "Report of the Select Committee on Investments for the
   Savings of the Middle and Working Classes", 1850, Qu.837.
2) "The Economist", 1850, p.537.
3) W. R. Greg, op.cit., p.451. Among those supporting
   this hope were J. S. Mill, Charles Bray, J. Ludlow,
   Richard Cobden, Charles Kingsley, to mention only a few.
4) "Partnership with Limited Liability", p.60.

be the first results, and would be quickly followed by
elevation of character, dignified bearing and increased
self-confidence and self-respect." [1]   "Worn out doctrines
of class legislation" must go; [2] henceforth they were to be
one big happy family all sharing in the profits.

In view of the very real gap that did exist in England
at that time, this type of argument was very difficult to
oppose, but it was nevertheless done very effectively. It
was pointed out that the working class demands throughout
the first half of the nineteenth century had been based on
a "Labour Theory of Value" reasoning.   They asked for a
share in the joint product, not a dividend on what they
could save and invest in a business.   "A worker does not
say to his employer, 'I have saved £150 out of my wages,
let me add that sum to your capital and take the proportion
of the say £4,000 profits that my pittance bears to your
thousands' but it is 'I have contributed to produce that
£4,000 profit at least as efficiently as your capital has
done, why should I not have a proportion of the result?'" [3]

---

1) Ibid., p.62.
2) Edward Warner, M.P., "The Impolicy of the Partnership
   Law", 1854, p.28.
3) Swinton Boult, "Trade Partnerships", 1855, p.10. Boult
   was first secretary, then director, of the Liverpool,
   London and Globe Insurance Company.

The big manufacturers were particularly hostile to
these "benevolent" arguments.   'A Manchester Man' argues
that while the working class in America might save through
limited liability "because of the higher condition of the
hands there, ours have been too much weighed down by
poverty,"[1] and if they could save they are not the type
who would.   Others looked behind the "benevolent" argument
to find some ulterior motive on the part of lawyers and
others who were supporting limited liability.   It was
pointed out that the working class was not really interested
in limited liability as such.   Even Greg, a supporter of
the amelioration argument writes, "The poor care little
about it; the amounts which they would venture would
generally be their all."[2]   Swinton Boult agrees with this
and suggests that "... it is the 'rich man' with 'mixed
motives' for whose special advantage it (the principle) is

---

1) 'A Manchester Man', op.cit., p.48, but cf. W. R. Greg,
op.cit., p.405, who shows that in 33,223 societies in
the 'fifties thus saving were 3,052,000 members whom
he suggests were mainly working class.

2) W. R. Greg, op.cit., p.449.   J. S. Mill, of course, also
saw this and he explained his position further. "I think
that the great value of limitation of responsibility as
relates to the working classes be not so much to
facilitate the investment of their savings, not so much
to enable the poor to lend to them who are rich as to
enable the rich to lend to those who are poor." (1850
Report, Qu.847.)

to work."$^{(1)}$ Bouverie moving the 1855 Bill in the House of
Commons was sufficiently a realist to leave this argument
out of his speech altogether and to deal solely with the
possibility of attracting the rich and at present idle
landed classes.$^{(2)}$

In the stage just above the working classes, that of
the lower middle classes of traders and professional men,
the argument of co-operation was used with more realism.
But though they could and did join in enterprises with
richer classes it cannot be maintained that "friendships
without number" sprang up. Swinton Boult was nearer the
truth when he described the co-operation in these terms,
"... he (the small capitalist) must yield himself up,
trusting where he is not trusted, and be shorn of every
attribute of a partner except that of being liable to lose
his all before he is deemed properly qualified to enjoy
the desired participation."$^{(3)}$

---

1) Swinton Boult, op.cit., p.11.
2) "Hansard", 1855, CXXXIX, p.320. "... he anticipated that
   in the course of very little time the gentry of England
   would not be indisposed if the risk now attached to it
   were diminished, to advance money ... to carry on trade."
   "The law deterred ... that very class of persons who of
   all others it was most desirable should join them -
   namely men with large means." This deference to the
   interests of the landed classes so soon after the Corn
   Laws and the Factory Acts naturally annoyed the manufacturers. Edmund Potter wrote, "What the aristocracy a
   boon, needing protection from the trading class, and
   this, too, suggested by an old Free Trade member!" ("A
   Reply to the Rt. Hon. E. P. Bouverie, M.P.", 1855, p.14)
3) Swinton Boult, op.cit., p.12.

The defenders of limited liability were correct when they suggested that it would bring additional amounts of capital into business, but their hopes of the creation on this basis of a profit sharing commonwealth were based on two fundamental misunderstandings. One, on the real nature of the working class demands, which, as has been pointed out above, were for a proportionate share in the joint product with capital, not a dividend on their small savings. Second, since wealth and class divisions were already in existence, "laisser faire" legislation would not remedy these divisions but would only tend to accentuate them. For although unlimited liability was attacked on these very grounds, "unlimited liability has tended to create feelings of enmity and distrust between the richer and poorer classes; for it clearly affords advantages to the one that it denies to the other,"[1] this argument ignores that limited liability could be and would be used by both. "It is in the nature of Free Trade that whatever mathematical advantage is to be obtained at all is more accessible to the rich speculator than the poor one."[2] The

---

1) "Chambers's Journal", 1855, Vol.24, p.196.
2) A. Crump, "Theory of Speculation", 1874, p.98. Edmund Potter was fully aware of this. In "Practical Opinions", p.15, he wrote, "It is a fallacy to suppose that limited liability could benefit the small working class capitalist; it would lead him into error. The larger capitalist has infinitely more knowledge ... he would take all the best and safest investments and leave his less able and less informed competitors the worst."

hopes of an idyllic England floundered on the rock of
mathematical advantage.

In the general welter of discussion on the pro's and
con's of limited liability as a solution to some of the
problems raised by the development of capitalism in
England, the chief question of whether industry needed
capital and whether limited liability would be a means of
supplying it, was rather overlaid. The three questions
discussed above, formed platforms for rival ideas rather
than for the working out of forms of action; the passing
of the principle of limited liability was really dependant
on the answer to the twin question of "Was there sufficient
capital for industry and were there sufficient investments
for capital?"

Capitalism had grown in this country by the method of
accumulation and re-accumulation by the single entrepreneur
or small partnership of entrepreneurs. This method had
been pre-eminently successful. Large fortunes had been
made, and with the adaptation of the working classes to the
factory system and the improvement in transport it seemed
that this method would likewise prove successful in the
future. The manufacturers were confident and proud of

their success. "I have the greatest possible faith in the
results of individual industry and energy. On the contrary
I see irresponsibility and association work so badly, so
expensively, so recklessly and so dishonestly," said the
"mouthpiece of the cotton lords".[1] And for the future,
"we advocate the employment of capital of the owner, the
legal owner, by himself, with all its attendant risks and
liabilities."[2] They had to agree that the joint stock
principle with limited liability might be necessary in some
cases where the scale of the undertaking was so vast that
private capital could not possibly supply the need, e.g.
railways, docks, gas, etc., but there was no need for this
method in general manufacturing and trading. They added
the interesting argument that if limited liability was ever
necessary as a method of attracting capital to
enterprises, it should have been adopted in the first stages
of capitalism, not now when there are fortunes made and
men ready to undertake at their own risk productive schemes.[3]

---

1) Edmund Potter, "Portrait of a Manufacturing District",
   1856, p.12.
2) William Hawes, "Unlimited and Limited Liability", 1854,
   p.31. Hawes was chairman of "The Committee of the
   Merchant Traders for the Amendment of the Law of Debtor
   and Creditor". His attitude was naturally very "pro—
   creditor" on this matter.
3) Swinton Boult, op.cit., p.34.

This was the background from the entrepreneurs' point
of view of the problem of whether industry required capital.
That there was enough capital going into industry was the
general opinion of observers. The 1854 Commissioners
report that they "have not been able to discover any
evidence of the want of a sufficient amount of capital for
the requirements of trade."[1] One or two people agreed
with Charles Buxton, M.P., in saying, "the partnership law
cuts the throat of ten thousand useful undertakings,"[2] but
the main criticism was not that of stifling enterprise but
of unnecessarily diverting capital, and of not looking to
the requirements of the future. W. S. Lindsay, the
shipping M.P., agreed that there is plenty of capital but
"the law prevents a free and natural distribution."[3] And
for the future, "if it is alleged that manufactures and
commerce find abundant for their successful pursuit, in the
hands of individuals in this country ... I will answer
England cannot stand still."[4]

1) 1854 Report, p.5.
2) Charles Buxton, "The Cream of the Pro's and Con's of
   Partnership Law", 1854, p.10.
3) W. S. Lindsay and R. Cobden, op.cit., p.14.
4) Edwin Moss, "Remarks on an Act of Parliament for the
   Formation of Companies with Limited Liability", 1856, p.9.

The manufacturers were on the whole against the
introduction of limited liability.   The Manchester and
Liverpool Chambers of Commerce both had long discussions
on the matter and rejected it.   Other Chambers of Commerce
were asked to write memorandums for the 1854 Mercantile
Law Commission on the subject and Belfast, Dundee, Glasgow,
Huddersfield, Leeds, Leith, and the Manchester Commercial
Association opposed limited liability.   They saw no
necessity for such a measure.   "No doubt the principle is
one admirably suited to the meridian of Paris and may bloom
in the streets of New York, but it does not seem likely to
be useful in London and Manchester."[1]   Samuel Cunard sums
up their attitude with regard to this when he opposed the
grant of a Board of T rade charter to a rival shipping
company.   "I do not pretend to say that nothing should be
done by corporations ... we contend that they should not be
wantonly created unless the magnitude of the undertaking
renders a corporation necessary."[2]   This did not occur in
the opinion of the Cunard firm until twenty-five years later.

At the same time, however, there was some fear of

---

1) Thomas Potter in "Transactions of Manchester Statistical
   Society", 1858, p.120.
2) Quoted by E. W. Field, op.cit., p.96.

competition in the opposition of the big manufacturers to
limited liability.   The attitude of these sections in the
rare cases of the Board of Trade considering the grant of a
charter to an industrial company brings this out clearly.[1]
But this cannot be called a struggle between large and
small capitalists.   It was the small capitalists who would
be hit first and who would be swallowed up by a limited
liability company.   Lord Hobart shows this in outlining
the sphere of limited companies,"... there are other
undertakings which though they may be carried on with some
profit by means of a small capital they cannot be carried
on so profitably by a small capital as by a large one."[2]
And again, "thus we find a Candle company with a million
capital - which means neither more nor less than making
serfs of the small traders in this branch of business."[3]

    There was fear of competition, but not fear of big
against small, it was both big and small against the
competition of men using the combined capital of several

---

1) Cf. A. Graham, "The Impolicy of Limitation of the
   Responsibility of Partnership in Manufactures and
   Commerce", 1838, p.19. A spinning company was applying
   for a charter. He writes, "Let the cotton spinners
   look to it!!"
2) Lord Hobart, op.cit., p.12.
3) Edmund Phillips, op.cit., p.35. This was Price's
   Candle Company.

(1)
hundred wealthy investors.

The general position of the industrialists was then, that they saw no need for such legislation and, to a certain extent, some dangers if it were passed in the form of strong competitors. On the basis of this the more vocal members built up a series of arguments dealing with the rights, morality, futility and dangers of such legislation.

On the investors' side (the question of were there sufficient good investments for capital) the position is not so simple. The investors were not organised in Chambers where they could put forward their views clearly and decisively. To understand their position it is necessary to trace the accumulation of capital in the hands of other than the entrepreneur class, to see what outlets were available for that capital, and to show what pressure there was, articulate and inarticulate, from investors for a change of the law.

---

1) The manufacturers used a very confused argument on competition. They urged first that limited liability was unfair and would lead to unfair competition and overproduction. Then they would contradict this and argue that limited liability would not work. Cf. E. W. Field, op.cit., quoting Cunard and other private shipowners.

We have mentioned above the existence of a non-
entrepreneurial class in the big commercial and trading
centres like London, which was rather isolated from the
industrial developments of the North.   The wealth and
size of this class is shown first of all by the size and
dispersion of the holdings of the National Debt.   This
group of about a quarter of a million people [1] form as it
were a solid base of the Victorian investment market,
though its function was not altogether static.   It also
formed a gateway to the likewise impersonal but more
exciting market of industrial and foreign securities. [2]   This
active factor came into play more and more as the nineteenth
century progressed, for wealth accumulated and increased
but the National Debt did not.   The overflow of these
savings went into monetary institutions of all kinds, banks,
discount houses, etc., and the more adventurous fringe into
the joint stock company and speculative markets.

Savings banks intended for the working classes were
reported to be attracting wealthier customers because of the

---

1) The figure for 1856 was 268,359 fundholders, but it is
   difficult to say exactly how many people this
   represented due to duplicate holdings and holdings of
   the trustees, etc.
2) L. Levi in an article in the "Journal of the Royal
   Statistical Society, Vol.23, March, 1870, p.10, suggests
   that many of the fundholders became the investors in the
   limited liability companies after 1856, a decrease being
   recorded in the number of fundholders.

rate of interest they allow on deposits. [1]   Banking
facilities were so much needed by investors and industry
that joint stock banks could grow rapidly without, in this
period, taking customers away from the similarly successful
private bankers. [2]   The deposit and current accounts of
the four chief London joint stock banks increased from
1840 to 1860 over twelve-fold.

In 1840	-	£3,348,188
In 1850	-	£11,913,388
In 1860	-	£38,732,429 [3]

Similar increases took place all over the country. Further
this growth in banking facilities, especially the practice
of the joint stock banks in allowing interest on deposits,
reacted on the tendency to invest. Hoards were broken up.
Money in one sense became more "liquid".   So the increase
in capital noted in this period was not only the result of
accumulation but also of capital in a more available form.

In the late 'forties and early 'fifties this
development of the banking side of the money market was
paralleled by a development in insurance companies and

1) A. G. Bowie, "Romance of the Savings Banks", 1898, p.26.
2) S. E. Thomas,"Joint Stock Banks to 1860", p.552.
3) H. Ayres, "Banks and Banking under Limited and Unlimited
   Liability", 1863, p.6.

discount houses. "Something little short of an 'Insurance Mania' has prevailed during the last few years",wrote a contemporary in 1856.[1] Discount houses though not increasing very rapidly in numbers until after 1856 were securing larger resources for their work.

The growth of these monetary institutions, banks, insurance companies, discount houses, etc., illustrates both the rapid increase of capital available for industry and the refusal of the manufacturers to adopt the limited liability principle. If they needed capital they could obtain it easily enough from these institutions, and the scale of their needs was not yet sufficient to make it cheaper to go direct to the investor rather than through an intermediary. John Howell described the rise of these institutions:-

> "... Our persistent refusal to admit limited
> liability for many years, except by charter,
> had had the effect of calling into existence
> great Banking and Bill Brokering establishments
> which, acting as viaducts and levying heavy
> toll, offered the principal though not the only
> means of linking capital and labour."[2]

They were not the only means, and the chartered

---

1) C. Walford, "Insurance Guide and Handbook for 1857", introduction.
2) John Howell, "Partnership Law Legislation and Limited Liability", 1869, p.4.

companies, the companies incorporated by Act of Parliament
and the unlimited joint stock companies played an important
role in establishing direct contact between the investor
and some new industries, and so building up an "investment
attitude". The funds and the banks were important in
providing the investor a place of deposit where his money
would be secure yet yield a return. Railways and the other
joint stock companies provided for a wider range of
investors, a semi-active role in the economic system and
consequently a higher return.

Further the railway company development had tended to
consolidate the investors as a class. Possession of capital
which could be invested in the London and North Western for
10% had broken down to some degree the difference of origin
of the investor. Investment had become a fairly respectable
occupation for landed gentry and merchant alike. "The
Times" in 1851 and E. P. Bouverie in the House of Commons
in 1855, both pointed out that investment was now providing
an occupation for the unoccupied and hoped it would draw
the industrialist and landed classes together. [1] The "era of

1) "The Times", quoted in A. Scratchley, "Industrial
   Investment and Emigration", 1851, p.ix, and Bouverie in
   "Hansard", loc.cit., p.319.

universal investment" had not by any means arrived by the
'fifties but the ground for it was being laid.

This was the background from the investors' angle of
the discussion on limited liability. There was a distinct
degree of isolation from the key industrial areas of the
country but through the funds, banks and joint stock
companies, such as railways, the investor was both finding
an outlet for his savings and imbibing an "investment
outlook". The decisive pressure for the immediate change
of the law came from the narrowing of investment outlets
in the 'fifties and the opposition accumulated over fifty
years to the danger of a dormant partner being liable for
debts of the company "to his last shilling, his last acre."

In the 'fifties the spirit and means of investment
still remained, though the railway and joint stock form
through which it had found a partial outlet,had almost
disappeared. Railways were said to be in the "zero of
depression and the thraldom of insecurity." [1] The
dividends of the established lines had sunk far below
their former golden era of 10%. Of the 55 companies given
in "The Times" by Mr. Yeats for the year 1854-1855

---

1) Civis, "The Railway Question", 1856, Preface, p.iii.

representing a mileage of 5,156 miles, only 8 were paying
above 5% and 21 of them were paying below the current rate
on Consols (£3-8-0).[1]   The average dividend on the total
capital in railways in the United Kingdom in 1855-1856,
nearly £300,000,000, was only about £4-0-0 per annum.
Equally important with the fall in dividends was the fall
in the demand for capital coming from the railways. In
the five years 1846 to 1850 the annual amount of money
authorised to be raised for railways had fallen from
£132.6 millions in 1846 to £4.1 millions in 1850. And in
the next five years 1851 to 1855 the annual average was
only £9.5 millions, and there were no signs of an increase.[2]
The seriousness of this to the investor can be seen by
reference to the estimates of the National Savings which
ranged from £40,000,000 a year to £65,000,000.[3]

This stagnation, or impending stagnation affected
investors in joint stock companies and fundholders alike.
Lord Hobart wrote in 1853:-

"There is no prospect of any large addition to our

---

1) Quoted from "The Times" by Civis, op.cit., p.51.
2) H. Ayres, "Financial Register", 1857, p.393.
3) £40,000,000 given in the 1854 Commission's Report;
£65,000,000 given in "Partnership en Commandite", 1848,
p.xlii.

> National Debt; the numbers of railway companies
> is not likely materially to increase; most of
> our towns are provided with gas and water com-
> panies; and with regard to companies acting
> without limited liability, there seems no
> disposition on the part of the public to add to
> their number or importance which are both
> inconsiderable."[1]

Subsequent events have shown that his prophecy as to the

future of railways and gas companies was wrong, but his

attitude reflects the outlook of the investor of that

period.

The first and main demand of the investors in the

'fifties was for increased outlet for their savings,for the

removal of the "impediment that now interferes with the

investment of capital";[2] either by increasing the number of

companies which were granted charters, or, if this led to

monopoly, then, to let incorporation be universal. The

second demand, which is only a different aspect of the

first was for limited liability. As E. P. Bouverie said,

the investors were wealthy men who did not want to lose

their all in the failure of one company. The experience

in joint stock banks was a particular warning in this

_____

1) Lord Hobart, op.cit., p.11-12.
2) William Hawes, op.cit.

respect.   Between 1846 and 1857 43 joint stock banks
failed with liabilities amounting to £40,819,000. Further
they were not particularly interested in the running and
management of concerns. They regarded themselves as
shareholders, not as partners or proprietors. Herbert
Spencer in his brilliant essay on railway investors shows
the degree to which they were content to sit back and
receive dividends and sign proxy forms, leaving the rest
to directors and managers. [1]   They wanted a remunerative
investment rather than a part share.

The answer given to these demands was that "the
capitalists do not want it (limited liability)." [2]   The
banks and the entrepreneurs themselves provided sufficient
capital. And on the moral plane Bellenden Ker's judgment
was, "I think it would be very prejudicial to encourage
the middle and lower classes to become speculators ... I
have a very strong feeling that the best investment is in
the three per cent Consols." [3]

This was the core of the discussions on limited

---

1) Herbert Spencer, "Railway Morals and Railway Policy",
   "Edinburgh Review", October, 1854.
2) "A Manchester Man", "A Reply", p.12.
3) Quoted in "The Westminster Review", p.40; cf. this 3%
   with the statement that ordinary profits in business
   were 30% to 40% in Edwin Moss, op.cit., p.9.

liability. The industrialists had capital and they invested
it in their partnerships. The commercial, trading and
professional classes similarly possessed capital but their
outlets were narrow and limited. The Professor of Political
Economy at Oxford summed up the position before the 1854
Commission. "The deficiency complained of is not that of
lack of capital, but of _investment of capital_."(his italics) [1]
And he went on to show that it was the latter classes of
people he was considering. There was no common ground for
discussion between these two rival forces. The introduction
of moral and other issues tended to confuse rather than
clarify the issue.

The 1850 and 1854 Commissions had failed to find a
solution. But the increasing pressure from the investors
in the 'fifties combined with the fact that the House of
Commons tended to represent the investing classes rather
than the big manufacturers [2] led to a partial united front
of the professional classes, the traders and a section of
landed interests to form a majority in the House and to

---

1) 1854 Commission, Appendix p.230-231. E. W. Richards.
2) "There were many professional gentlemen, members of the
House, ... wanting secure and remunerative investments
for their savings."

pass the Acts of 1855, 1856 and 1862.

The next twenty-five years of joint stock company development in England was dominated by this victory of the investing classes over the industrialists. The other hopes, fears and ideals of the promoters of the legislation had only a transitory effect on the development of the company form. The ideal of attracting the working class disappeared almost immediately with the introduction of high share denomination with uncalled capital. The hopes of limited liability solving crises were laid to rest almost as soon. And the discussion of "a right or a privilege" passed completely into academic abstraction when the principle was almost universally adopted.

CHAPTER II

The Development of the Limited Liability System in Industry,

1856 to 1885;   the Reasons for its Adoption in Particular

Industries;   and the Extent and Character of the

System in 1885.

The previous chapter has shown that while the
manufacturers and industrialists were on the whole well
provided with capital by the partnership and banking
systems, a certain number of entrepreneurs and a large
number of investors were not satisfied. This pressure for
a change in the law, coming from the rapidly growing
"wealthy middle and industrious classes"[1] and assisted by
the general feeling of all but industrialists that "small
partnerships would not meet the demands of modern enterprise",[2]
succeeded in carrying the day on the legal issue. A period
of quiet development between 1856 and 1862, which London
contemporaries tended to ignore,[3] led to a new burst of

---

1) Arthur Scratchley, op.cit., preface, p.ix.
2) "Journal of the Society of Arts", Vol.XV, November 30,
   1866, p.30.
3) Both the "Bankers Magazine" and D. Morier Evans described
   the Act in this period as "a dead letter", but there
   were 2,000 odd schemes started.

discussion in the 'sixties, a considerable simplification
of the law in 1862, and a big increase in the number of
company promotions.

The discussions ran along the same lines as those of
the 'fifties, though the emphasis had changed.   Where
limited liability had been expected to ameliorate the
conditions of the working classes by drawing labour and
capital closer together in the same happy enterprise, it
was now more frequently suggested that it would enable
philanthropic housing, dining and drinking schemes to be
established (with the natural small profit).   Chartism
had receded from the scene, trade unionism was slowly
turning towards sickness and burial benefits, and in 1861
the Post Office Savings Bank Bill was passed which provided
by 1864 over 3,000 branches where the working class could
deposit their small savings at $2\frac{1}{2}$%. [1]

On the other side the desire of the middle and upper
classes for a remunerative outlet for their savings was
more frequently stated.   "Every year adds to the large
amount of floating capital constantly waiting for profitable

---

1) "U.K. Post Office Green Papers", No.30.

investment ... dissatisfied with the meagre profits
obtainable by joining old commercial enterprises it is not
surprising – indeed it is the most natural thing possible –
that the owners of unemployed capital should strike out
fresh paths, plans and projects for themselves." [1] Or again,
"The Economist", "The popular voice exclaims 'why should
not we be also merchants in every sense of the term?'". [2]
It is interesting to note that the confidence of these
classes led them now to think of "fresh paths" and not
merely of joining the old established undertakings with the
security of limited liability.   An additional stimulus to
find a new outlet at home was given in the 'sixties by the
American Civil War and "the very ticklish state of affairs
on the Continent", which reduced foreign investment and led
to a "vast amount of English capital lying idle" [3] and "a
real plethora of money" [4] ready for investment.   But there
was little or no change in the attitude of the industrialists.
Their opposition was not so vigorous, but only slowly as the
necessity for more capital developed and the advantages of
the system became clearer did they adopt limited liability.

1) "Shareholders Guardian", November 17, 1863, p.20.
2) "The Economist", August 22, 1863, p.931.
3) "The Observer", September 21, 1862, p.5.
4) "Shareholders Guardian", March 1, 1864, p.132.

This increase in the supply of capital available for investment without a corresponding increase in the demand from the industrialists influenced the character of the limited liability companies formed in the early 'sixties. Instead of a large number of industrial companies being formed to carry on the consolidation of the Industrial Revolution at a greater pace, the chief types formed were financial and speculative. The isolation of this new group of investors from the industrial centres of the day is clearly illustrated by the formation of the credit associations, the purpose of which was to act as an intermediary (or a"collector of capital first and a distributor of capital second")[1] between the source of capital and the demand for it. Although the collection proceeded apace by means of these and similar institutions, the demand from industrial entrepreneurs was not so readily forthcoming with the result that, after a few years of speculation with little accomplished, the whole facade crumbled and collapsed in 1866 and 1867. The "plethora of capital" was replaced by what a governor of the Bank of England called "the exhaustion of the nation's capital",[2] the circle was

---

1) G. W. Norman, "Papers on Various Subjects", 1869, p.130.
2) Ibid., p.134.

complete, and limited liability had had its first trial of fire.

However, while this pressure from the middle and upper classes for an outlet for their investments had led to the formation, usually by members of these classes, of the [1] colourful but shortlived projects of the 'sixties, and until the decade of the 'eighties this desire for investments at a high rate of interest irrespective of the real demand for capital continued to be a feature in some degree of each successive "burst" of company flotation, there was taking place at the same time a decisive change in the attitude of industrial concerns towards limited liability. It was this change which had the most far-reaching effects on the business organisation of this country and it is on this change that we shall concentrate most attention.

First, we have to determine what factors there were operating which would lead to the formation of a limited liability company (whether "new" or "converted") and, secondly, the influence of these factors on the organisation of British industry between 1856 and 1885.

There are in general four problems confronting an

---

1) We discuss the role of these classes in forming companies later.

industrial unit which were most effectively solved by the
adoption of the company form.   Firstly, there is a
necessity to increase the capital of a concern beyond the
resources of a partnership. This increase can, of course,
up to a certain stage be obtained slowly by widening the
partnership but the limited liability system is advantageous
in terms of security and speed both to the investor and to
the concern.   Secondly, there is the semi-fraudulent and
semi-sound desire to avoid the dangers of complete
bankruptcy attendant on the partnership form. Thirdly,
when a new concern is being formed it should be easier to
raise capital through the organised capital market than by
trusting to the vagaries of the personal partnership
connections. Fourthly, there is the desire of the leading
partners to retire personally from the management but at
the same time to leave their capital in the concern and
receive profits on it.
(1)

We are not concerned with the reasons for bogus
promotions. Some light has been thrown on them above,in the

1) These four reasons were put forward at various times in
most of the discussions on the uses of limited liability.
They are almost identical, but not quite, with those set
out in "The Limited Liability Companies Directory", 1866,
p.14, "Mercantile positions in which the Company form
recommends itself."

discussion on the investor, but here we are only dealing
with those business units which are sound from an economic
point of view.

The first two factors given above, namely, the need
for more capital beyond partnership means, and the desire
to "limit responsibility", are the positive factors affecting
the transition of business organisation from the partnership
to the joint stock form. As either of these or both grow
more powerful, so will the speed of the transition increase.
The other two factors, namely, the establishment of a new
concern and the desire of partners to retire, will, of
course, affect the extent of the company system over a long
period of time but their nature is passive rather than
positive. These two problems were in existence before
the right to limited liability was introduced and their
solution through the formation of a company was more a
matter of adopting the means available at the time rather
than anything inherent in the principle of limited liability.
This does not apply to the new concerns which needed an
initial capital beyond the means of the partnership
organisation. This acted as a positive reason for
adopting limited liability and is included under the
heading of factor one.

This analysis ignores the role of the investor. His attitude towards investment, towards different types of investment, and towards the management of the company would act as a general incentive or deterrent to the formation of companies at different times. For our purpose here, however, it is permissable to ignore the year to year fluctuations in the amount of money coming forward for investment and the fluctuations in the character of the securities which the investor demanded, and to assume a steady supply of capital where the company promotions were sound. The details of this assumption are dealt with fully later. On similar grounds we have ignored the effects of the trade cycle on the formation of companies. These fluctuations, it is held, would increase or decrease the influence of any one or more of the factors given above, but would not and did not introduce any additional factor into the above reasons for adopting the company form of business organisation.

There is a third proviso to make before we go on to discuss the working of these factors in this period, and that is, that these factors often overlapped in the case of individual concerns. Nevertheless we think it is possible and necessary to the understanding of the development of

the company form to define the relative importance of each
of the factors in the periods under discussion.

There were five main fields of the limited liability
company development in this period from 1856 to 1885; the
shipping, iron and steel, and cotton industries, general
industrial and commercial undertakings, and banking and
finance.   This excludes the use of the system for overseas
development.   We propose to take each of these fields in
turn, describing the changes which took place in the form
of industrial organisation and analysing the influence of
the factors given above in bringing about the adoption of
the company form.

The shipping industry in the middle of the nineteenth
century was organised roughly into three distinct types of
business unit. First, there were the large chartered
companies, e.g. the Peninsular and Orient Line, the Royal
West Indian Mail, the Pacific Steam Navigation Company, the
General Steam Navigation Company, which had been incorporated
because of the necessity of keeping in touch with the
distant parts of a growing empire and because the size of the
organisation needed, and the risk of these journeys were
often too great, to be undertaken by an individual or a
group of capitalists.   Second, there were a few very large
private concerns which also concentrated on regular lines

and services. The feature of these firms was the energy
and spirit which characterised the individuals who had
built up the firms. Men like Samuel Cunard, Burns, McIver,
and Napier, had worked their way up in the concerns and
bought out their partners until they had complete control
of huge lines and had amassed great fortunes.[1] Both the
above types of organisation were maintained in some degree
in their semi-monopolistic position by the grants of
"postal subventions" from the Government for carrying mails.
The third type of organisation was found in its purest form
in the cargo ships, the "free traders". Here the capital
of the ship was divided among a number of partners, in the
early stages into "eights", later under the Merchant
Shipping Act of 1854 into "sixty-fourths". "The chief
members of the group were frequently men who had some
connection with various aspects of the shipping business,
ship builders, ship brokers, chandlers, etc. ... if they
could not put down between them the whole cost of the
vessel they could dispose of a certain number of the 64ths
among their family, friends and business associates."[2] At

---

1) e.g. in the Cunard Shipping Company. "The original
   shareholders were by degrees bought out by the founders,
   until the whole concern became vested exclusively in the
   three families of Cunard, Burns and McIver." ("History of
   the Cunard Steamship Company", 1886, p.16) The period
   referred to is 1840 to 1850.
2) C. W. Fayle, "World Shipping Industry", 1934, p.260.

this date, these cargo ships were made of wood and propelled
by sail. The 64th system was successful when applied to
this type of ship as the capital was not so large as to
necessitate going beyond the 64th limit, the division of
shares spread the very high risk, and the local nature of
the "investment" allowed ample supervision and trust of the
"managing owner" on whose enterprise and ability the whole
success of cargo ships depended.

Into this rather idyllic picture came a tremendous
development of world trade and a series of revolutionary
inventions. The development of English shipping between
1860 and 1914 in terms of amounts of cargo and number of
passengers carried is too well known to describe here.[1] By
itself, it would have led to a big expansion of the number
of shipping concerns: Coupled with the technological
changes it led to a transformation of the basis of
organisation of the shipping unit.

The technological changes were briefly these. In the
'fifties began the large scale displacement of wood for iron
in the construction of the ships. At the same time began
the development of the compound engine which replaced sail

---

1) This is admirably done in A. W. Kirkaldy, "British
   Shipping", 1914, and E. Crammond, "British Shipping
   Industry", 1917.

and was without a rival between 1860 and 1880.[1] The
compound engine together with the iron hulls gave the first
impetus to the later overwhelming success of the cargo
steamer, for it led both to an increase in freight per ship
and a decrease in operating, though not capital, costs.[2] To
carry the story on further, from 1885 steel began in its
turn to replace iron in the construction of ships until by
1914 almost 98% were steel, and between 1885 and 1900 the
triple expansion engine with the twin screw replaced the
compound engine with a single screw. The twentieth century
saw the quadruple expansion engine with the quadruple screw
which was being replaced just before the War by turbines.[3]

The effect that these technological changes had on the
organisation of the shipping unit can be best seen by
describing the position in 1885. The big chartered
companies still remained, but they were now supplemented in
the passenger and mail carrying trades by large limited

---

1) "Iron tonnage exceeded wood and composite in those ships
   added to the Register of the United Kingdom in 1860. The
   amount of steam tonnage exceed sailing tonnage in 1865."
   ("British Merchant Shipping", p.39). "Success with the
   compound engine was reached in the late 'fifties and for
   over twenty years was without a rival." (Kirkaldy, op.cit.,
   p.168.).
2) Fayle, op.cit., p.247. Also p.261, "Compound engine first
   enabled steamer to compete successfully with sailing
   vessel in general cargo trade."
3) Crammond, op.cit., p.3, and Kirkaldy, op.cit., p.167 et
   seq. In 1885 Lloyd's first general steel ship rule's
   were introduced.

liability companies.   The type of vessel used by these
lines was very costly to build and as success could not be
made by one ship, a whole fleet was necessary.   Consequently
in order to raise the capital to build and maintain such a
fleet, the company system was adopted.   In 1885, 19 of
these companies with a total loan and share capital of
nearly £15,000,000 controlled one-fifth of the total steam
tonnage of the United Kingdom. [1]   The actual ownership of the
ordinary shares, or at any rate the direction of the
company, tended still to be in the hands of the type of
individuals whom we mentioned above as "working their way
to the top of the firm". [2]   The risk attached to shipping
and the tremendous changes which the industry was undergoing
continued to give a marked opportunity to the energetic
"captain of industry", but the capital necessary to keep
pace with these changes and opportunities had exceeded
even such men's powers and they were forced to appeal to
the public for additional resources,

---

1) "The Statist", 1885, p.600.
2) The leading individuals of this period around whom
   companies were formed and lines built were Donald Currie
   (Union Castle Line), Alfred Jones (Elder Demster Line),
   James Anderson (Orient Line), Frederick Leyland, Ismay,
   Charles Booth, and many others.   The hard work and
   accumulation that characterised these men is described
   in Clement Jones, "Pioneer Shipowners", 1934.

We have shown above that already in the 'fifties the
cargo ship was acquiring some importance. The increase in
world trade, the opening of the Suez Canal, and the
technological changes increased and consolidated this
importance, and at the same time the method of organisation
had changed. The 64th system was dying together with the
sailing ship, and the steamers were usually owned by a
limited liability company. In the boom periods of shipping
in the first few years of the 'sixties, the early 'seventies,
and from 1879 to 1886, most of the new organisations that
were being formed to exploit the iron and compound engined
steamers, were limited companies.[1] Other companies were
formed either directly from an old 64ths partnership taking
over the existing property, or were formed to purchase
shares in 64th partnerships and eventually to control the
ships.[2] In the last period, 1879 to 1886, the "single"
ship company was a favorite form. These were always
limited liability companies and were formed partly by the

---

1) The opening of the Suez Canal in 1869 gave a big fillip
   to the iron, compound engined steamers as the old sailing
   vessels could not compete on this new route.
2) An example of the latter type of company was the "Mutual
   Steam Shipping Company Limited", 1880. In its prospectus
   it offered to "exchange a 64th share in a steamer at its
   net cash value for a fully paid up share at par in the
   Company" which it suggested would give the holder of the
   share "marketability and a more certain dividend". "The
   Accountant" in 1887 devoted an article to the advantages
   to be gained by a limited company buying up the 64 64ths
   of a ship. (p.320 et seq.).

owners of small "fleets" who split up their lines into so
many individual companies and partly by groups of men who
previously would have formed 64th partnerships but who now
recruited their capital from a much wider field.

The factors that lay behind this spread of the limited
liability form to shipping, stand out clearly. First and
foremost, the rapid and costly technological changes had
rendered individual capital insufficient for the establishment of a line. This is most marked in the case of the
large passenger lines. The famous Cunard line which became
a limited liability company in 1878 and issued shares to
the public in 1880 wrote in its prospectus in the latter
year, "The growing wants of the Company's Transatlantic
trade demand the acquisition of additional steam ships of
great size and power involving a cost of production that
can best be met by a large public company." The capital of
the company was £2,000,000, of which two-thirds was issued
to the public. A year later the first Cunard steel ship
was built and launched.[1]

This need for capital greater than could be supplied
by the partnership was also an important determinant in the

---

1) These details from the prospectus of the Company and from
the "History of the Cunard Company", op.cit., pp.16-18.

transition of the smaller vessels and lines which carried
on cargo trade, from the 64ths system to that of the limited
liability company.   A few partners could equip and
maintain a wooden sailing vessel but the costly changes made
this system increasingly difficult and approaching the
impossible.   A contemporary wrote in 1882 of these
difficulties of 64th ownership,

> "Owing, however, to the multiplication of large
> iron ships propelled by expensive engines, there
> has been an increasing tendency for several
> years to divide the ownership of such vessels
> amongst the largest number of separate owners
> permissable under the law ... one result has been
> to complicate the shipping register to a very
> considerable degree. It is now possible under
> this section for one ship's register to show as
> many as 320 owners." [1]

The 64ths system was becoming unwieldy and inadequate. [2]

The actual transition to the company form was partly the
result of this increasing cost and partly, in the case of
these small ships, the result of the second factor, namely,
the desire to avoid or escape undue risk.

---

1) T. J. Pittar , "The Law and Practice of Merchant
   Shipping", 1882, p.59.
2) The transition from wood and sail to iron and steam in
   cargo trades had doubled both the cost per ton and the
   size of the vessel. In "Phillips Investors Annual", 1887,
   it is estimated that a wooden ship cost £9-11 per ton and
   a steamer £16-24 per ton. The size had risen from c.500
   tons in the 'fifties to c.1000 tons in the 'eighties.
   One sixty-fourth share had increased from c.£75-100 in
   the 'fifties to £300-350 in the 'eighties.

The great advantage to ship owners of the limited
liability system was that in the event of an accident
involving a compensatory action by another ship owner, the
amount that could be paid was limited. If the "limited
liability" ship had been responsible for a collision but
in this collision it had been sunk, then the owners of the
other vessel could get no compensation at all unless the
limited ship in question was only one of a fleet of ships
owned by the same company. It was in order to close up
this latter loophole that the conversion of a line of
steamers into so many "single ship companies" became so
common in the 'eighties. Not only was the capital for a
ship easier to raise by the company form but also the risk
for the owners was less. (It must be reiterated here that
we are considering the adoption of limited liability from
the point of view of the entrepreneur only, and not from
that of the investor. There were many additional reasons
why the limited liability ship company should be preferred.)

The third factor which would influence the use of the

1) These were the reasons given for the formation of single
   ship companies by W. R. Price, London shipowner, before
   the Royal Commission on the Depression in Trade and
   Industry (later referred to as 1886 Royal Commission on
   Depression), Qu.10,156, and by Sir T. Farmer, Qu.15,127 ff.
2) e.g. smaller value, easy marketability, etc. These are
   discussed later.

limited system, that of starting a new concern, played quite a large part in shipping. While very few of the large companies which were established in this period were entirely new undertakings, they were almost all the outcome of the conversion of a firm or partnership, and a number of completely new units were started to run ships of the ocean tramp class. The limited liability organisation was the only course open to the founders of these concerns for, as shown above, the 64th system was proving rapidly unworkable for any steamer of normal size.

The last factor, that of conversion into a company with the retirement of the proprietor of the private concern, was of little importance in shipping. In contrast to iron and steel, as we shall show later, the prospectuses of the shipping companies appealing for public subscriptions never gave as the reason for the formation of the company, "the late proprietor wishes to retire", or, "... has died and his relatives wish to dispose of the property." The reason most frequently given was that quoted above in the case of the Cunard company,"... the need for additional capital."

To sum up then, the position in the shipping industry showed a fairly close correlation between the change in the method of organisation and the big technological and

commercial changes that took place in the industry in this
period.[1] The increase of the scope and the cost of carrying
on a shipping line led to the demand for a much larger amount
of fixed capital. The risks were too great for this capital
to be supplied by the banks and other financial institutions
and so it was necessary to make a general appeal to the
public. This applied equally to the large capitalists who
were engaged in the costly passenger trades and to the
smaller capitalists who were concerned with less expensive
cargo trades. Two further factors influenced the spread of
the company system in the latter sphere. The first was the
ability to spread the higher risks more effectively through
the company and the second was the need of the new concerns
that sprang up to make use of the changed technique for
an initial capital of a size which made the company the
only possible form of organisation.

The iron trade had been one of the key centres of the
Industrial Revolution. Its tremendous expansion had been
financed for the most part by the accumulations of landed
gentry and of individual capitalists. Big fortunes had
been made by those associated with the trade. In 1865 "The

---

1) The term "method of organisation" here as above is
applying only to the legal and outward character. The
"internal" position, that is in whom rested the control,
etc., will be discussed later.

Fortnightly Review" wrote, "It is well known that within
the last forty years it has doubled itself ten times with
an annual rate of increase of 20 or 30%. Of course, this
gigantic growth represents a corresponding rate of profit
and justifies McCulloch's remark that 'larger fortunes
have been made in this than any other department of
industry'. Recent events have in the past few years raised
these profits into still more fabulous proportions."[1] The
basis of the organisation in the trade up to the 'fifties
and 'sixties was partnership between wealthy capitalists.
The joint stock attempts had not been many and had been
"lamentable in results".[2] The capital cost of the rapidly
enlarging blast furnace and the big working costs involved
in the puddling processes had kept down the number of
small works and had encouraged large scale units. The
returns of the Factory Inspectors for 1870-1871 on the
number of workpeople employed in 127,000 workplaces in
Great Britain,showed that the average number of workpeople
per works for "iron making" was 219. The only industries
that ranked above this were jute,with an average of 291 and
iron-shipbuilding with 570.[3]

1) "The Fortnightly Review", 1865, p.103.
2) J. H. Clapham, op.cit., Vol.II, p.135.
3) Ibid., p.117.

The changes that took place in the iron industry
between the 'fifties and the decade of the 'eighties were
briefly a change of area, a change in the technical
processes and the introduction of large scale steel making,
and a change in the form of business organisation. The
change in area was the development of the North East coast
from the fourth in order of importance of the iron ore
producing areas in the country in 1855, to easily the first
in 1885. At the latter date it produced between 30% and
40% of the total amount of iron ore raised in this country.[1]
The rise in steel making from a special and laborious
process in the 'fifties to a position, where in the 'eighties
it was rapidly taking the place of iron for use in railways[2]
and steel ships were becoming a general possibility, was[3]
due to the successive introduction of the Bessemer converter,
the Siemens "open hearth", and the Gilchrist Thomas "basic"
processes. The Cleveland iron district and the Sheffield

---

1) Figures in J. H. Clapham, op.cit., Vol.II, p.49.
2) L. Bell, "Principles of the Manufacture of Iron and Steel",
   1884, p.378. "Steel ... must be henceforward looked upon
   as the proper material for railroads."
3) In "The Iron Trade", 1886, p.42, Lothian Bell points out
   that shipping had already displaced railroads as the
   chief source of the demand for iron. But ships at this
   date were also turning to steel, and in 1894 56% of the
   steam vessels employed in foreign trade were steel.
   (E. Crammond, op.cit.,p.2.)

manufacturing district were the two areas leading the way
to the transition to steel.

The method of business organisation changed at the
same time.   The company began to take the place of the
partnership.   For the country as a whole 41% of the concerns
working blast furnaces given in the first Mineral Returns
in 1882 were limited liability companies.[1]   In Middlesborough
and district, and in Sheffield, the importance of the
company was still greater.   In 1883, of 32 firms in the
Cleveland district working blast furnaces, 16 were limited
companies controlling 74 of the furnaces in the area, 16
were private concerns controlling only 49 furnaces.[2]
Sheffield had become in 1886 "one of the two most important
centres of joint stock" (Oldham was the other)[3]   with 44
companies and a total paid-up share capital of £12,065,757.[4]
The feature of these iron and steel companies was their very

---

1) In the Mineral Returns for Great Britain, 1882, there were
   195 concerns working a total number of 843 blast furnaces.
   Private concerns numbered 115 with 465 furnaces, i.e.
      "   "   "   59% with 56% of the blast furnaces
   Limited companies numbered 80 with 378 furnaces, i.e.
      "   "   "   41% with 44% of the blast
                                                   furnaces.
2) C. T. Jones, "Increasing Returns", p.283, in statistical
   appendix gives these details.
3) "The Accountant", 1886, p.570.
4) Ibid., 1887, p.17.

high capitalisation. Of the 1,585 companies listed in
Burdett's "Official Intelligence" for 1885, the 102 iron,
steel and coal companies had a higher average capital than
any other group except railways. The total paid-up share
and loan capital per company averaged between £300,000 and
£400,000.[1]

We shall now make an analysis of the factors operating
in the iron and steel industry which led to this use of the
limited liability company rather than the partnership method
of organisation in some 40% of the concerns.

First, there is no doubt as to the steadily increasing
need for fixed capital taking place over this period. Blast
furnaces increased in size,[2] and, although the Bessemer
process for steel making increased in some ways the need for
working capital to pay for the imported ore, at the same
time it laid emphasis on large scale plants for steel making,
which emphasis was redoubled by the Siemens and Thomas
processes.

But this increased demand for capital did not lead
immediately to the adoption of the joint stock form. For

---

1)See Appendix E.
2)J. H. Clapham, op.cit., p.50, gives details of the
  doubling of size and increasing of capacity four times of
  blast furnaces between the late 'forties and the
  'seventies.

where the banks had been hesitant to lend in shipping
because of the risk, they were willing and did lend in the
iron industry. We have given above some examples of this
connection between the Northern banks and industry. One
further can be added. In 1872, "the Yorkshire Banking
Company, and also concerned was the Yorkshire City and County
Bank, granted a loan of £26,000 specifically to institute
the Bessemer process."[1] It is interesting to add by way
of contrast to this that a year later Walter Bagehot,
banking prophet of the new school, was writing, "Caution,
I had almost said timidity, is the life blood of banking."

The need for additional capital beyond the resources
of a partnership was an important factor in the conversion
of concerns to the limited form, but the ability to supply
some of this capital by other means slowed down this
adoption. The very large fortunes and accumulations that
were already in existence among the iron manufacturers and
the willingness of the banks to lend for long term meant
that the company form was only adopted when the concern needed
a capital greater, on an average, than say a quarter of a

---

1) J. E. Wadsworth and W. F. Crick, op.cit., p.226.

million pounds.[1] This ability of the partnership system
to supply fixed capital for iron and steel works to amounts
up to this figure is a marked contrast to other industries,
and the fact that by 1883 about 40% of the iron and steel
concerns were limited companies illustrates the great extent
to which capitalistic methods of production, "more round
about" methods, leading to a very big demand for fixed
capital, were already in use in this industry.

The influence of the second factor, the desire to "be
on the safe side" on the part of the proprietors of
concerns which adopted the limited company, is hard to
determine. R. L. Nash in 1880 suggested that the "mania"
for conversion of private concerns in the iron industry
between 1870 and 1875 was due in part to this. "A host of
private firms seeing their opportunity effected a sale of
their properties to joint stock companies at highly inflated
prices."[2] Nash, of course, was only looking at the problem
on the surface, for, although the "inflated prices" existed,
due to the big rise in the price of iron, the vendors in
most cases did not take all the purchase price out in cash,

---

1) This figure is estimated from the average capital of
these companies in 1885 - £300,000 to £400,000 - and D.
Chadwick's estimate that the existing partners supply
c.70-80% of the capital of a new company in this industry.
("Report of Select Committee on the Companies' Acts of
1862 and 1867 VIII", 1877, Qu.2077 - later referred to
as the 1877 Report).
2) R. L. Nash, "A Short Inquiry into the Profitable Nature
of our Investments". 1880 p 103

but left a considerable portion of it in the company in the
form of shares. They were dictated,apparently, partly by a
desire to be limited in their responsibility if the boom
broke and bankruptcies set in.[1]

T his desire to be on the safe side can be accepted
as   a contributory factor to the necessity of
appealing for a larger amount of capital. That the two
worked hand in hand is seen in part by the comparatively
small amount of capital that was actually subscribed from
outside in the formation of one of these companies. David
Chadwick puts the figure at between 20% and 30%.[2] Standing
out above this factor and second only in importance to the
necessity of raising additional capital,was the factor of
the entrepreneur or the leading partners wishing to retire
with their well earned fortunes and only retaining a
limited responsibility, from the point of view both of
amount and legal consequences, in the concern.

---

1) David Chadwick, a "financial agent" who took part in the
   promotion of a large number of iron and steel conversions
   in the 'sixties and 'seventies, in his evidence before
   the 1877 Committee on the Companies' Acts also suggested
   that a number of vendors attempted conversions because
   their firm was on the downgrade and the partners wished
   to limit their responsibility. He says as many as forty
   made propositions of this nature to his firm alone, and
   39 of them were refused assistance. (1877 Report, Qu.2042).
2) 1877 Report, loc.cit.

In the prospectuses of these companies, especially
those formed in the late 'sixties and early 'seventies,
this is repeatedly given as the reason for the formation of
the company. There were slight variations in the reasons
given but the general undercurrent was the same. Some
examples will make this clear. "The proprietor is desirous
of retiring from the principal management", Darlington Iron
Company, 1872; "owing to the death of Mr. Aaron Gould, the
late owner, the Trustees have sold the property to the
company", Bilson and Crump Meadow Collieries, 1874; "the
proprietor desires to retire", Brittania Iron Works Company,
1872; "owing to the recent death of one partner and the
serious illness of another...", Earle's Shipbuilding Company,
1871; "owing to the death of the late proprietor...", South
Cleveland Iron Works, 1872; and the retirement of Sir John
Brown was given as the reason for the formation of John
Brown and Company Limited. The most explicit prospectus on
this question was that of Mercy and Cunningham of Glasgow,
who controlled iron works in Lanark (1872). "Mr. Cunningham
died in 1865 ... the present contract of Copartnery expires
in 1879 and Mr. Cunningham's Trustees who are bound to
realise his estate as speedily as possible, must withdraw
his capital from the business at the earliest opportunity.

Mr. Mercy does not feel disposed to add to the large
interest which he already holds in the undertaking and as
neither of his sons desires to engage in commercial
pursuits he prefers gradually to withdraw from active
business. It would be almost impossible to find private
capitalists to contribute the capital necessary for such an
enterprise and it has therefore been resolved to place the
present proposal before the public."[1] The capital
proposed was £1,000,000 in shares and £500,000 in debentures.

This prospectus reveals admirably the problems that
were facing the partners in large undertakings in the
second half of the nineteenth century. Whereas in previous
years the death or illness of a partner was rarely sufficient
reason for abandoning the whole project, for the capital
invested by one partner could be replaced by other men, or,
in the case of an actual dissolution, the units were
sufficiently small to have little effect on the industry
as a whole, in the 'seventies the position was radically
different. The capital accumulated and re-invested in the
concern by the partners had reached a size in the iron
trade where its replacement by another capitalist was
impossible. The men with capital on this scale were for
the most part already deeply involved in undertakings of

1) From the prospectus of the company.

their own. And on the other hand, the dissolution of a
partnership like Cunningham's and Mercy's, which represented,
apparently, at least half a million pounds of fixed capital,
would have made a major impression on the industry. The
only alternative was the joint stock form and for those just
coming into the business and for those "wishing gradually
to withdraw from active participation", limited liability
with the joint stock form was just as much a necessity. The
inclusion of the remark about the "sons not desiring to
engage in commercial pursuits" among the reasons for turning
"limited", implies that it was not solely a case of being
unable to find another partner: the whole spirit of business
was undergoing a change as well.

David Chadwick in his evidence in 1877 agreed that this
factor of "retirement" was leading to limited liability
companies. "Men with large interests in some businesses
desire to limit that interest and the only mode to do it is
by forming a joint stock company."(1)

The company method of organisation was not used in the
iron and steel trades to any great extent to form entirely
new units. Large scale steel developments were almost

---

1) David Chadwick before the 1877 Committee (1877 Report,
   Qu.2074 et seq.)

always pursued by firms or companies already in existence
in the iron trade. The production of steel often meant the
issue of more capital or the conversion of the firm in
order to bring in more capital, but rarely was an entirely new
unit started. In the sphere of working out new inventions
it is interesting to note that Bessemer in 1858 formed a
(1)
partnership to do this, but Gilchrist Thomas and Percy
Gilchrist in the 'seventies, after purely laboratory research,
conducted experiments with the Blaenavon Company Limited
(2)
and successfully with Bolckow Vaughan and Company Limited.

To sum up, the reasons for the adoption of the company
method of organisation in the iron and steel trades were as
follows. While the demand for additional capital resulting
from technological changes and greater scale of production
was important, it was tempered somewhat in its effects by
the very large private resources of the iron and steel
"captains" which had accumulated in the forty years previous
to the introduction of the company system and by the
willingness of the banks, up to the time of the City of
Glasgow crash in 1878, to lend money on long term to both

---

1) J. H. Clapham, op.cit., p.55. Vol. II.
2) "Thomas and Gilchrist, Bolckow and Vaughan, 1879-1929",
   1929, p.7.

companies and partnerships in the iron trade. On the other
hand, however, the very size of the accumulations which
enabled private individuals to continue in the trade,
alongside of a different attitude towards industry on the
part of the younger generation, led, of necessity, on the
death or removal of one or more of these "captains",to the
formation of a joint stock company with limited liability.
Neither the desire to limit the entrepreneurs' risk, nor
the establishment of new units played a very large part in
the introduction of the limited system into this trade.

The third industry in which there was a quite rapid
transformation in the method of business organisation
between 1856 and 1885 was cotton. At the time the "Oldham
Limiteds" received more attention than any other sphere in
which the company form developed, partly because of the
concentration of this new form in Oldham and partly because
of their fierce competition with private enterprise, but
there has not been any detailed account of the reasons for
this rapid growth of companies in Oldham. [1] We shall attempt

---

1) This is in spite of the confident assertion in "The
Co-operative Wholesale Society Annual", 1884, that "when
the history of the joint stock movement comes to be
written - especially that part of it which pertains   to
industrial enterprises - the town of Oldham will occupy no
inconsiderable place in that narrative." (p.193).

as with the previous two industries to analyse the influence that the four factors outlined above had on the adoption of the company form in cotton.

The inventions in the cotton trade associated with the names of Arkwright, Crompton and Lee, led to the establishment of the factory system in this spinning side of the trade at a far earlier date than was the case in other industries. This did not, however, imply the necessity of a joint stock form of organisation at an early date. The fixed capital needed in a cotton factory in the 'forties and 'fifties was not beyond the resources of an individual's accumulation or those of a partnership. "The builder of the mill", it was said, referring to the cotton mills of the 'fifties, "would find himself at least three-quarters of the capital required." [1] And in this period, although many new mills were built as the high margin of profit attracted entrepreneurs, there was not a tendency for the amount of fixed capital per mill to increase. In fact the average number of spindles per factory fell from 10,868 in 1850 to 10,525 in 1862. [2] The private individual or the partnership form were able to

---

1) J. C. A., "Limited Liability and Cotton Spinning", 1886, p.17.
2) J. S. Jeans, "England's Supremacy", 1885, p.194.

finance on their own the expansion of the cotton trade and
to supply "the shirts for the backs of millions", even if
the millions did not always purchase the shirts. The joint
stock form except in a few co-operative mills,[1] which do
not here concern us, was unknown and cotton was regarded as
the least likely industry to need it.[2]

There were no major inventions in the cotton trade
between the 'fifties and the 'eighties but the cotton famine,
the development of labour saving devices, and the increased
demand, effected an important change in the organisation of
the individual units. The famine led, though with
considerable fluctuations, to a narrowing of the margin of
profit.[3] Many firms found they could no longer compete
with the larger factories and a gradual process of weeding
and absorbing took place. This influenced in part the
increase in the average number of spindles per mill which
rose from 10,525 in 1862 to 15,399 nine years later,
and there was a further increase to 16,531 in 1878.[4] But

---

1) Examples have been given above.
2) Cotton is cited by the industrialists in 1851 as the
   least likely industry in these terms, "What would be
   thought of an application for a charter with limited
   liability from a company of proprietors to erect mills!"
   (quoted in E. W. Field, op.cit., p.94).
3) J. S. Jeans, op.cit., p.195.
4) J. S. Jeans, op.cit., p.195.

hese figures apply to the industry as a whole throughout
he country. In Oldham,"the real seat of the industry," the
verage number of spindles per mill had risen to 65,342 in
(1)
he middle of the 'eighties for the"limited" mills. The
ncreased demand for cotton goods had the effect, particularly
n the 'seventies of increasing the number of new mills
eing built. These were taking the place of some of those
hat had been absorbed, but from the start they had a high
verage number of spindles per mill.

But the real basis for this turn towards larger mills
as the increasing efficiency of labour. With the
(2)
ntroduction and success of the self acting mule more
pindles could be operated per mill hand. This process,
hich Schultze-Gaevernitz described as "the replacement of
(3)
abour by capital", is shown very clearly by the statistics
or the number of spindles in operation throughout the
ountry and the number of workpeople engaged in the years
861 and 1885. In 1861 there were 30,381,467 spindles and

) G. von Schultze-Gaevernitz, "Cotton Trade in England", 1895,
   p.67. This, if anything, is an underestimate. The
   average spindles per mill of the 72 limited companies in
   Oldham given in "The Co-operative Wholesale Society Annual",
   1884, is 71,300 (p.188).
) Samuel Andrew, "Fifty Years of the Cotton Trade", 1887, p.8.
) Schultze-Gaevernitz, op.cit., p.85 et seq.; he suggests
   the result is the disappearance of the class struggle!

248,000 spinning operatives; by 1885 the figures had risen
to 41,298,110 spindles but the number of spinning operatives
had fallen to 240,000 (1880-1882)[1] . Put in percentages
there was an increase in spindles of 36.5% and a decrease
in the number of spinners of 3.2%. The most efficient
methods of production demanded a relatively higher
proportion of fixed capital in terms of spindles, than of
working capital in terms of labour. Oldham was the centre
where these methods were most widely adopted at the
beginning.

To do this two things were needed - firstly, a greater
amount of capital per mill, and secondly, new machinery
and a different organisation of the mill. The necessary
increase in capital per mill has in effect been shown above
in the figures of the increased number of spindles to a
mill.   For with a spindle costing on an average £1
throughout this period[2], a mill with 20,000 to 30,000 spindles

---

1) These figures are taken from J. H. Clapham, op.cit.,
   Vol.II, p.81, and "Some Economic Developments during the
   last Hundred Years in the Cotton Trade" (a paper read
   before the Manchester Statistical Society, 1934), p.6.
2) This is only an average. In 1867 Samuel Andrew said the
   cost per spindle was 18/-. In the boom period, 1870-1874,
   the cost rose according to J. C. A., op.cit., p.5, to
   30/- to 35/- per spindle in a fireproof mill. In the
   'eighties it was down again to £1. This increase in the
   early 'seventies explains Ellison's statement that the
   cost in the 'eighties had fallen 20% to 30% per mill.

needed a capital of at least £20,000 to £30,000, and the
mills in the 'eighties in Oldham with 60,000 to 70,000
spindles needed at least an equivalent amount of capital
in pounds. This calculation is borne out by the estimates
given in the 'fifties that £20,000 to £50,000 were necessary
in a cotton spinning mill,[1] and in the 'eighties the average
capital of 240 mills in Oldham, limited and unlimited, was
c.£60,000 while the average share and loan for the "limited"
mills (72) was £75,000.[2]

The re-organisation of the machinery in order to make
use of the labour saving devices was most satisfactorily
achieved by building a new mill. The difficulties which
were present,say in the iron and steel industry to such a
course, for example, the scarcity of land with minerals, the
high overhead costs of a mine, the long period which
elapsed between sinking the mine and using the ore, etc.,
were not present in cotton. A mill could be built, equipped
and started working within about two years,[3] the cost though
increasing,was insignificant compared with a mine, transport

1) This is the estimate given in Field, op.cit., p.94. The
seven cotton companies that were formed in 1867 had an
average capital of £24,571 ("Journal of the Institute of
Bankers", 1886, p.508).
2) Calculated from the figures given in "The Co-operative
Wholesale Society Annual", 1884, p.188.
3) Ibid., p.189.

and steam-driven machinery had solved the location problem,
land was still cheap around Oldham, and, in addition, other
improvements besides those of machinery could be introduced
such as fire-proofing which could not be used in an old or
"converted" mill.

These changes in the cotton industry leading to the
weeding out of the small mill, the increase in the number of
spindles per mill, and the increase of fixed capital costs
relative to labour costs brought about a change in the
method of organisation of the cotton unit, particularly
in those areas where these changes had been most marked. "A
comparison of the position of the cotton trade to-day (1889)
with what it was some thirty years ago shows a decided
change in one respect - i.e. in the firms conducting the
business. Many of the old private firms have disappeared
and their places taken by companies."[1] Put in a statistical
fashion, in Oldham 71 out of the 156 firms engaged in
cotton spinning, i.e. 45%, were limited liability companies,
in 1884, and they owned over 50% of the spindles in the

---

1) C. P. Brooks, "Cotton Manufacture", 1889, p.8, and cf.
"Cotton" (journal of the cotton trades), 1876, p.270,
"During the last twenty years our entire system has
changed. We do not now establish but 'float' a concern
... cotton masters have become 'promoters' and 'directors',
bookkeepers 'secretaries', and profits 'dividends'."

(1)

whole town. The figures for most of the Lancashire
spinning area, including Blackburn, Bolton, Burnley, Bury,
Manchester, Preston, Rochdale, Stockport, and other smaller
places, show that out of 553 spinning firms, 156 were limited
companies, i.e. 28%. The "limited" company was far less
frequent in the concerns doing both spinning and
manufacturing and those engaged only in the manufacture of
cotton goods. The figures for all these firms (spinning,
manufacturing and spinning, and manufacturing) show that
(1)
of 1,610 firms 298 were limited companies, or about 18%.

The factors underlying this change of organisation
from the private firms of the 'fifties have been set out
explicitly or implicitly above. We shall now discuss and
summarise the influence of each of the four main factors.

First, there was the necessity due to the increased
size of the mills and the displacement of labour by capital
for a greater amount of capital to be devoted to the fixed
plant of a mill. The average amount of capital needed for
a mill was almost doubled between 1850 and 1885. It was

---

1) These figures are taken from "The Cotton Spinners and
Manufacturers Directory", John Worrall, Oldham, 1884.
They are fairly representative for Great Britain, for
there were only 355 limited cotton companies in existence
in 1884 ("The Co-operative Wholesale Society Annual",
1884, p.203).

found easier to raise this larger amount of capital by the
joint stock rather than by the partnership method. For,
while the capital needed for a mill in the 'seventies and
'eighties was small compared with that needed for the iron
and steel units,[1] and in the latter industry the sum would
certainly at this date have been raised by a partnership
and not joint stock, the position of the "entrepreneur" in
the two industries was entirely different. In the iron
trade the very size of the units and the interest of the
landed classes had led to a growth of family tradition in
ownership and family accumulation. The works were known
by the names of their owners for the most part. Fortunes
were made and kept. In cotton, on the other hand, the
nature of the trade led to much greater freedom of competition.
Entrepreneurs could easily step in and build a mill in a
time of high prices, realise a fortune, and then almost as
quickly lose a good part of it again. Mills were known by
the name of the area in which they were erected and only
rarely by the name of the owner. The phrase, "cotton lords",
had just as much national significance as "iron masters",
but whereas in the latter case well known names appear in

---

1) Cf. the figure of over £250,000 needed for the most up
   to date iron and steel works with £75,000 to £100,000
   for the most expensive new mill.

the lists year after year, in the former the names change
rapidly. This factor alongside the early development
of a small investing class in the cotton areas through the
creation of big urban centres with their hordes of merchants,
shopkeepers, publicans, etc., meant smaller effective
individual fortunes and a total greater spread of capital
looking for investment. The natural response of the
entrepreneurs to the larger need for capital was not to
search for a few men who could supply say £25,000 each, but
to draw in the £100's of both the merchants of the
commercial cities and the shopkeepers and foremen of the
industrial towns.(1)

The influence of the second factor, that of concerns
adopting limited liability in order to be secure in case of
failure, played a small part in cotton. For the "outside"
investor this limitation of responsibility was, of course,
important but on the entrepreneur who was already engaged
in production this factor had little influence.

The use of the limited company as the form of

---

1) We discuss the type of investor in cotton mills later.
Though contemporaries were not agreed on the extent to
which the working class invested they were all struck by
the comparative smallness of the savings that desired
investment in cotton. "As long as there is an abundance
of money awaiting investment in small sums, limited
liability cotton mills are likely to continue and
increase." ("Cotton", 1876, p.271).

organisation for a unit which was just starting production
was widespread in cotton. As we showed above, the changes
in the organisation in the cotton mills in this period led
not only to an increased demand for capital but also for
new machinery and new mills. The combination of both these
factors meant that whenever a new mill was built in order
to make use of the technological changes it was usually
built and run by a limited liability company. Almost 60%
of the "limited" mills in Oldham in the 'eighties were
"new mills and new machinery."[1]   "Turnover" companies
were few in number and neither successful nor popular.
Because of the increased capital and new organisation
required, the limited liability company was the form that
was most suited to quick economic exploitation of these
developments.[2]

The absence of the family tradition in ownership of
cotton mills meant that the number of cases where a company

---

1) "Cotton", 1877, p.431, gives 41 of the 71 limited
   liability mills in Oldham in that year as having started
   "with new mills and new machinery", and remarks that
   "turnover companies are not patronised so well by a long
   degree."
2) This is seen from the profits. "It is now generally
   admitted that the profits of companies are higher than
   those of private firms." ("Prospectus of Heywood Cotton
   Spinning Company", 1874). While this statement about
   profits did not remain true up to the 'eighties, it was
   accepted that limited companies were quicker to make use
   of the technological changes and that "private firms did
   not keep pace with the times." (1886 Royal Commission
   on the Depression, Appendix A, p.308).

was formed owing to the"retirement of the proprietor who
wished nevertheless to retain some capital in the concern"
were few.   An example was the retirement of the well known
Joshua Hoyle, whose mill was turned into the Park Street
(Heywood) Cotton Spinning Company Limited in the 'seventies,
but it was an exception.   The "turnover" companies were
usually mills bought outright by the promoter of the
company and not converted with the continuance of some of
the capital of the former proprietor.

In the cotton trade, then, the two most powerful
influences which led to the spread of the company system
were the need for more capital than could be supplied by
the ordinary Lancashire partnership and the starting up in
the trade of a large number of new concerns which adopted
the company system from birth.   The factors behind these
were the changed method of organisation leading to the
increase in the number of spindles per mill, the relative
decline in the number of workers, and consequent on these
changes the necessity for new mills and new machinery.   The
adoption of the company form by the entrepreneur in order
to lessen his risk or in order to allow him to retire with

a regular income, played little part in cotton.[1]

There are two more spheres of the development of the
company system to be considered. The first was in the
general industrial and commercial field. Under this
heading fall a host of miscellaneous manufacturing concerns,
e.g. railway wagon builders, hotels, amusements, cemeteries,
chemicals, breweries, and so on. Their very differentiation
makes it almost impossible to obtain reliable information on
their method of organisation or their adoption of the
company system, but there are one or two general trends that
can be noted.

.In the 1885 Burdett's "Official Intelligence" this
group constitute the largest group of companies listed (507)[2]

---

1) A further reason has been advanced for the spread of the
limited liability system in cotton spinning as against
its comparatively small use in manufacturing (e.g. in 1884
of 579 firms manufacturing cotton goods in Lancashire,
only 45 were limited liability companies - "Cotton
Spinners Directory"). S. J. Chapman, "Lancashire Cotton
Industry", 1905, p.44, follows Adam Smith and suggests
that less individual initiative was needed in spinning as
there was no great fluctuation in the colour or design of
the goods demanded. In manufacturing, on the other hand,
these fluctuations formed a major part of the trade,
therefore individual partnership with energetic personal
management remained supreme. But the capital factor must
not be neglected. In 1883 it was estimated that "weaving
may often be carried on with a capital of £20-£50 per
employee. In spinning the average is £250-£300 per head."
("The Co-operative Wholesale Society Annual", 1883, p.161-2)
2) See Appendix E.

and they show the smallest average capital. As this sample
would tend to include only the best known and largest of
this group, the total figures for this type of company spread
probably into thousands with a comparatively small average
capital per company. A number of these companies had been formed
to develop entirely new projects. This was particularly true
of the group which sprung up to deal with the needs raised
by railway development, railway wagon companies, hotels at
railway termini, etc.; the entrepreneurs in these cases
had few, if any, trade connections before starting the
project and took recourse to the limited company system in
order to raise the capital required. They were later
described as being "singularly successful".[1] The same
applied to projects such as housing schemes, restaurants,
public amusements and cemeteries. The last three types of
enterprise were considerably assisted in their trade by
having their capital spread over a wide field. A prospectus
of one of the amusement companies stated in 1864, "It will
hardly be disputed that there is no class of enterprise
which derives greater benefit from the application of the
Limited Liability Principle than that of public places of

---

1) J. D. Walker & -. Watson, "Investors and Shareholders'
   Guide", 1894, p.189.

entertainment, wherein the creation of a number of
shareholders having a common interest in the prosperity of
the concern is obviously equivalent to the extension of a
connection." The connection in the case of cemetery
companies was perhaps not so immediately important but was
expected to play a role in the long period.[1] With these new
concerns the lack of trade and personal connections of the
entrepreneur starting in a new field, the direct trade
which a wide shareholding would bring to the undertaking, and,
of course, the lessening of the high risk factor to the
entrepreneur of a new project, were the main reasons for the
adoption of the limited form.

The conversion of existing private concerns accounted
for a number of these miscellaneous companies. The two main
periods of this type of promotion were the early 'sixties
and the late 'seventies and 'eighties. By 1865, according
to "The Shareholder's Guardian", it had reached the
dimensions of a "mania" and the whole idea of thus employing,
what they had called a year and a half earlier "the great

---

1) Cemetery companies when offering shares to the public put
   forward as an inducement to invest the exchange of a
   number of shares for a vault or grave when necessary!

principle of limited liability", was repugnant to them. [1] This
general antagonism to small firms adopting limited liability
was very current in this period and converted companies
which were competing against private enterprise and which
had been "More familiar with the bailiffs than with the
purchasing public", [2] were regarded with great suspicion. In
the late 'seventies, however, conversion was beginning to
be accepted. Unlimited liability had been "struck a death
blow" [3] in more fields than banking by the failure of the
City of Glasgow Bank in 1878. Before the Royal Commission
on the Depression in 1886, the Registrar General of Joint
Stock Companies reported that in the five years 1879 to 1884,
"during which the practice has principally prevailed", 560
concerns were converted to the company form - 400 of which
were still in existence, showing that the bailiff element
was still present but not overwhelming. [4] Representatives of
the smaller industrial areas before the same Commission also
reported that while they considered that limited liability

---

1) "The Shareholder's Guardian", 1864, March 1st. "Limited
   Liability is therefore established as a great principle",
   p.132. The antagonism to "conversions" appears in almost
   every issue.
2) Ibid., 1864, December 14th, p.41.
3) "The Statist", 1885, Vol.XVI, p.147.
4) Royal Commission on the Depression, 1886, Qu.668.

had not had very much influence on trade (they were thinking
of new companies established in their trades), they agreed
that the companies that had been formed "were mostly
conversions".[1] While it is impossible to discover the
reasons for all these conversions, whether they were necessary
because "the results achieved and the prospects before them
now warrant an extension of their operations to an extent
beyond private means",[2] or whether they were the results of
a desire to escape the responsibilities of the "barbaric law
of partnership", there were unmistakeable signs that the
private company, which issued no shares at all to the public
at large, and which was formed purely in order to avoid risk,
was beginning to appear in this general industrial and
commercial group.[3]

The last sphere of company development that we shall
consider is its use in the financial, credit and banking
fields. The credit and financial associations of the

---

1) Ibid., e.g. Birmingham, Qu.1525 et seq.; Belfast, Qu.7027
   et seq.; and to some extent in Paper Trades, Qu.14,495.
2) From "Prospectus of Brunner Mond & Co., Ltd.," 1881.
3) It was suggested before the 1877 Committee that there
   was "a great number of companies formed that do not become
   public at all", Qu.317, and the chairman of the Institute
   of Bankers in 1884, Richard B. Martin, made a distinction
   between public and private companies, "I am speaking of
   those small private companies that do not come before the
   public." ("Journal of the Institute of Bankers", 1884,
   p.13 et seq.).

'sixties were, as we mentioned above, the direct response
and result of the desire for an outlet for savings from a
number of successful merchants, traders, and professional
men, in the big centres, who were almost completely out of
touch with industrial areas and industrialists. Their
pressure had led to limited liability, and the limited
liability company form in the credit associations was
regarded as axiomatic.   The profits were for a short time
very high and the risks all the time very great. But in
banking traditional views on responsibility had to be met
and answered before "Limited" could be added after the
names of the big joint stock banks. Their risks were
sometimes as great as those of the finance companies, but
their responsibilities were not only to the shareholders
but to the general public as well.

A partial victory was won in the Limited Liability Act
of 1858 which applied only to banking concerns, but
security for the general public was still maintained to some
degree by the regulation requiring high shares only partly
paid up. After the 1862 Act, which made the same practice of
registration apply to both banking and other companies, there
was a promotion "burst" in limited banks. "Limited Liability
in banking", it was said in 1863, "has now become the rule

and not the exception"[1], but this generalisation was true
more of the new banks that were established and of the banks
which carried on foreign business rather than of the already
established home joint stock banks. To them limited liability
was still regarded as a sign of insecurity. The failure of
the City of Glasgow Bank in 1878, however, changed all this.
The shareholders of this unlimited bank had to pay about
£2,750 on each £100 share which they held.[2] With this
example in front of them and with the assistance of the
special legislation in the following year, shareholders and
the general public now readily accepted the idea of limited
banks. Reserve liability and unpaid shares still continued,
but the basic principle of limited liability was accepted
in banking by the 'eighties. While in the new banks in the
'sixties, the need for capital had been the reason for the
adoption of the company form with limited liability, the
main factor in banking, and that which came most to the fore in
the 'eighties, was the desire to limit the responsibility
of the shareholders of existing banks.

To conclude this chapter we shall outline the extent
of the limited system in 1885, summarise the reasons for

1) H. Ayres, "Banks and Banking", 1863, p.23.
2) "Journal of the Institute of Bankers", 1908, p.498.

its development, and with the help of contemporaries attempt to analyse the character and effect of the limited companies.

From being "established as a great principle" in 1864 the limited liability joint stock company had in 1873 "become one of the great powers of the world. It furnishes every civilised community with light, with water, with food and drink of many descriptions and a thousand other articles indispensable to the wants of modern civilisation ... it touches closely the fears and hopes of millions and moderates even the·terror of death by vast insurance associations firmly grounded on the law of probabilities."[1] In the 'eighties contemporaries were even more impressed by its influence. In 1886 "The Statist" produced an article which in inspiration closely paralleled,the "Made in Germany" book of E.E. Williams in 1896. "We are cradled in limited liability cradles, nursed in limited liability milk, taught in limited liability schools. As youths we smoke limited liability cigars, ..."[2] and so on. However the exaggeration as well as the inspiration was paralleled for the actual figures of the number of companies do not give the same

1) "The Financial Register", preface, 1873 edition.
2) "The Statist", 1886, p.670.

impression of universality.   On April 30th, 1885, there
were 9,344 companies believed to be in existence in the
United Kingdom with a total paid-up capital of £494,909,862.[1]
Professor Clapham has pointed out that this number,
considering that a percentage of the companies were carrying
on their businesses abroad, and that some were very small,
compares very unfavourably with the number of textile
factories in existence in that year - 7.465 [2]   Another
comparison of the importance of the company system of
management in the economic life of the country as a whole
was given before the Committee on Partnerships in 1872.   It
was then suggested that the Bill to register partnerships
would affect between 200,000 and 300,000 such contracts.
But this figure is possibly an exaggeration, as it was given
by Edmund Potter still valiantly defending partnership
against any kind of interference.[3]   Richard Seyd in 1876
estimated that the "total number of firms in the United
Kingdom engaged in Financial, International, Wholesale and

1) "Companies 45th General Annual Report", 1936, p.14.
2) J. H. Clapham, op.cit., Vol.III, p.203.
3) "Report on the Practicability of Registration of Trade
   Partnerships," 1872, XII, Qu.663, and "Hansard", 1871,
   CCVII, p.1191.

Manufacturing Commerce, amounted to between 60,000 and 70,000."[1]
Many large, e.g. in mining, and many small, e.g. in
"mechanical and small retail trades",partnerships are
excluded from this figure. These estimates are, of course,
extremely rough, but taking c.100,000 as the number of
important partnerships in this country in 1885,we see that
limited liability companies accounted for at the most at
that date between 5% and 10% of the total number of important
business organisations (excluding one-man concerns and
public utilities).

In particular industries, however, the percentage was
much higher - the limited liability company system did not
develop evenly. "Only in a small number of our national
industries have such companies been numerous and large,"[2] but
in these industries - shipping, iron and steel, and cotton -
their influence by 1885 was considerable. We have already
shown that of a total number of 553 cotton spinning concerns
in Lancashire 156 or 28% were limited liability companies.
Of the number of concerns working blast furnaces throughout

---

1) Richard Seyd, "Record of Failures and Liquidations in
   Financial Wholesale and Manufacturing Branches, 1865-1876",
   1876, preface. An analysis of Seyd's figures of the
   number of firms engaged in wholesale and international
   trade in the City of London was given in A. Crump, op.cit.,
   p.142. This showed that of 7,873 firms with a capital of
   £199.3 mn. only 30 were limited liability companies.
2) "Journal of the Institute of Bankers", 1886, p.506.

the country 41% were limited companies. And in steam
shipping while the figures are less determinate we have seen
that at least 20% of the total tonnage was controlled by
limited companies in 1885. The real figure is probably
nearer 30% to 40%. Further, it is noticeable that
particularly in shipping and iron and steel the firms that
were limited were far and away the most important in those
trades, judged by size of unit and amount of fixed capital.

The spread of the company system in these industries
which were the "key" centres of British capitalism stands
out as the most significant event in this period, 1856 to
1885. For it was from industrialists in these trades that
the greatest opposition to the limited company had come.
Further, they had been convinced that even if the right
were granted there would be no adoption of the limited form
in "their" industries. Edmund Potter wrote in 1856 that
while he expected the limited system to gain sway in small
and marginal industries in Stoke, Leicester, Coventry and
Nottingham, "the iron and cotton trades would be the least
touched, because I think in these districts that there is
a clearer knowledge of business and a clearer insight into
the difficulties of sale."[1] But the representatives from

---

1) "A Manchester Man", "Practical Opinions", 1856, p.27.

Nottingham and Coventry and similar towns reported to the
1886 Royal Commission on the Depression that "there were no
limited companies in their district", and in the industries
apparently noted for their "clear knowledge" of business the
company system was well established. Concentration on the
possible fraud that could develop from the use of the
limited company had blinded men like Potter and John Bright
to the positive use which the company could be in recruiting
additional capital for a concern, and the necessity for
this capital had changed the sphere of company enterprise
from being concerned merely with the "accessory" industries
to capitalism, like public utilities and transport, to that of
embracing the leading concerns of the key fields of
British capitalism.

A second feature of the spread of the company system
was the amount of capital that had been brought into
industry and trade from outside the resources of the
individual entrepreneurs. The comparative isolation
between the commercial centres and the major industrial
areas which we noted in the 'fifties had been broken down
to some extent by the limited liability company. The
preparedness of merchants, traders, and professional men in
the large urban centres and of landowners in the decaying
agricultural areas to lend capital, was gradually being met

by the necessity of the industrialist to "borrow", and
assisted by the limited company and the activity of agents
like Chadwick, these two were being brought together.

It was a gradual process. The figure of nearly
£500 million paid-up capital in limited companies in 1885
does not all represent new capital brought into industry.
David Chadwick said that so far as the companies with which
he dealt ware concerned, big industrial companies, the amount
of "new blood" was only between 25% to 30%,[1] but this did not
apply to all companies. Finance, railway wagon, hotel,
mining, and similar companies were usually started "ab initio"
and it must also be remembered that new capital had been
subscribed and projects developed that were out of existence
by the 'eighties, the first date when reliable estimates of
the amount of paid-up capital in companies were made. H. A.
Shannon calculates that the rate of mortality in public
companies within five years of their formation was 35.9%
for those formed 1856 to 1865, 37.1% for 1866 to 1874, and
36.2% for 1875 to 1883.[2] These factors make any accurate
estimate of the new capital which entered industry through
the limited liability system almost impossible, but a third

1) 1877 Report, Qu.2075-6.
2) H. A. Shannon, "Economic History Review", October 1933,
   p.302.

of the 1885 total would show that, in that year at least,
there was about £150 million in industry and commerce coming
from "new" sources. It was this power of recruiting capital
from sources outside the usual partnership circles that
(1)
impressed contemporary observers of limited liability.

The extent, then, of limited liability in the economic
organisation of this country as a whole was in 1885 quite
small. But in certain industries of basic character as
high a percentage as one-third of the firms were limited
and contained in this number were some of the largest and
most important units. Also these companies had recruited
to industry a certain amount of capital from outside the
usual partnership sources.

We have discussed the reasons for the adoption of the
company system in particular industries affected at some
length above. We now wish to summarise the reasons for
the country as a whole. The most important reason was that
of the need to obtain capital on a greater scale than could
be supplied by the partnership organisation. And behind
this were the technological changes, particularly important
in some industries but also of general importance throughout

---

1) e.g. the 1886 Royal Commission on the Depression, Qu.663,
J.S. Purcell, the Registrar of Joint Stock Companies;
Qu.1678, representatives of the Birmingham Chamber of
Commerce; and Qu.3440, Thomas Vickers.

the country, leading to the need for bigger units, greater
fixed capital, and more round about methods of production.
It was the possibility of this form of industrial development
that the opposers of limited liability had overlooked. Lord
Overstone had asserted before the 1854 Commission that
"security of trade depends rather upon prudence and
discrimination than upon the positive amount of capital."[1]
By the 'eighties the position had changed. Then it was the
positive amount of capital that counted, or as the "Tyne
Coal Company" wrote in its prospectus, "the fittest means of
ensuring success in these undertakings depends on the
liberality with which capital is embarked in them."[2] No
matter how "prudent" and "discriminating" an entrepreneur
was, he could not run a fleet of steamers or control ten or
more huge blast furnaces without an appeal for capital from
outside his resources and the resources of his immediate
friends. For such an appeal to be successful, limited
liability had to be granted to the shareholders. In shipping,
iron and steel, and cotton this necessity was greatest and
these industries led the way in the adoption of the limited
company system.

---

1) Quoted in "The Bankers' Magazine", 1854, p.358.
2) From the "Prospectus of the Company".

The desire on the part of entrepreneurs to avoid
the risks of partnerships leading them to adopt limited
liability, was not of great importance in this period. It
was confined to some of the "single ship" companies, and,
particularly after 1878, to banking, mining, and a number
of "converted" private firms.

The use of the limited company to raise capital for a
new enterprise or to work out a new invention was also not
general. The 1877 Committee reported that very few
companies were established to work out new inventions,[1] but
on the other hand new companies of any considerable size,
e.g. railway wagon, hotel, mines, and new cotton spinning
companies, were finding the limited method the most
effective. On the whole it can be said that although
division of risk was now possible through the limited system
the inventors did not find it particularly easy to raise
capital for their untried projects. After the "investors"
boom in the 'sixties there was a tendency to invest
cautiously, and the more the company system spread in the
older industries the easier this became. The consequence
was that, although entirely new projects were still put
before the public, the "inventors" had to employ financial

---

1) 1877 Report, Qu.1634.

agents and promoters to boost the company, leading to the
general impression that new concerns were dangerous investments
and that a large percentage of the capital raised did not
go to the working out of the new project but to the
promoter in return for services rendered.[1]   The happy idea
of the 'fifties of an inventor floating a company by himself
and working with the capital of other "limited" adventurers
was rarely a reality.

The last factor, that of the desire on the part of
leading capitalists to retire and leave their capital safely
in the concern, was in this period only of serious
importance in the iron and steel industry. Its influence
was not very general.[2]

The major part of the development of limited liability
system in this country up to 1885 was due then, to the
increase in the amount of fixed capital needed in the
individual units of some industries and the inability of
the private partnership system to supply this additional
capital.   In the next thirty years of the development of

1) Cf. "Journal of the Society of Arts", 1866, p.23.
2) Cf. G. C. Allen, "The Industrial Development of Birmingham
   and the Black Country", 1927, p.355, "The strenuous
   individualists ... had passed away and the inevitably less
   vigorous, interested or prejudiced second generation was
   turning the private concerns into limited liability
   companies."

the company system this factor while remaining important was
considerably supplemented by a growth in the strength of the
other influences outlined. It was the increase in the
influence of these other forces that led in   part to
the great divergence in spirit and use of the limited
liability company in 1914, compared with the aims and ideals
of its founders in the 'fifties and 'sixties.

In 1885 this divergence had not progressed very far.
There was a very strong feeling, corroborated in practice,
that the limited system should be used only in cases where
the partnership form was insufficient.   A second
characteristic in keeping with the spirit of the arguments
in the 'fifties was that the company should not be formed
where there was private enterprise in the field.   The
Rt. Hon. E. P. Bouverie, when introducing the Limited
Liability Act of 1855, said that "he believed that the change
he proposed would prove the wisdom of Adam Smith's doctrine
and would show that in ordinary trading undertakings the
Joint-Stock companies could not compete with private traders." (1)
Up to the 'eighties contemporaries agreed with him in both
theory and practice. Small firms were "bitterly hostile" to
any new limited company in their field, and from R. L. Nash (2)

---

1) "Hansard", Ser.3, CXXXIX, p.328.
2) A. Crump, "A New Departure in the Domain of Political
   Economy", 1878, p.178.

to "The Bankers' Magazine", it was stated that the "great

mission of the limited company was outside the scope of
(1)
private enterprise" and any companies that dared to defy
(2)
this rule were expected "to go to the wall and perish."

There were, however, some other hopes and ideals which

the company system in its development up to 1885 had not

fulfilled. It had not brought the working class and the

capitalist together in one joint enterprise. "The Limited

Liability Act of 1862 was a scheme inaugurated for the

benefit of the working class but which has been misapplied
(3)
in many instances," wrote C. P. Brooks rather sadly in 1889.
(4)
Very few joint enterprises were established   though

---

1) "The Bankers' Magazine", 1881, p.457, and cf. R. L. Nash,
op.cit., p.102, "Where private enterprise can compete with
joint stock enterprise the former is usually the more
successful." David Chadwick, who was helping to promote
some of these very companies had to use the other part of
Adam Smith's argument about "routine". He promoted
"Laurie and Marner", a retail store, and wrote, "A
legitimate and promising field for joint stock enterprise
is furnished by trade concerns producing articles in
regular demand and not liable to spasmodic variation in
the nature or extent of their business" ("Chadwicks
Investment Circular", 1874, p.220).
2) "The Bankers' Magazine", 1860, p.411.
3) C. P. Brooks, op.cit., p.7.
4) Some were established in the early 'sixties in cotton, e.g.
"Bury Co-operative Manufacturing (Cotton Spinning)", 1860,
and "Belthorne Co-operative Manufacturing (Spinning,etc.)",
1861, and John Briggs concerns at Whitworth and Crossley's
company in the woollen trade. These were not run by a
co-operative society but genuine attempts at "limited
liability co-operation", though they were few in number and
doubtful in result. J. H. Clapham, op.cit., Vol.II, p.145,
says of the whole country that such attempts were, to
1886, "negligible".

throughout the same period the co-operative consumers and
producers societies were progressing quite steadily. Some
reasons for this failure were given at the very beginning
in the discussion in the 'fifties. The increase in the
amount of fixed capital necessary in each unit, had not made
the possibility of working men with the aid of limited
liability becoming capitalists any more real in the 'eighties.
"The Co-operative Wholesale Society Annual", in 1883,
remarked, after pointing out this position in cotton:-

> "And what is true of the cotton trade is equally
> true of all other trades where large capitals are
> required. Every new improvement in machinery
> causes a larger amount of capital per head to be
> required, and thus the possibility of actual
> workers in this and many businesses ever employing
> themselves with their own and borrowed capital
> added, becomes more difficult every day." [1]

But this was not all. A further reason was put forward in
a pamphlet published sometime in the 'seventies or 'eighties:-

> "Joint stock companies are trading corporations
> established to carry on business for the benefit
> of those who set them up, by means of any contract
> which the recognised rules of justice enforced by
> the courts of law permit. Co-operative societies
> on the other hand are trading corporations formed
> to carry on business in accordance with principles
> of justice more perfect than those now enforced by
> the courts of law." [2]

---

1) "The Co-operative Wholesale Society Annual", 1883, p.167.
2) E. V. Neale, "The Distinction between Joint-Stockism and
   Co-operation", no date, p.2.

A philosophy of life was now gradually developing among the
working classes which in addition to their lack of capital
was proving an additional reason for eschewing the happy
utopian idea of workers and capitalists together.

Besides this hope not realised,there was one fear
equally unrealised. The fear was that the limited system
would bring about the demise as a class,of the sturdy
"captain of industry" who had, in their own opinion, made
England what it was in the middle of the nineteenth century. [1]
Arthur Crump, a rather fanatical opponent of limited
liability was ready to see signs of this happening in the
'seventies. "Business in general is not so dependant on
personal exertion and immediate ability as it was in former
days." [2] In London the prevalence of the "guinea pig"
directors, who got more than their fair share of publicity,
led many people to agree with Crump. But this was certainly
not the tone of the witnesses before the 1886 Royal Commission
on the Depression in Trade. The witnesses from the northern
industries reiterated time and time again that the direction

---

1) e.g. "The Railway Banking Almanak", 1866, p.77, "The noble
   race of old English Merchants and men of business would
   become extinct under the levelling pressure of Joint
   Stock ubiquity."
2) A. Crump, "A New Departure", p.XII.

and management of the companies were usually the same as
in the former partnership.   The limited company system
had meant that the technical ownership of the concern was
in more hands but had not changed, at this date, the groups
of leading entrepreneurs.   Cotton, however, was apparently
an exception.   The witnesses at the 1886 Commission claimed
that "they (limited companies) are bringing in a class of
shareholders who are not cognisant with the trade"[1] and
"they are destroying the resident body of employers, the
middle class, and substituting for them a non-resident
corporation."[2]   While there is a certain amount of truth
in these allegations, it must be remembered that these
witnesses were private spinners and violent opponents of
the limited companies.   The struggle for existence had
tended to warp their objective judgement.   On the other
hand, in areas where the competition was not so great
witnesses, who themselves were running private concerns,
agreed that limited liability had not affected the
management of the unit.[3]

1) 1886 Royal Commission on the Depression, Qu.5506.
2) Ibid., Qu.5589.
3) e.g. Sheffield, "the management remains the same", ibid.,
   Qu.1429, and Belfast, "to a very large extent the capital
   is held by the persons who were owners of the mills at
   the time they were converted into companies", Qu.7027.

The limited liability system had by 1885 slowly spread
as an alternative to the partnership form of business
organisation in Great Britain.   While certain important
industries were considerably affected, the country as a
whole had not adopted the system to any great extent.   The
spirit of the Acts and the discussion around them, with
certain exceptions, continued in general to guide the course
of this gradual spread.   The recruitment of part of the
capital from new sources had necessitated an outward change
in the form of business organisation but had not, at this
date, affected basically either the large interest which the
leading entrepreneurs had in their units or the method of
control and direction of these units. The partnership
system had been forced to give way to the company form in
some of the key units of capitalism but the picture was only
slightly different from the picture given of industrial
organisation in the 'fifties.   The largest units were now
as then joint stock companies.   The small units were private
partnerships, and banks were assisting both with short and,
to some extent, long term loans.   A Watt had still to find
his Boulton but the intervention of Mr. Chadwick had made
the process easier and in some ways more certain.

   There were, however, some contrary tendencies to be

een. The banks were by the 'eighties no longer showing
uch a readiness to act as partners in industrial concerns.
hey were moving further and further away from the concept
f long term loans and were concentrating on an efficient
ational short term credit system. At the same time
ndustry was finding that debentures and other securities
ere as easy to raise as bank loans and more satisfactory
o the company. Secondly, although the recruitment of
dditional capital for industry had not to this date
ecessitated a very wide flung net,for the trade and distant
ersonal connections and the merchants brought in through
en like Chadwick were sufficient, there were signs of a
ifferent tactic being adopted. The high share denomination
nd its largely uncalled character so common in the first
ew years of company development, and especially in the
ndustrial companies, was disappearing in favour of the
mall paid-up share which had a much wider appeal and
ntailed less investment per investor in the company.
hirdly, in spite of the hopes that the company system would
ot compete with private enterprise there were signs of the
private" company trading directly in those fields where
rivate concerns had been supreme.   These developments were
ot important until after the 'eighties. They should,

however, be noted as small but significant trends away
from the general analysis given above.

We now go on to discuss the period from 1885 to 1914
when there was both a rapid extension of the limited system
throughout all forms of business enterprise and a definite
change in the character of the business unit and in its
direction and control.

CHAPTER III

The Development of the Limited Liability System in Industry,
1885 to 1914; the Changes in the Reasons for its Adoption;
and the Extent and Character of the System in 1914.

It has been noted above that the failure of the City of
Glasgow Bank in 1878 was regarded as the "death blow" to
unlimited liability. This date, the beginning of the
'eighties, did mark the turn of public opinion from an
attitude of doubt and even hostility towards the limited
companies to one of support and acceptance of this form, but
there were other factors besides the change in public opinion
that led to the general adoption of the system. First,
there were the four factors whose influence we have seen in
the first period and which continued to constitute the main
pressure away from the partnership form. Secondly, there
were changes within the company form itself which led, from
the point of view both of the investor and the entrepreneur,
to a greater adaptability of the company form to all types
of enterprise. These two factors, combined with the
general acceptance of the company, interacted on one another
to transform by 1914 the methods of business organisation in
this country compared with the position sixty years previously.

More important still, the character of the company itself
was changed in the last thirty years.

The course of the internal developments in the company
system, resulting in a changed character and the increased
adaptability of the company will be dealt with only in
passing.   Later chapters are devoted to a detailed study
of these questions.   Here we intend to sketch in outline the
adoption of the company system, the general changes that
took place in its form, the reasons for this spread and
change of form, and, lastly, to summarize the role of the
company system in the economic life of this country in 1914.

Some data on the adoption of the company by industrial
and commercial units in this country between 1885 and 1914
has been given by Professor Clapham in the third volume of
his "Economic History of Modern Britain".[1]   We wish to add
little to this account in terms of quantity.   We shall
concentrate on two main trends in this spread of company
organisation - the spread to large firms and units, and its
adoption in the smaller marginal concerns.

Firstly, in the large concerns the limited liability
system continued to be adopted in those industries which we

---

1) J. H. Clapham, op.cit., Vol.III, 1938, pp.201 et seq.

noted above as having by 1885 about one-third of their units in the company form, i.e. cotton spinning, iron and steel, and shipping.   In cotton it was reported in 1891 that "a deputation representing a large section of the industrial population of Lancashire and Yorkshire", which interviewed the Board of Trade in that year, "felt that all their great enterprises had passed or were passing into limited liability companies."[1]   In Oldham in 1893 the percentage of spindles owned by limited companies in that town had risen to 80% compared with the 50% of 1884,[2] and the "gold rush" in cotton, 1900 to 1907, with widespread mill building saw the triumph of the public limited company in cotton spinning.   In the iron and steel trades similar adoption of the company system was taking place.   At the 1899 annual meeting of the Associated Chambers of Commerce the delegate from Sheffield could report that "in Sheffield more than four-fifths of the whole of the industries connected with the iron, coal and steel trades were under limited liability."[3]   This is borne

---

1) "The Manchester Chamber of Commerce Monthly Record", 1891, February 27, p.36.
2) G. von Schultze-Gaevernitz, op.cit., p.68.
3) "The Chamber of Commerce Journal", 1899, April Supplement on "The Annual Meeting of the Associated Chambers of Commerce."

ouᴸ by the figures of the number of blast furnaces owned
by companies.   In 1900 of 604 blast furnaces 506 or 83%
were owned by companies.   In 1910 of 508 furnaces, 457 or
(1)
90% were owned by companies.   The figure given above for
1882 was only 44%.   In shipping comparable figures are
difficult to obtain, but the fact that between 1894 and
1913 the aggregate tonnage of vessels under 2,000 tons had
fallen by half while the aggregate tonnage of those above
2,000 tons had increased fourfold shows the growth in the
(2)
size of the vessels   and illustrates the statement that
"shipping firms had grown to a point (in 1914) at which it
was impossible for any one man to finance them out of his
(3)
own resources."   The limited liability company was the
(4)
solution adopted.

---

1) Figures for 1900 from J. H. Clapham, op.cit., Vol.III,
   p.262; figures for 1910 from "The Mineral Returns". At
   this latter date private blast furnaces existed only in
   the unimportant areas of iron-making, e.g. Derbyshire,
   South Staffordshire and Worcestershire. In the important
   areas where Clapham had noted 31 out of 383 blast furnaces
   still owned by old style partnerships in 1900, in 1910
   there were only 4 owned by this method out of 285. The
   total number of separate concerns that were in existence
   in 1910 was 109 of which 92 or 84% were limited companies.
2) Figures of tonnage from E. Crammond, op.cit., p.3.
3) A. W. Kirkaldy, op.cit., p.166.
4) This is shown in part by the remark of "Fairplay" in 1892
   that "all triple boats are limited", p.617, and in 1919
   almost 80% of the concerns in the Liverpool Steam Shipowners Association, the largest organisation of this type
   in Great Britain, were limited companies.

It was in this period, 1885 to 1914, that the coal
industry caught up with the other basic industries in the
extent of its adoption of the limited form. "Coal mining
was, compared with some other industries, quite late in
coming under the sway of the joint stock company type of
organisation"[1], due in a large part to slow increase in the
need for fixed capital compared with working capital. It
was only when the shafts became much deeper, calling for
additional pit-head machinery, that the limited company was
used. Outcrops could be worked by a partnership but they
could not work large coal fields and deep mines. Another
factor was the tendency in this later period to combine coal
mines under the ownership of one firm. Part of this
development of the combination movement was vertical; iron
and steel and shipping companies bought up coal mines and
this played some part in the spread of the joint stock
system for such vertical combinations were invariably limited
companies.

Outside the basic industries the company system spread
rapidly in manufacturing, commercial, transport and
distributive trades. Breweries are probably the most

---

1) W. H. Williams, "Capitalist Combinations in the Coal
   Industry", 1924, p.5.

conspicuous single example of the conversion of a whole
trade from the partnership form to companies in almost two
decades. The size of the companies and methods of promotion
rendered the transformation in other established trades less
noticeable but it was none the less real.[1]

The new industries that developed in this period usually
adopted the company form from the beginning as a matter of
course. This did not mean that such companies were started
"ab initio" with a straight appeal to the public and a
democratic vote on who was to direct and manage the company.
Such industries, e.g. motor cars, bicycles, and other forms
of transport, chemicals, electricity, etc., already
possessed their aspiring "captains of industry" and their
full quota of financial sharks, and the system of "purchasing"
an embryo organisation by the new company was a far more
common practice than that of raising capital publicly in
order to start an undertaking. Whether the aspiring captains
kept control of the company through possession of founders or
ordinary shares and only sold the public the pre-ordinary
voteless stock, or whether the promoter regarded his duty as
done once the company had been "sold" to the public, depended

---

1) "The Investors Monthly Manual", 1895, p.226, gave prominence
   to the spread of the company system in "warehouses and
   'stores' in 1894-1895."

on the particular circumstances of the concern. [1] However,
the role of the company system in providing capital for
entirely untried undertakings must not be altogether ignored. [2]
In the case of foreign enterprises this role was quite
marked. The important consideration here is that for some
"new" and most "semi-new" projects, the company rather than
the private partnership was regarded as the most satisfactory
method of raising the capital needed.

Another factor which led to the increase in the importance
of the company system, if not to an actual increase in the
extent of company organisation, was the development towards
amalgamation and combination. It is unnecessary here to
go into the details of this movement or to estimate its
extent or to determine its causes. This has been done

---

1) For example, some of the bicycle and tyre companies
   promoted by Hooley were bought from the owners and sold at
   almost double the price to the public. There was little
   more in it than that. On the other hand, in electricity a
   group of promoters in the British Electric Traction Company,
   e.g. E. Garcke, Lord Rathmore, Sir Charles Rivers Wilson,
   always kept control of the founders of ordinary shares in
   the electric companies that they promoted (details in "The
   Electric Trust", 1903).
2) W. H. McCrostie in "The Trust Movement in British Industry",
   1907, p.320, considers this use of the company as the most
   important. "The special sphere of joint stock company in
   the modern world has been the exploitation of new industries
   whether originating in patents or in the development of
   foreign sources of raw materials," and he goes on to give
   the examples of nitrates, tea-planting, rubber plantations,
   jarrah wood, etc.

(1)
adequately in many volumes, but its importance to the use of
the company system is that this development towards
amalgamation could only have been carried on with the
assistance of the limited liability legislation. It would
have been impossible for a few men in partnership to raise
the capital necessary in a combination such as the Salt Union,
the first British joint stock industrial combination, with its
capital of £4,000,000, or the Fine Cotton Spinners and Doublers
Association Limited with a share and loan capital of £8,000,000.
The importance of the limited liability system to the
establishment of this structure of combinations and monopolies
can be readily seen when the effects of the withdrawal of this
"right" are considered. At the present day it could be
assumed that the announcement of unlimited liability for the
shareholders in, say, Lever Brothers would not have in the
long run a catastrophic effect; there would seem to be no
alternative investment. But at the very beginnings of the
trend towards combination and monopoly the withdrawal of the
right to limited liability might well have slowed down this
development, even if it would not have stopped it altogether.

This is the first main trend of company organisation in

---

1) e.g. McCrosty, op.cit.; Carter, "Tendency towards Industrial
Combination", 1913; H. Levy, "Monopolies, Cartels and Trusts",
1927 edition; and J. Morgan Rees, "Trusts in British
Industry", 1922.

the period, 1885 to 1914 - general adoption in all large
(1)
concerns, whether old or new, and a big strengthening of the
importance of the company in the country's economic life by
its development through the use of this form of monopolies and
combinations.

The second trend is the use of the company in the small
units. We suggested above that up to 1885 the main use of
the company had been in large enterprises. Only here and there
were very small ones adopting the system. Investors were
hostile to the idea, and the general opinion was that a firm
competing with private enterprise, owing to the lack of
personal direction, was bound to fail. A rapid change took
place both in the idea of the proper sphere of the company
and in its actual practice.

By 1894 the existence of a private company was already
recognised in the Courts. The rough definition was that of
a company which did not issue shares to the general public.
The Select Committees of the House of Lords in the closing
years of the nineteenth century were very busy discussing
what was reported on all sides as the "growing practice of
private concerns to convert themselves into 'private' companies".

---

1) Of the 5,337 companies listed in Burdett in 1915, 469 of
them had capitals of £1,000,000 each.

The Act of 1907 was forced officially to recognise the
difference between these companies,which were to be called
private, and those issuing shares to the public, which were
to be called public, but this was only a legal recognition of
a growing practice for twenty years. [1] The numbers of these
companies formed had risen from an estimate of 23% to 33% of
the total number formed in 1890 and 1895 to 77% in 1914. [2] The
number of official private companies on the books of the
Registrar-General in the latter year was 48,492 compared with
14,270 public companies.

This big growth in the number of small private companies
makes any general figures of either the number of companies in
existence or their average capital unreliable as a guide to
the importance of the company system. For example, between
1885 and 1915 the average capital paid up per company fell

---

1) The actual recognition of the distinction was due in a large
part to the demand for balance sheets to be given to all
shareholders. This was considered as "unfair" to the small
private companies as the ordinary partnership firms against
which they were competing did not issue balance sheets, so
the only solution was to distinguish between the "public"
and "private" companies.
2) The Registrar General of Joint Stock Companies gave 23% of
1,588 companies formed in the first six months of 1895 as
being private or family concerns ("Report from the Select
Committee of the House of Lords to Report on the Companies
Bills", 1896, IX, Qu.1402 - known later as 1896 Report).
D. H. Macgregor in "Economic Journal", December, 1929, gives
33% as the number of private companies on the register in
1890.

from c.£59,000 in 1885 to £55,000 in 1895 and a further fall
to £41,000 in 1915.   On the other hand, the average capital
of the companies listed in Burdett's "Official Intelligence"
for those years, which were mainly public companies, showed
an increase in average paid-up capital from £209,000 in 1885
(1)
to £263,000 in 1895 and £324,000 in 1915.   These figures
show the two different trends in company organisation.   It
can be noted that this tendency towards the formation of
private companies and the tendency of the capitals of these
companies to fall were the chief factors that prevented any
attention being paid to the role of limited liability in
assisting the formation of combinations and monopolies.   It
appeared that the company system was, if anything, assisting
the "survival of the small firm" and that any attempt to
curtail its operations by such a measure as the withdrawal
of the "right" of limited liability of the shareholders would
have hit the small concern equally as hard as the large one.

The reasons for this widespread use of the company
system by 1914 are also best discussed under the two separate
heads of the factors influencing the formation of the large
companies and those influencing the formation of the small
private ones.

---

1) From figures given in Appendix E.

Under the first heading, the large companies, the need
for capital greater than could be supplied by a purely
private partnership was still the major factor both for new
companies and for concerns which wished to expand the scale
of their operations. The greater scale of production and
the more round-about methods of production that had been
developed in a few units in several industries in the period
1856 to 1885, became a general feature of most industries in
this latter period. The increase in demand had made large
scale methods economical in both the producing and distributing
trades and the increasing efficiency of labour enabled more
capital per unit of labour to be used.

In new industries, for example, electricity, chemicals,
motor cars and bicycles, the units either had of necessity
to start large scale capital expenditure from the beginning,
e.g. the plant, cables, land and buildings necessary for an
electricity unit, or the demand for the product and the
growing mechanical efficiency and accuracy rendered the
transition from small scale to large scale a very rapid
process, e.g. chemicals and new transport industries. In the
former case the capital could only be supplied by a limited
liability company from the start (or, of course, by a
municipality but in both cases the majority of the capital
must be raised by impersonal investment). In the latter

case the company stage was often preceeded by an experimental
private partnership or private company stage, but sooner or
later the wide recruiting of capital became necessary.

A second factor that was influencing the use of the
company system in the large companies was the comparative
ease with which capital could be raised and, at the same time,
the equal ease with which the control could be kept in a few
hands.   We discuss this in detail later, but this factor was
of considerable importance both in the conversion of old
companies, e.g. breweries and some iron and steel amalgamations,
and in new companies where the entrepreneur, though unable to
raise the capital sufficient for large scale production himself,
wished to keep a guiding hand on the development of his
project.   A limited liability company system made this
easier than in an extended private partnership.

The use of the limited form   by the
entrepreneur of a going concern to avoid possible loss or to
retire with "peace and honour" and a regular income, was not
of great importance in the large companies.   Many concerns
did, of course, convert themselves when they were on the
down-grade.   The persistent campaign in the investors' Press
warning all and sundry not to purchase shares in a converted
company except after careful consideration, or, as "The

Statist" put it, "don't buy a pig in a poke"[1], is evidence
that this did exist.   One must, however, be careful to
distinguish between the existence of fraud which is present
in any economic system and a general significant trend.
"Bogus" promotions were prevalent in both the small and the
large companies but the conversion of a concern in order to
avoid the risks of complete ruin through bankruptcy was more
prevalent among small than large companies.[2]   The retirement
factor still cropped up from time to time as the reason for
the conversion of a private firm, but it generally only
applied to concerns of some magnitude   where the leading
entrepreneur had a large personal interest.   These, as we
have seen above, had already been converted in some number
before 1885 and the influence of this factor in the later
period, though present, was passive and not of great
importance.[3]

The reasons for the big growth of private companies can

---

1) "The Statist", 1887, II, p.11.
2) This was the opinion of witnesses before the Committees
   held in the 'nineties, e.g. Justice Vaughan Williams,
   addendum, p.xxiii, in the "Report of the Departmental
   Committee appointed by the Board of Trade to enquire what
   Amendments are necessary in Acts relating to Joint Stock
   Companies under Acts of 1862 to 1890", LXXXVIII, 1895
   (known after as 1895 Report).
3) The 1895 Report referred to this factor of capitalists
   retiring and said, "To what extent this is done it is
   impossible to ascertain, though the number of such companies
   must be large", para.64.   They were, of course, considering
   both large and small companies.

be discussed under two heads, which are, firstly, the
reasons for the conversion of existing small firms into
private companies, these being the majority of the private
companies, and, secondly, the reasons for the formation of
entirely new private companies.

The strongest element in the conversion of firms was
the desire to avoid the dangers of the partnership law. "A
private individual has always got the fear of the
Bankruptcy Court - the Court is before him, the Poor House
is before him, his all is at stake, his character is at
stake."[1] But with a company it was altogether different.
Failure meant a brief sojourn in that now national
institution, "Winding-up", and out again with only a little
financial loss and hardly any stain on the character. In
fact in some cases there might even be a profit, if the
vendor had taken out debentures on the company. Although
it is very difficult to express this desire in economic
terms, it played an effective part in the transition to the
company form, but before this could be generally adopted
public opinion had to be convinced that a company was as
good as a private firm. Goodwill was of great importance

---

1) 1896 Report, Qu.1339.

to the small concern.   The change in public opinion started
in 1878, as we have shown above, and rapidly grew until
H. W. Jordan, partly truthfully and partly for advertisement,
could say in 1915, "Probably it would be true to say that
as a general rule more confidence is reposed in a company
                    (1)
than in a firm."

Other factors acted as an additional inducement to a
private concern to turn "limited".   The first of these was
the "superior facilities for borrowing which are open to a
           (2)
company."   Any private partnership that raised a loan had
to have it registered under the Bills of Sale Act, but not
so a company. Debentures, as we shall show later, could
be raised on all property and, through a floating charge,
on property and assets of the future. The registration was
only necessary at the headquarters of the company itself
and other creditors could be ignorant of its existence.
There were also signs of the branch bank managers showing a
greater readiness to lend to a company which they knew was
definitely worth something rather than to a partnership.
The decline of provincial and local banks, the proprietors

---

1) H. W. Jordan, "Private Companies", 1915, 3rd edition.
2) C. W. Turner, "Treatise on the Conversion of a Business
   into a Private Limited Company", 1907, p.9.

of which had known all the partners of a local concern by their Christian names, had resulted in a less hospitable attitude towards such organisations.[1]

These two advantages of a company over a partnership, namely, less risk in case of failure and greater ability to raise capital on loans, combined with the popular acceptance of the idea of the "limited" company led to large scale conversions into companies. Other transitory factors increased this number. For example, it was pointed out before the 1895 Committee on the Companies Acts that at least 200 private companies were formed by one man with his dummies signing the memorandum of association in order to "pursue the career of a druggist." In this way he escaped prosecution for being unregistered.[2] But while this type of use of the Companies Acts could be stopped, the whole principle of the right to form a company with limited liability, no matter if there was one or fifty real shareholders, could not be challenged so easily.[3]

The entirely new companies that adopted the private

1) This point is made very strongly in "The Commercial Review", 1914, p.189, in an article entitled, "The Threatened Existence of the Small Trader".
2) 1895 Report, p.157.
3) An attempt was made in the famous Salomen case by Justice Vaughan Williams but the tide against him was far too strong.

limited liability company form were promoted either to work
out a new project in which a few people were interested or
to act as subsidiaries of larger public companies. In the
first case the motive was that of limiting the risk that
attaches to a new idea,[1] in the second the motive was largely
the concealment of profits made by the larger company. The
former was, of course, directly in accordance with the
spirit of the 1862 Act, but the importance of this type of
company was small.   More and more it was the research
laboratories of the large amalgamated companies that were
working out the new schemes and new machinery for industry.
The day when a Watt had to find his Boulton had gone. In
the twentieth century he applied for a post as research
chemist or scientist with one of the big companies. The
promotion of a private company either as a shield for the
profits of a larger concern or, as in some cases, as a "kite
flyer" in a new development, had not proceeded very far
before the War.   It was in the post-War round of financial

_____

1) This type of company started with the shares held by a few
   people, then if the project was successful they would
   widen the basis of their proprietory. This is reported as
   being quite a common practice for entirely new and sometimes old concerns which adopted the company form. Cf.
   1895 Report, para.3, "It is frequent experience that a
   company is formed in the first instance by a small number
   of members – and when the business is developed and more
   capital is required it is offered to the public", and the
   1896 Report, Qu.647.

bubbles and labour troubles that it reached its zenith.[1]

One further type of private company should be mentioned: that of a large concern adopting limited liability but issuing no shares or debentures to the public, the shares all being held in a few hands. The Company Law Amendment Committee in 1906 gave several examples of this type of company, e.g. Huntley & Palmer, Crosse & Blackwell, J. & J. Colman, and in shipping there were Harland & Wolff, Alfred Booth & Company, and John Bibby & Sons. They differed from the other large private concerns that went "limited" in that whereas, for example, the brewery companies issued preference and debentures on the market to the public, these companies remained entirely private with no public issue at all. It would seem that this type of company was the height of evasion of the spirit of the limited liability Acts. The partners were the same, the capital was the same, the direction was the same, the company form merely entailed the continuance of the firm after the death of the original partners. This continuity had been effected before, though

---

1) The number of officially private companies had risen to 81,909 and the number of public had fallen to 9,109 in 1924. "Subsidiary" companies to develop new projects or to hide the profits of the "parent" company are now recognised as a normal development.

not with such large concerns, through the successions of
sons or relatives in the partnership, so why not now?
Perhaps the root of the matter lies in the changed attitude
towards business on the part of these sons and relatives.
A seat on the board of directors with the week-end free was
more attractive now than the pressure and hard work of
constant accumulation and careful watching of the firm.

The general adoption of the company system in the
period 1885 to 1914 was, in the main, the result of two factors.
Firstly, the increased large scale demand for products
combined with the technical changes in the methods of
production meant that individual units of production needed
a greater amount of fixed capital than could be supplied by
either a small group of capitalists or the banks. Secondly,
the limited liability system afforded a relatively more
secure position, in terms of possible loss, to the
entrepreneur than did the partnership.

The first factor led to the use of the company system
in large firms and units. The formation and extension of
such units was no longer dependant on the powers of
concentration and accumulation of capital by the leading
individual entrepreneurs, but by the centralisation in the
hands of a company, of the accumulations of several hundreds

of capitalists the necessary capital was readily and
comparatively easily raised.   The second factor led to the
use of the limited company in the small units.   The
dominant need in these units was not centralisation of
capital but security.   (1)   The capital of these units for
formation and extension was usually dependant to a large
degree, as before in the partnership stage, on the accumulations
of the individual "captain" assisted slightly by the greater
borrowing power of the company.   But, as a contemporary put
it, the chief advantage for these companies "was the
protection afforded by the Limited Liability Acts."   (2)   It
would appear from the use of the word "protection", that
limited liability was now more a privilege than a right, but
at the same time the widespread use of the system was
removing the exclusiveness which is the hall-mark of privilege.

---

1) It is difficult to ascertain the reasons for this use of
   the limited company in order to increase security. On the
   one hand it is urged that this tendency was "inmoral" and
   "unfair", hard on the creditors, etc. - in other words the
   adoption of limited liability by these concerns was merely
   a device. On the other hand the "joint stock system
   favours the creation of businesses carried on on a large
   scale and renders the existence of smaller establishments
   more difficult" ("Dictionary of Political Economy", 1892-6,
   p.370).   It had favoured the creation of semi-monopolies
   and made competition in these trades difficult and
   competition in those trades untouched by combines very
   over-crowded, in general increasing the risk factor -
   hence the desire for security through limited liability.
2) "Duncan on Investment and Speculation", 1894, p.50.

By 1914 then, the ability of the limited company to give both a greater power of centralisation of capital and a greater security than the partnership system had led to the triumph of the company in almost all spheres of economic life. It was accepted as a fit method of organisation for both the small and the large units, for both those industries that were subject to fluctuating and changing demand and those whose work was routine. [1] Sixty years of development had broken down the opposition of industrialists and fanatical individualists, and had convinced both the creditor and the investor that from the point of view of security the company was equal, if not superior, to the private firm. Viewing the economic life of the country as a whole, the limited liability company had become without a rival the avenue through which the savings of the community went into both the "key" and marginal industries. The banks, as contrasted with, say, Germany and Great Britain sixty years before, did not play a major part in the financing of industry.

---

1) This spread to industries with a fluctuating demand was more a question of practice rather than of theory. Alfred Marshall in his "Principles" was still faithfully repeating Adam Smith and describing joint stock companies as being "too sluggish" for this type of enterprise.

"The flow of money into business has been made more
direct. In the collection and distribution of the
surplus capital of the country the banks do not play
quite so great a part as they previously did. Some
portion of what would formerly have been deposited
with them, and by them lent out to traders now goes
direct into the hands of the companies."(1)

Although by 1914 this picture was changing slightly under

the influence of the big campaign for banks to assist more
(2)
in industry, and the increasing tendency for insurance

companies at least to purchase the pre-ordinary stock of
(3)
industrial companies.

This widespread use of the company as both the usual

means of carrying on business and the usual avenue for

savings had brought with it a change in the character of the

company. We do not wish to discuss this change here in

detail: it is inextricably bound up with the changed

attitude of investors towards the company, with the changed

type of shares, and the changed mechanism of investment.

Certain trends, however, became clear particularly in this

---

1) "Dictionary of Political Economy", op.cit., p.371.
2) The pre-War competition with Germany led to a great deal
   of attention being paid to their methods of financing
   industry, and leading economists and financiers suggested
   that a similar link-up between banks and industry would
   be advantageous in this country, e.g. H. S. Foxwell,
   "Papers on Current Finance", 1919,   and L. Joseph,
   "Industrial Finance, 1911.
3) There was in addition to the insurance companies buying
   securities a growing interlocking of directors between
   banks and insurance companies ("Journal of the Institute
   of Bankers", 1897, II, p.521).

last period, 1885 to 1914, which it is necessary to mention
before going on to deal with these other questions.

First, it became evident in this period that the new
companies that were set up did not consist of a group of
adventurers who, by combining their capitals, could start a
new profitable project. New companies were for the most
part old units converted, with the vendor supplying over half
of the capital. This is seen from the figures of the new
companies between 1885 and 1915. Between 1885 and 1890 the
public subscribed just over half of the total amount of
paid-up capital of the new companies registered in those
years, but between 1890 and 1915 with only one exception
(1905) every year saw the public subscribing less than half
the total capital considered as paid-up. In one year (1904)
the public subscribed only 25% of the £30,696,000 of capital
considered as paid-up on new companies in that year. [1] In
addition to this it must be remembered that in a number of
cases part of the monies subscribed by the public went to
the vendors in cash, in part payment for their property over
and above the payment for the property by paid-up shares.
Against this, however, debentures and loans were issued to
the public which do not appear in these figures which are

---

1) See Appendix A.

concerned only with shares.

The reasons for this high proportion of the capitals of new companies going to the vendors are twofold. First, there was the conversion of the private firm into a limited company mainly in order to make use of the additional security afforded by the limited form. As we noted above, this type of conversion was particularly prevalent in this period and accounted in part for this high proportion going to the vendors. Secondly, in the case of new "public" companies with the widening of the basis of investment it was becoming increasingly difficult to attract investors to an entirely new project. T here was far more certainty of them subscribing if part or all of the buildings or factories were in existence and it was purely a question of supplying capital to work them. The investors were not prepared as they had been previously to wait for a lengthy period while the buildings were being built before they received the profits.[1] Consequently, it became more and more the practice for a new company to take over the property either from an existing partnership or from a company which had started the construction of a unit. This tendency of

---

1) This difficulty was overcome in some industries, e.g. cotton, by the paying of interest during construction or by guaranteeing dividends.

new companies which were appealing widely to the public for
capital, to be in reality a purchase of some existing plant
is shown by the figures of such companies that were issued on
London; for the companies that were issuing on London were
definitely not the "private" type which figure largely in
the total figures of the whole country, which we gave above.
In the five years 1899 to 1903, 70% was the average amount of
capital that went to vendors in cash or shares of all new
companies which were issued on London in those years and
which were to be engaged in "home" enterprise. For the years
1904 to 1908 the average percentage was 45, and 1909 to 1913
the percentage was 40.[1] The option of cash or shares to
vendor should be noted, for in the figures given for the
country as a whole we were only considering shares to vendor;
in these companies issued on London the vendor would, if the
issue were successful, tend to exercise his option of cash,
thus making the new company in effect a purchase of an
existing concern with a certain amount of additional working
capital.

---

1) These figures are calculated from the table given in G. L.
   Ayres, "Fluctuations in New Capital Issues on the London
   Money Market, 1899 to 1913", unpublished M.Sc. (Econ.)
   thesis, 1934, p.40-41. The fall in percentage going to
   vendor can be explained in part by the power after 1907 to
   pay underwriting commission direct and not through the
   vendor.

There are two conclusions that can be drawn from these facts. Firstly, while there was a very big increase in the numbers of new companies registered, the yearly additions of paid-up capital resulting from the formation of these companies in no way represented that amount of new capital drawn into industry or that amount of capital applied to new capital construction. The adoption of limited liability as a "protection" and the changed attitude and composition of the investing classes had meant that the new company was now a secondary organisation which either purchased outright an existing business unit or was the result of the conversion by the proprietor of an existing unit. The second conclusion is that in these new companies the vendor appeared to have a controlling interest in the company. The amount of shares subscribed by the public tended to be less than those going to the vendor.

The second general trend in company organisation which became clear in this period, 1885 to 1914, was contrary to that suggested above. The existing companies in each year tended to become more and more important as the channel for the savings of the investing classes as compared with new companies in that year, and at the same time, while the actual entrepreneurs or directors in these companies became possessed, of necessity, of a smaller and smaller proportion

f the total capital of the company, the company itself
began to take on a self-perpetuating character.

It is difficult to obtain reliable figures covering
the whole country for the amounts of capital subscribed by
the public to "new" as compared with "old" companies. But
some indications of the increase in importance of "old"
companies can be gathered from the annual register of the
number of companies with their paid-up capitals, and from the
issues on the London market.

The annual returns show the number of companies in
existence and their total paid-up capital. The number of
liquidations, both voluntary and compulsory, of old companies
have, of course, to be deducted from this annual figure of
the total additions. But in the thirty years between 1885
and 1914 the annual amount of share capital added by "old"
or existing companies exceeded the amount lost through
liquidations in nineteen years - 1885 to 1886 to the extent
of £32.9 mn., 1889 to 1891 £94.7 mn., 1900 to 1908 £97.7 mn.,
1910 to 1914 £372.3 mn. [1] In the four years 1911 to 1914 the
amount added by old companies after deducting losses through
liquidations exceeded the amount added by new companies. In

---

1) These figures are taken from "The Annual Returns of
Joint Stock Companies".

addition it must be remembered that the issue of debentures which, as we shall see later, was now a favorite mode of raising capital, is not included in these figures.

These figures tend to show that after 1900 the existing companies were becoming of greater and greater importance in the capital market compared with new companies. This can be further illustrated, though not with absolute accuracy, by introducing into these figures the returns of winding up, voluntary and compulsory, which were published from 1892 onwards. The following method was used. In one year, e.g. 1895, the total amount of new capital on the register added was £83 mn. The total paid-up capital of new companies in that year was £102.9 mn. From these figures we see that for existing companies the liquidations exceeded their new issues by £19.9 mn. But the total amount of capital involved in liquidations in that year was £33.7 mn. Therefore existing companies had cancelled the balance of liquidations by raising new paid-up capital to the extent of £13.8 mn. In another year, say, 1905, the old companies not only cancelled liquidations to the extent of £50.0 mn. but added to the total amount of paid-up capital on the register £10.2 mn. This latter figure is found by subtracting the total amount of capital paid-up on new

companies in that year, £38.8, from the total amount of
additions to paid-up capital of all the companies in
existence in that year, £49.0 mn.   Using these methods we
have set out a graph in Appendix B showing the whole period
1892 to 1914.   The conclusions to be drawn are that from
1892 to 1900 the capital issues in each year by new companies
were greater than those of existing companies.   For the
period 1901 to 1914 the capital issues of existing companies
in each year were very much greater than the issues of new
companies, from 1910 onwards being almost seven times as
great.

The figures of new and old company issues on London are
strikingly in favour of old companies.   Between 1899 and
1913 there were issues totalling almost £500.0 mn. on behalf
of old and new companies for home investment (excluding
government and municipal issues).   £326.0 mn. was the
amount raised by old companies or 65%.   From the point of
view of new capital investment, of the remaining 36% which
were the issues of new companies a large percentage of this
was going to the vendor, whereas in the old companies the
amount raised was usually for new capital construction
(after allowing for underwriting expenses).   After deducting
the amount of capital going to vendor in shares or cash the

inal total of the amount of issues of new companies was
72,000,000 or 14%. (1)   These figures for London alone cannot
e considered as a picture of the country as a whole. As
e shall show later, the London market had a heavy bias in
avour of securities of existing companies and new "home"
ompanies had difficulty in finding sponsors. But since
he figures give the total amount of "old" issues each year
s compared with "new" issues with no deduction for the
osses due to liquidation, they give a clear picture of the
mount of capital demanded by old companies each year as
gainst that demanded by new companies in the chief financial
market of Great Britain.

Both these sets of figures tend to show that, in spite
of the big increase in the number of "new" companies formed
each year, the process of consolidation and amalgamation of
the "old" companies had rendered these of equal, and in the
eriod before the War of greater, importance than the "new"
nes as the source of the demand for capital from the
investing classes.

Two further tendencies in these "established" companies
ecame marked in this period. First, they tended to acquire
a momentum of their own. It was claimed by some opponents

) Figures calculated from a table given in G.L. Ayres, op.
cit., p.40.

of the limited system that the spirit of individual
initiative was disappearing from business as a result of
the extension of the limited system. But this was posing
the wrong question. It was more a matter of the company
itself now taking on these qualities of the former "captains
of industry". The company, though appearing impersonal
"with neither a soul to be saved nor a seat of honour to be
kicked", was no longer dividing all the profits made, after
allowing for depreciation, to the adventurers joined in the
company. Large accumulations of reserves were appearing.
"The Economist" gave figures of a selection of important
companies just before the War which show that in 1907 21%
and in 1914 26% of the profits made were put to reserve.[1]
F. E. Lavington asserts that the boot and shoe industry in
Kettering and Northampton was mainly financed by the
"re-investment of accumulated profits."[2] The small
association of adventurers with limited responsibility had
gone and in their place was appearing a gigantic organisation
with a staff of thousands and managers and directors whose

1) Quoted in E. Burns, "Modern Finance", 1922, p.32-33, and
   "The Economist" suggests this percentage is an understate-
   ment.
2) F. E. Lavington, "The English Capital Market", 1921, p.278.

livelihood was dependant on the continued existence of the
company. This was the quite natural outcome of large-scale
production but it is an important factor to consider when
comparing the partnership and company methods of organisation.
It is too often said that the partnership was personal and
the company impersonal: in one sense this is true but if
it is suggested that consequently there is nothing to keep
the company together the reverse seems to be the case.

The second development in these large established
companies was the smaller and smaller proportion of the
total capital of the company that was held by the directors.
We shall discuss this in detail later, here it is only
necessary to note it as the outcome of the tendency of old
companies to raise additional capital on a scale that could
not be supplied by the original shareholders or directors.

To conclude this chapter on the development of the
company system up to 1914, we see that there were two
divergent lines of development both of extent and character.
The company form was adopted in large and small units,
assisting on the one hand   amalgamations and combinations
and on the other hand, giving security to the small
competitive producer.   There was the use of the company
form to centralise the capital of thousands of capitalists

in one organisation alongside   the   use of the company
as the form of organisation for the individual capitalist
or small group of capitalists to accumulate capital on his
or their own.   Thirdly, the control and existence of the
large companies was moving from dependence around one man
or   group of men who owned the majority of the shares,to a
group who were dependant more on the continued existence of
the company than on the rate of dividends declared. Against
this the smaller companies, particularly the newer ones,
were more under the control of the vendor, as seen by his
taking over fifty per cent of the shares,than at any previous
period of company development. Lastly, the demand of the
investor for return on capital as soon as it was invested,
instead of waiting for projects to be built and developed,
tended to move the whole sphere of company enterprise away
from new fields to that of extending old concerns or
purchasing existing property.

Some of these conclusions have only been sketched in
the preceding pages; the details lacking can only be
supplied by a study of the changes in the methods of
financing companies and the changes in the attitude and
composition of the investing class and their relations with
the company. We now go on to consider these questions in
detail.

P A R T   II

THE CHANGES IN THE FINANCIAL ORGANISATION
OF LIMITED LIABILITY COMPANIES BETWEEN
1856 and 1914 ;   THE CHANGES IN THE
DENOMINATION AND CHARACTER OF THE SHARES,
AND THE USE OF PREFERENCE, FOUNDERS, AND
DEBENTURE   ISSUES.

CHAPTER IV

The changes in the denomination and character of the
shares of limited liability companies 1856-1914.

The share denomination of a limited liability
company and the character of the share (whether fully
paid or not), form a useful guide to the general attitude
towards, and the spirit of, company organisation.   The
denomination of the shares is, as it were, the shop
window that the company presents to the intending investor;
it will vary according to the type of investor who is
available in the investment market, and according to the
type of investor that the company desires as its shareholders.   The amount paid up will vary similarly according
to the amount of capital needed in the early stages of
forming the company, the uses to which the uncalled
capital can be put, and the degree of interest in the
management that it is desired or hoped that the shareholders will take.

The decade of the 'eighties again can be taken
as a dividing line between two different developments
in the denomination and character of the share.   The
period, 1856 to 1885, as we have seen above, was
significant for the spread of the company form in financial
and speculative concerns, mining and hotels, and in the
'seventies it was adopted to a certain extent in the

asic industries, i.e. cotton, iron and steel, and
shipping.   This diversity of development, which was
accompanied as we shall see later by a diversity in the
type of investor, is reflected in the changes in share
denomination.

The second period, from 1885 to 1914, saw the
general and all-embracing spread of the limited liability
company as a form of business organisation in both large
and small, monopolistic and marginal enterprises.   Over
the same period the investors were moulded into a more
and more homogeneous whole, not from the aspect of
equalincomes and equal investments, but in their
attitude towards the company.   (1)   The share denomination
and character of the share in this period tended likewise to a general uniformity;   similarity in different
industries and companies rather than diversity.

This is the outline of the development.   We intend
to treat both periods in detail, to analyse the exceptions
as well as the major trends, and to attempt to draw some
conclusions from the change in share denomination as to

---

1)   We discuss the changed attitude of the investor
     towards the company in detail in a later chapter.

the development of the company form, the types of investor,
and the relation of the investor to the company.

Between 1856 and 1885 the general average of share
denominations was high when measured with modern standards,
but throughout the period it tends to fall, though unevenly,
to the 'eighties when the "new departure"[1] of the £1 share
fully paid, starts it's run of popularity.

Between the 1856 Act and the "great winding up" in
1866 there were violent fluctuations between company and
company in share denomination, and the general average
reveals a slight rise.   Over 60% of a selection of
3,720 companies registered between these dates and
believed still to be in operation in 1865, had shares
to the value of £10 and over.   Three hundred and eight
of the companies had shares of £100 and over.   The
tendency to rise after the 1862 Act is seen from an
analysis of these figures.

Of 2,040 companies formed between 1856 and 1863
inclusive, just over 50% had shares of £10 and over.
Of the 1,680 formed in 1864 and 1865 alone, over

---

1) "Burdett's Official Intelligence", Vol. 1, 1882, Preface.

(1)
70% were £10 and over.   The "coming to town" of
companies from the provinces, the formation of finance
companies and banks, and the conversion of some very
wealthy iron and steel works were probably the causes
of this increase.

But this general average does not sufficiently
present the fluctuations.   There were more than thirty
companies formed with share denominations of £1,000 and
over, the chief types being iron and coal (ten), land
development (seven) and cotton (three).   The three
largest were the Powell Duffryn Steam Coal Colliery Company (1864)
and the Majorca (1863) and Almenera (1864-1865) Land
Companies, each with shares of £5,000.   At the other
extreme Irish companies were fairly frequent with shares
of 10/- and the Irish Liberator Newspaper Company (1862)
had shares of 5/-.   (2)

This tendency to an increase was reversed by the
financial panic of 1866.   The companies still in
existence with high shares attempted at first by private

---

1) See appendix C for full details. This sample of 3,720
    companies is over fifty percent of the total number
    registered.
2) Examples from the Limited Liability Joint Stock Companies
               List, 1864-1866.

legislation and then by the general Act of 1867 to reduce
their share denomination.(1)   New companies being formed
learned from the difficulties of the earlier ones.   But
the average share denomination did not sink spectacularly.
The witnesses giving evidence before the 1867 Committee in
favour of share reduction, regarded a £10 share as the
lowest denomination that an ordinary company would wish
to use. (2)   Throughout the 'seventies this formed the
general average around which the shares of different
industrial and commercial types of company fluctuated.

The success of the cotton companies and the "single
ship" companies in raising capital easily with shares of
£5 and £1 in the late 'seventies and 'eighties encouraged
a reduction in other spheres.   In 1882 Skinner could
write in the introduction to his Year Book, "It is the

_____

1) Loftus Fitz-wygram, "Limited Liability made Practical.
   Reduction of Capital of Companies and the Subdivision
   of Shares", 1867, p.10, refers to several companies preparing
   private Bills to obtain special sanction for a reduction in
   shares, though the House of Lords, led by Lord Redesdale
   refused every case.   Under the Act itself, however, only
   seventy-one companies had reduced their capital by 1877
   ("Report of select Committee on the Companies Acts of 1862
   and1867" VIII. 1877 Qu. 30 - later referred to as the 1877
   Report), but the general pressure for a reduction is seen
   in the "Report of Select Committee on Limited Liability
   Acts, X" 1867,(later known as 1867 Report) and in actual
   liquidations of companies which reformed under slightly
   different names with reduced share denominations.   This
   whole question links closely with that of uncalled capital
   on shares which will be dealt with later.
2) 1867 Report, e.g. Newmarch's draft Bill for reduction of
   capital "not a less amount than £10", p.32, and cf.
   Fitz-Wygram, op.cit., p.16.

feature of the present financial period that fully-paid
shares chiefly of £1 are quite the vogue." [1]   In the next
decade the triumph of the £1 share was complete.

   The character of the share - whether fully
paid up or not - shows a parallel course of development.
Uncalled shares were a major characteristic of the finance
of companies in the period 1856 to 1866. Of 1,252 companies
formed between 1856 and 1865 and beleived to be still in
existence at the latter date, 43% had unpaid shares in
one degree or another. The unpaid portions were not
generally the result of calling up the capital slowly,e.g.
as in the extreme case of the Airedale Building and
Manufacturing Company Limited in Yorkshire where the shares
were £210-0 each on which one shilling was called monthly.
The companies usually had no intention of calling up the
other portions, and it was a common announcement in the
Prospectus, " It is not intended to call up more than 25 L
per share (100 L)" [2], or "It is not anticipated that more
than 10 L per share will be required (on a 20 L share)" [3].
After the crisis of 1866 when companies were forced against
their anticipations and intentions to call up the unpaid
portions of shares,causing,according to contemporaries,

---

(1) W.R.Skinner "Stock Exchange Year Book and Directory",1882
  preface.
(2) Prospectus of the "London and Colonial Bank Limited",1865.
(3) Prospectus of the "East Rosedale Iron Company Limited",1866.

great hardship and distrust of limited companies, this
method fell into disfavour.   When calls of £30 and £40
per share were made in some cases[1] there was a general
cry that this " limited liability was unlimited in fact".[2]
This, along with the smaller share denomination, tended to
lessen the proportion of unpaid shares in the 'seventies,
but again the transition was not sweeping.   Certain types
of companies found it convenient or necessary to continue
with high share denominations and a very small proportion
paid up.   In 1885 of the 1,585 companies given in Burdett's
official intelligence in that year, 60% of the issued capital
was paid up, leaving the average amount unpaid on each share
at 40%.[3]

But this is only the average trend in the denomination
and character of the share; there were wide differences
between individual industries.

Apart from the companies that were formed as small
co-operative concerns usually for small scale manufacture,
local retail trading or workmen's clubs, the largest group
of companies with a very low share denomination and fully
paid up were those engaged in mining.   Between 1856 and

---

1) Loftus Fitz-Wygram, op.cit., p.8.
2) W. Bartlett & H. Chapman, "A Handy Book for Investors", 1869.
3) See Appendix E.

1865, 408 (135 abortive) companies were formed to carry on mining at home and abroad.[1] The majority of these had shares of £5 and under; a large number of the gold mining companies favoured the £1 share. These were usually fully paid up within six months of the company's formation.

Cotton companies developed a special type of share. In the first period of cotton company formation, 1860 to 1865, there were roughly two types of denomination. Some were very high, e.g. J. H. Bates (Albert Cotton Mills) Company Ltd., 1864-1865, with shares of £1,000 each, the Minorca Spinning Company of Rochdale, 1862, with shares of £350 fully paid, and Oldham Cotton Spinning Company, 1860, with shares of £150 each fully paid. At the other extreme there were co-operative spinning companies, e.g. Bury Co-operative Manufacturing Company (Spinning), 1860, with £5 shares fully paid, and Belthorne Co-operative Manufacturing Company (Spinning), 1861, with £1 shares fully paid. In the next burst of cotton company formation, 1870 to 1875, the "Oldham Limiteds" era, a type of share was established which was adopted by most cotton companies

1) H. A. Shannon, " Economic History" , Jan. 1932, p.396 ff.

up to 1914; a share of £5 with £1 to £3 paid up. Of 71
cotton spinning companies in Oldham and district working in
1883, 80% had share denominations of £5, and only 13 were
fully paid.[1] Of the 355 cotton spinning, manufacturing and
doubling companies registered in the United Kingdom between
1873 and 1882, 58% had shares of £5.[2] The companies not
adopting this denomination, e.g. 39 companies had shares of
£100 and over, were usually manufacturing companies or
companies formed to carry on both spinning and manufacturing.

The shipping industry shows interesting contrasts in
share denomination. As shown above, there were three chief
periods of shipping company formation, 1863 to 1866, 1871
to 1872, and 1879 to 1882. The average share denomination
tended downwards from £50 in the 'sixties to £10 in the
'eighties, but there are two divergent lines running through
each period. Companies that were formed to take over old
private lines, or to amalgamate lines, tended to have a
high share denomination. The shares were slightly smaller
than those under the 64ths arrangements,[3] but they were

1) From the list given in "Co-Operative Wholesale Society
Annual", 1884, Manchester, p.176.
2) Ibid., list on p.204.
3) We estimated above that the average value of a 64th share
was between £75 and £100.

likewise not easily negotiable and were usually bought to
hold.   The other type of company that was attempting to
develop new lines, cargo boats, or new inventions, had a
much smaller denomination.   In their prospectuses they
attacked the high share and 64ths system as keeping investors
out of shipping.   The British Ship Owners Company Limited
in 1864 points out that their shares of £20 each will "not
yield a good return as investment, but will possess the
very important advantage of being readily convertible." [1]
This appears again in the prospectus of the Nautilus Steam
Shipping Company Ltd. in 1881.   "The value of a single
sixty-fourth share of a steamer of medium size amounts to
such a sum as to practically exclude entirely the investor
with a moderate amount of capital at his command." [2]

The conversion of successful shipbuilding and
engineering works, which is a feature of this period was
invariably accompanied by shares of a high denomination.
To take a few well-known names, Earle's Shipbuilding Works,
1871, Humber Iron works and Ship Building Company, 1864,
London Engineering and Iron-Ship Building Company, 1864,
Tyne Iron Ship Building Company, 1864, and the London and

1) Prospectus of company.
2)   "   "   "   "

Glasgow Engineering and Iron Ship Building Company, had
shares of £50 each.   The shares of these companies and of
both types of ship-owning companies usually had a high
percentage paid-up.   The boom in shipping in the 'eighties
saw £10 shares very common, though some of the established
lines that were converted into "private" limited companies
had large shares.   The " single ship" companies, tramps
and cargo boats, were, for the most part, formed with small
shares, £1 to £5 shares fully paid up.[1] In 1885 the 52
shipping companies given in Burdett in that year had 82%
of their issued capital paid up.   This was a higher
percentage than any other industry.[2]

   The iron, steel and coal companies started in the
'sixties with the highest average share denomination of any
group of companies, being between £50 and £100.   The high
shares of £100 and upwards were rarely more than 50% paid
up, and from these companies came the greatest pressure in
1867 for power to reduce the nominal value of the shares.[3]
After the experiences of the first decade the next period
of formation of companies of this type, 1870 to 1875, showed

---

1) 1886 Royal Commission on the Depression Qu. 10,791.
2) See Appendix D.
3) 1867 Report, cf. Evidence of Chadwick, auditor and agent
   to this type of company, q u. 838-950.

a smaller nominal capital and a smaller share denomination.
The usual shares were between £10 and £50, of which 2/3rds
was called up sooner or later as the company required the
capital. The formations in the 'eighties followed the same
course, but it was noticeable, in contrast to other types
of company, that the £1 fully paid up share was practically
non-existent in iron, steel and coal companies down to 1885.
The average percentage paid up in 102 iron and coal companies
given in Burdett in 1885 was 77%,[1] which was a contrast to
the position in the early 'sixties, but this still shows a
good proportion uncalled and so the transition to fully
paid up shares must not be ante-dated.

Banking, investment, finance, land and insurance
companies can be taken as a group, for the characteristics
of their shares denominations were determined by the same
underlying factors. The Bank Act of 1844 allowed Joint
Stock Banks to be established on the condition that their
shares were of at least £100 each with £50 paid up. The
1858 Act giving limited liability to banks also contained
this regulation as to the denomination and character of
shares. Though this was withdrawn through the 1862 Act,
the tradition of high unpaid shares remained for banking

---

1) See Appendix D.

and followed by other financial companies.   Of the 58
banking companies given in the 1875 Stock Exchange Year
Book and Directory only seven had fully paid up shares,
and of those unpaid only in one case was more than half of
the share called up.[1]   Financial Credit Associations and
Land Companies were particularly conspicuous for their high
nominal capitals and high unpaid shares.   And it was
stated at the 1867 Committee "nothing was more common for
insurance companies ... with shares of 100 L and only 5 L
or 10 L called up."[2]   In the 'eighties the nominal share
values were lower in these companies but the gap between the
nominal and paid up portions remained.   In 1885 in banking
and insurance of 144 and 87 companies respectively, only
24.6 % and 21.8 % of the issued capital was called up.
In the finance and land companies, however, the formations
in the early 'eighties had brought their average percentage
paid up capital up to 61% for 226 companies.   Both the
figures are of the companies given in Burdett for that
year.[3]

Why was there this general downward tendency in share
denominations, why were there such variations, and what

1) W. R. Skinner, " Stock Exchange Year Book and Directory" ,
   1875.
2) Report of 1867 Committee, Qu. 1305.
3) See Appendix D.

light do they throw on the spirit of the business organisation
and on the investor in the companies?

In the first twenty-five years of company formation in
this country after the 1856 Act, the denomination of the
share was of the utmost importance to the company.
"Probably no point ought to be more anxiously weighed than
the nominal amount of the shares into which the capital of
the company is to be divided."[1] It has been suggested that
the high denomination and uncalled character of the shares in
the 'sixties was an accident, that " limited liability was
not understood"[2], but evidence seems to show that the
variations in the shares were just as much a part of the
process of attracting capital to the company from a group
of given investors as were the variations in the type of
share (founders, preference, etc.), which were used after
the share denomination had fallen to the general level of
£1 fully paid.

First the tradition of partnership practice and the
experience of railway and canal companies and other joint
stock organisations had an important effect on the shares
of limited liability companies. The difference between a

1) Loftus Fitz-Wygram, op.cit., p.7.
2) Cf. Wm. Hawes, "Journal of the Society of Arts", Vol.XV.,
   November 30, 1866, p.23, and 1867 Report Qu.1008.
   W. Newmarch..."the public did not really understand what
   the operation of limited liability was".

partnership and a limited liability company in this period
to a large section of investors was not that less was invested
in a company, but that in event of failure liability was
limited to the amount paid up and the uncalled portions.
"The last shilling and the last acre" did not disappear in
the bankruptcy court.   The early joint stock organisations,
though they had a wider basis than a partnership, were
established on similar lines and with similar ideas as to
what constituted an investment.   To take one example, the
Liverpool and Philadelphia Steam Ship Company in 1850 had
"shares of £9,000 each and more."[1]   Canals, banks and
railways were a closer approach to the conception of an
impersonal company, but as noted above, it was laid down by
law that bank shares should not be less than £100 each and
the shares of canal and railway companies were rarely less
than £25 each.   The effect of this tradition is seen in the
1855 Act which prohibited shares with a denomination smaller
than £10.   This was repealed in the 1856 Act but the idea
remained.   As late as 1888 Lord Bramwell, an ardent advocate
of limited liability, said in a lecture, "I can never understand
the meaning of the £1 share ... why not £10."[2]

---

1) Example given in E. W. Field, op.cit., p.91.
2) "Journal of the Institute of Bankers", 1888, Vol. IX.,
   p.382.

A second important "tradition" affecting the denomination and character of the share, was the fear of speculation.
This had constantly been raised in the discussions around
limited liability and the companies using the limited form
were on guard against this criticism.   The best method, it
was thought, was high shares and uncalled reserve.   "The
unpaid portion of the shares constituting a continuous
guarantee fund beyond the control of Directors and Managers ...
practically establishes a security of the _highest_ order."[1]
"The security of the uncalled capital ... one of the chief
arguments in favour of limited liability."[2] In the
pamphlets, articles, and evidence given before commissions
on limited liability, high shares with a fair proportion
uncalled were accepted by friend and foe alike as a natural
consequence of the principle being adopted.   John Brooke,
representing the Huddersfield Chamber of Commerce, which
was opposed to limited liability, expressed this feeling
when he said, "if you limit the responsibility of joint
stock companies ... then make it three times the amount which
is paid up."[3] William Hawes, another opponent, says

1) "Law of Limited Liability and its Application to Joint
   Stock Banking Advocated", 1863, p.11.
2) "Journal of the Royal Society of Arts", loc.cit., p.52.
3) "Report of the Commission on Mercantile Law", 1854, p.159.

"a fixed proportion of capital should not be called up except in very special circumstances."[1]

In 1867 the legalists tended to confirm the early expectations that small shares would lead to speculation and rashness.   Justice Romilly noted that

> "the smaller the amount of the shares the less 'bona fide' is the company; that is the experience we have in the Court.   There are very few of the companies which are wound up which have 100 L shares; the companies which are wound up have 10 L and 5 L shares and the like."[2]

The Master of the Rolls agreed with this and said, "there is more fraud in the small than in the large companies."[3] Their experiences and beliefs supported the theory that the smaller the shares,the less responsible the body of shareholders.

These hopes and traditions were the background of the high denomination but the type of investor and the necessities of the companies were the immediate factors influencing its introduction and subsequent decline.

The typical shareholder of the early joint stock companies was wealthy, tended to confine his investments to two or three companies and was interested to a certain

1) William Hawes, op.cit., 1854, p.41. He had changed his views in 1866, cf. " Journal of the Royal Society of Arts", loc.cit.,
2) 1867 Report, Qu. 1388.
3) Ibid., Qu. 1556.

degree in the running of these companies.   This applied
particularly to the shareholders in industrial concerns.
Limited liability was expected to encourage such investors.
"Under the measure of limited liability we shall secure a
better class of shareholder, not less practically sure will
be the continuous election of the best men for Directors."[1]
Other types of investors were not readily available, they
were an uncertain element, whereas the wealthy type was
known in the locality or by brokers and financial agents in
London.   "When the Act first came into operation it was
usual to divide the capital of the new limited liability
companies into shares of large amounts, for the reason
principally that when they were placed in good hands the
capital was more easily raised."[2] It was suggested that
the desire to raise capital easily was partly speculative.
"The object of these large 100 L shares when they were first
brought forward was partly a very bad one; it was much easier
to get 5,000 shares of 100 L each subscribed for, and run
up to a premium when a company was brought out than it was
to get 50,000 shares of 10 L each subscribed for."[3]
But this criticism did not apply to industrial companies

---

1) "The Law of Limited Liability", op.cit., p.11 and cf.
   the "Bankers' Magazine" 1864, p.350. "The Limited
   Liability Act encouraged the wealthy shareholder."
2) Loftus Fitz-Wygram, op.cit., p.7.
3) 1867 Report, Qu. 1139.

which rarely applied for a Stock Exchange quotation.   For
them large shares meant stability.

> "A company comes and consults a counsel as to what
> shall be the value of the shares, and the answer
> invariably is 'if you want to have a large stable
> company, make your shares very large' ... there is
> not a shadow of doubt that a company with 10 share-
> holders of 1,000 L each is a much more stable company
> than a company with any number of shareholders with
> 1 L each."(1)

One reason for the high shares and the resulting
stability of the company was the interest the shareholders
took in the company.   The pamphlets and journals advising
people on investments did not expect them to be "interested
in more than two or three companies."(2) Local subscriptions
meant that those investing knew something about the nature
of the business carried on by the company.   The shares of
lower denomination tended away from this and were subjected
to criticism on this ground.

> "In undertakings such as the Great Ship Company,
> which come out in £1 shares is it not commercially
> absurd to intrust such a vast professional structure
> to the fostering care of petty tradesmen who know
> nothing of the technicalities of shipbuilding and
> shipowning trade, instead of seeking at least £100
> shareholders."(3)

The very existence of a large uncalled portion on each share

1) Ibid., Qu. 3043.
2) Cf. "The Investors and Stock Exchange Magazine," No. 1,
   January, 1863, p.2.
3) "Journal of the Royal Society of Arts", loc. cit., p.84.

was a direct incentive to interest in the activities of the
company. If there was any doubt about the honest running
of the concern, or the promises of the prospectus not being
fulfilled, the shareholders attempted to use legal methods
to absolve them of the necessity of paying up the ramainder
of their shares. Further difficulty of transferring shares
on which there was uncalled liability tended to keep the
composition of the shareholders stable and to interest them
in the concern.

The shares, however, were not all of a very high value.
The wealthy investor deeply interested in one or two concerns
was the most conspicuous person in the market, but there
were other sections of investors. The middle classes,
professional and trading, who were interested in the regular
dividends and marketability, and the section interested
mainly in speculation. William Hawes discussing the
advantages of limited liability points this out.

> "The more wealthy can unite to conduct large monetary
> and commercial undertakings, the shares in which may
> be of a high denomination; the middle classes including
> the members of all professions can unite in manufacturing
> and trading industries to their mutual benefit."[1]

The shares for this type of investor were lower and their
uncalled liability was less, though there was a good deal of

1) "Journal of the Royal Society of Arts", loc.cit., p.24.

opposition to small shares. "I suppose the lower you go
in the denomination of shares, the more ignorant people you
are likely to catch?"[1] This was the view of the Chairman
of the 1867 Committee.

In spite of all the talk of the importance of the
working class in the discussions around the introduction of
limited liability, they were almost forgotten as constituting
a section of the investing public once the Bill had been
passed. As shown above, one or two groups of working class
people got together to form a limited company with very small
share denominations, but the instances were few and there
was little co-operation between the rich investors and the
poor ones. The rich formed their companies with shares
of £100 and above, the working class with 10/- shares; the
soil between them remained "virgin of friendship". The
only possible sphere of industry where they could have joined
hands was in speculative mining where the shares were always
low, but investments in these companies would hardly have
improved the relations between capital and labour.

"The Shareholders Guardian" recognised that the working
classes could not invest in these companies with high shares,

1) 1867 Report, Qu. 786.

> "... let the idea of working men as ordinary share-
> holders be dismissed at Utopian" and the only alternative
> they could suggest was a vague scheme, - "Yet it seems
> to us that the plan of issuing preferential or debenture
> stock with fixed interest, or at all events without
> liability, in sums small enough to meet the case might
> be very easily manipulated."[1]

A very jaded picture compared to the idyllic England that
ought to have been brought about.

With the spread of limited liability in the 'seventies
and 'eighties, and with the increase in effectiveness of the
methods used to reach the investor, the share denomination
tended to fall. The wealthy investor did not disappear,
but there was a gradual change in his attitude towards
investment. The middle classes were convinced of the
possibilities of investment in limited companies and were
attracted into the investment market. The process was slow
and it was only half accomplished by the 'eighties but its
effects were becoming visible.

The panic of 1866, although it affected, so far as
bankruptcy was concerned, the small speculative and large
financial companies rather than industrial concerns, had
some far reaching effects on the wealthy investors.
William Newmarch before the Committee of 1867 gives some
impression of the insecurity they felt when they discovered

---

1) "The Shareholders Guardian", March 1st, 1865, pp.231-232.

that uncalled shares could be called up rapidly and even if
they were not called they were absolutely unrealisable.
"I should think that at this moment there is between 20
and 30 millions of actually paid up money which is more or
less in a state of suspended animation in consequence of
the unmarketable character of the shares."[1] Henry Pochin,
a merchant of Manchester and sometime Mayor of Salford
who had made his money by private trade and was now an
extensive investor in, and director of, many huge cotton and
iron and steel firms, described the difficulties with which
the investor was faced. "The shares of many companies are
incapable of being negotiated in any form ... the bankers
won't look at them as security for advances ... and investors
were forced to keep money lying in the bank at low rates of
interest against future calls."[2] After this experience
the wealthy investor tended towards a wider dispersion of
holdings, with smaller denominations and more paid up.

Witnesses before the 1867 Committee supported this
trend towards smaller shares in the blessed name of "security".
"The smaller the share the larger then becomes the basis of
the company. The creditor has a much better security with

1) 1867 Report, Qu. 528.
2) 1867 Report, Qus. 2298, 2301, 2311.

10 men holding 100 L. each than one man holding 1,000 L."[1],
and "I had much rather have five men at 10 L. a piece than
one man at 50 L."[2]

It was further suggested that a high share "far from
making the company fall into the hands of rich shareholders,
it tends to its falling into the hands of those who have
nothing to lose."[3] The traditional basis of security had,
it appeared, turned into a basis of insecurity.   Low shares
(but not lower than £10) would prevent a repetition of 1866.

The middle class investor was coming into the market
but he was afraid of high shares and uncalled liability.
David Chadwick spoke for a large number of them when he wrote
in 1870, "We are too much alive to our own interests to place
our trusts in Consols alone,"[4] but the essence of their
experience in Consols was marketability and no further
liabilities.   Shares "payable to bearer" had been discussed
in the 1867 Committee and their importance to the middle
class investor is seen from the welcome given to the idea by
a Bristol investment review.   The leading article claimed
that "Cautious people have avoided investment because of the

---

1) Ibid., Qu. 539.
2) Ibid., Qu. 995.
3) Ibid., Qu. 681.
4) "Chadwicks Investment Circular", issued monthly by
   Chadwicks Adamson & Collier & Co., 1871, p.30.

heavy unpaid liability ... payable to bearer shares would
remove this ... and would be a new and practically sound
innovation in our present system."[1] The article went on
to support such shares with an argument which was the exact
opposite of one put forward earlier in the 'sixties in
favour of high unpaid shares, namely, that it would make
the company more careful and less speculative. Before, the
argument ran - unpaid shares make the shareholders keep a
careful watch on the Directors. The new argument is -
"if there is no possibility of further squeezing the shareholders Directors would be more careful."[2] It is an
interesting reflection on the muddled and confused state of
economic analysis that every step and innovation in the
commercial world had to be introduced under the slogan of
"security."

We have reviewed two factors affecting the high share
denomination in the early period of company formation, and
have traced the changes in these factors which tended to
induce a smaller share and a greater proportion paid up.
Traditional security weakened and was attacked on its own
ground: the wealthy investor began to prefer a spread of

1) "Bowyers Investment Review", Bristol, April 7th, 1869,
   p.159. One of the first investors' papers in existence
   outside of London.
2) Ibid., p.159.

investments rather than concentration leading to smaller
shares and this trend was supported by the increase in the
number of middle class investors who were unwilling to invest
in the old type of shares.[1] There are two more influences
to be considered; the importance of uncalled shares in
obtaining credit for the company and the varying capital
needs of different industries adopting the company form.
These two factors accounted for the slow and uneven trend
towards the smaller shares.

Uncalled shares were used as a method of obtaining
additional capital or credit for the company in two ways.
The first was by issuing successive amounts of shares with
less and less paid up on each.   The second was by raising
loans and sometimes debentures on the security of the unpaid
portions.

The first method was fairly popular in the early decades
of company formation.   In 1864 "The Shareholders Guardian"
writes, "The pernicious practice has grown up whenever
additional working capital is required, of not making calls
on the existing shares but of issuing new ones and of requiring
a small payment to be made on them."[2] Wagon companies,

---

1) Loftus Fitz-Wygram op.cit., p.14.   "high shares tended to
   keep out the middle classes".
2) "The Shareholders Guardian", August 1st, 1864, p.300.

which were conspicuous during the first twenty-five years of
company development in discovering new ways of raising
capital, were in the forefront.   The North Central Wagon
Company Limited (1861), and the British Wagon Company Limited
(1869), each had by 1875 four different issues of Ordinary
shares with less paid up on each successive issue.   The
Yorkshire Wagon Company Limited (1863) in 1868 had three
issues:-

> A. shares of £10 each with £10 paid up.
> B. shares of £10 each with £5 paid up.
> C. shares of £10 each with £1 paid up.

A more common method was two different issues of Ordinary
shares with less paid up on the second.   This was quite
common in iron and steel companies.

The second method, raising loans and debentures on
the unpaid portions, was a very important development.
In the first period of company formation uncalled shares
were a direct security for the creditors of the company.
"Creditors are in clover",[1] was a remark that could be applied
widely to limited liability companies in the 'sixties.
However, security to creditors was only necessary if the
company had creditors, and a differentiation grew up and was

---

1) Wm. Hawes, "Journal of the Royal Society of Arts",
   loc.cit., p.24.

reflected in the shares according to the amount of credit the company needed. "Certainly where they do not require a large amount of credit ... they usually have small shares ... whereas large shares are very attractive to the creditor."[1] Ten years later when "you find now that nearly the whole amount of the shares has to be paid up within a reasonable time,"[2] David Chadwick pointed out that because of this need for credit, companies should still continue with unpaid shares. "In the case of a trading company I think it is very prudent and very proper to have from 25-33 or 40% uncalled out of the subscribed capital, without that they cannot stand in the market with proper credit."[3]

The next step in this development was the apparently harmless one of raising capital by loan or debenture rather than call on the shareholder.[4] "May I ask you what advantage it would be to a limited company to issue debentures? Simply that it prevents the shareholders being called upon for calls."[5] The Bolcow Vaughan Iron and Steel Company announced in their Sixth Annual Report, "It is intended by

1) 1867 Report, Qus. 2046-2047.
2) 1877 Report, Qu. 1252.
3) Ibid., Qu. 1953.
4) The method used by cotton companies of raising loans was peculiar to that industry alone. It will be dealt with separately.
5) 1867 Report, Qu. 1235.

the company to receive loans and debentures in preference
to making calls for the prosecution of additional works."[1]

But alongside of and out of this development grew up
the system of raising loans and debentures specifically on
the unpaid portions of shares, a system contrary to the spirit
of the 1862 Act.[2]

The position in 1867 for companies other than Land
companies was doubtful.   "... It is a question whether
unpaid calls can be made a security for debentures."[3]
But in 1870 the Bristol Wagon Company had apparently done
this successfully.   At the shareholders' meeting, the
Directors suggested the issue of preference shares.
A shareholder raised the alternative "of a further call on
the present shareholders as the amount of the shares was
not paid up ... the Chairman, Mr. Weston, replied that as
the amount of their shares yet unpaid was security for the
debentures they had raised, a call could not be made without
being applied to the reduction of the money they had borrowed."[4]

1) Reported in "Chadwick's Investment Circular", March 11th,
   1871, p.53.
2) This principle had however been recognized in the Mortgage
   Debenture Act of 1865.   This Act which gave the right to
   certain companies to issue transferable mortgage debentures
   laid it down that the company must have shares of a nominal
   value of not less than 50 L of which not less than one-tenth
   and not more than one-half must be paid up.   The regulation
   for the unpaid portion was definitely considering that this
   50% unpaid should be the security of the debenture holders.
3) 1867 Report, Qu. 1244.
4) Reported in "Bowyers Investment Review", June 29th, 1870,
   p.203.

The legal position remained somewhat unclear but the practice
was quietly and steadily adopted in the 'seventies and
'eighties.

An article in the "Law Quarterly Journal" by E. Manson
in 1895 expressed regret at the degree to which this
development had broken away from the spirit of the 1862
Act.

> "When the privilege of limited liability was conceded,
> it was conceded on the terms that the subscribed capital
> should be inviolable ... It was to be irreducible.
> That was the price of the privilege - the creditors'
> security. No doubt the Companies Act 1862
> contemplated a limited amount of borrowing. The
> Register of Mortgages shows that it did. But not a
> mortgage on its uncalled capital."[1]

Instead of the ordinary creditor knowing he was certain of
the issued capital as security, now he could only be certain
of the called up portion. And even this, with developments
in debentures that will be discussed below, became less and
less certain. The Parliamentary enquiries of the
'nineties became, as a result of these developments, a battle
ground between the needs of the companies to obtain capital
and the rights of the creditors. The company won, perhaps
due to their method of splitting the creditors into different
isolated groups.

---

1) "Law Quarterly Journal", 1895, No. XLII, p.187.

The last factor affecting the denomination and character
of the shares was the type of industry or trade the
company was pursuing. An analysis has been made above of
the chief share characteristics of the five major types of
enterprise carried on under the Companies Acts in this
period. We shall deal with each group in turn and show
the conditions peculiar to that group which contributed,alongisde   the other three factors,to determine the
nature of the shares.

The traditions influencing mining companies came
from two sources. In home mining, lead, tin, copper,
slate and some coal mines, the cost book system and private
partnerships with transferable and quoted shares had been
the usual system of organisation.[1] Shares in cost book
companies were held locally usually by landlords, smelters,
and, in some areas, quarrymen, and were usually of low
denomination.[2] Shares in partnerships were often "divided ...
in halves, quarters, eights, sixteenths, thirty-seconds
and sixty-fourths."[3] In foreign mining the Australian
and Californian speculations of 1851 and 1852 laid the

1) A. H. Dodd, op.cit., p.309.
2) The largest share in cost book mines given in the "Joint
   Stock Directory", 1866-1869, was £10-11-0.
3) J. H. Clapham, op.cit., Vol. I, p.434.

basis of a strong tradition of small capitals and £1
shares.

The limited liability mining companies of the 'sixties
and onwards followed these traditions. They were supplemented by the type of investor. He was either the small
local man in Wales or Devon and Cornwall taking shares in
a mine he knew well, or the speculative type who would
risk a certain amount but not too much. As the English
and Welsh mines were exhausted, so the steadier type of
investor disappeared and mines both at home and abroad
were regarded as frankly speculative. This influenced
the character of the share. The promoters of the
companies were concerned with having the capital paid up
immediately, they did not envisage a lengthy existence
with calls on capital as required.

A third feature was the smallness of the capital
employed. Of the twenty-eight mining companies given in
the "Joint Stock Directory" for 1866 with shares of £1
each, the largest capital was £150,000 and the average was
between £20,000 and £30,000. A small share was, up to
the 'eighties, always the bedfellow of a small capital.

The distinctive development in the cotton industry
towards £5 shares, only partly paid up, needs special

consideration.   The rise of co-operative ventures in
Lancashire in the 'forties, 'fifties and 'sixties naturally
had some influence on the limited companies set up in cotton
spinning.   Very prominent in speeches made by the few
Lancashire men supporting limited liability was the
argument that this co-operation would be enhanced and
extended if the Act were passed.   In this, more than any other
industry the idea of these new companies uniting capital
and labour was discussed and thought possible.

Second in importance to this general spirit of co-
operation was the type of investor available.   In Oldham
in the 'seventies there were three main groups.   First,
the machine makers, e.g. Platts and Leeks who were always
ready to help a new mill provided the machinery was
purchased from them, and around this group were the
engineers and architects of the mill.[1] The second group
of investors were those who either were in the cotton
business or formed the comparatively well-to-do section
who catered for the needs of the cotton operatives, "small
shopkeepers, publicans ... lodge keepers, overlookers ..."[2]

---

1) "It is a well known fact that the successful competitors
   for executing the work required in a new mill are those
   who will subscribe for the greatest number of shares",
   J.C.A., op.cit., p.9, and "R. C. on the Depression",
   1886, Qu. 5276.
2) "R.C. on the Depression", 1886, Qu. 5134.

The third group came from outside   Oldham itself,
merchants and brokers of Manchester and to a small extent
Liverpool, and in the case of some mills from all over
the country.[1]

The operatives themselves did not invest in shares
to any great extent. Andrew Samuel, described by
Schultze-Gaevernitz in 1893 as the "best authority on the
English cotton industry hereto",[2] wrote in 1887, "the
number of shares in Oldham limited companies by real working
men is infinitesimal."[3] He goes on to remark on the
failure of the Acts to link capital and labour.   "It had
been thought that the limited liability companies of
Oldham had done something towards destroying this old
emnity (between capital and labour), I earnestly confess
that I do not think that they have."[4] Another observer
reported to the 1886 Commission on the Depression, "As
a matter of fact the working people have availed themselves
of the opportunity (to invest) to a very limited extent."[5]

Even those who still vaguely hoped that the working
class were investing and sharing in the profits, were quite

1) Ibid., Qus. 5507-5508, and pamphlet by J.C.A., op.cit., p.8.
2) Schultze-Gaivernitz, G. von, op.cit., p.30.
3) Samuel Andrew, op.cit., p.10.
4) Ibid.,
5) "R. C. on the Depression", 1886, Qu. 5042.

emphatic that the operatives were not investing in the
mills in which they worked.   "The Co-Operative Wholesale
Society Annual", which still half-heartedly believed in
a limited liability Utopia, wrote in 1883, "In fact it is
well known to a few that a very small proportion indeed of
the male cotton operatives ever hold shares in the company
employing them."[1] A careful study of the holdings in the
five public cotton companies in Burnley revealed the same
fact.   Joshua Rawlinson reported that in these mills there
were only seven shareholders working in the mills in which
they held shares.[2]

Five shilling, ten shilling and one pound shares were
not necessary or possible for most of the cotton mills.
The size of the capital required and the type of investor
available ruled this out.   The five pound share, partly
paid, was the medium suited to the artisan class, the
Manchester merchants, and the machine makers.

The share was unpaid, partly as a measure of security
and partly because a quicker way of raising capital had
been discovered in loan capital.

Loan capital was subscribed in all kinds of amounts.

---

1) "The Co-Operative Wholesale Society Annual, 1883, p.167.
2) "R. C. on the Depression", 1886, Qu.5805.

The mill tended to become in some cases a savings bank
giving 5% for all and sundry inside Oldham and out.
Workpeople, shareholders, merchants and even trade unions
are said to have subscribed to the loan capital of the
mills.   "So great was the drain from every source into
the 'limited' system that savings banks began to experience
an empty chequer ... so that one savings bank ceased to
exist."[1] The transition from savings banks to holding
loan capital in mills was also noted   by Mr. C. P.
Brooks in 1889.   "In future trade will become ... a bank,
with a small rate of interest in which the wealth of the
smaller Lancashire capitalists will be locked up."[2]
Mr. J. Mawdsley of the Association of Cotton Operatives
before the 1886 Commission doubted the extent to which
operatives subscribed even loan capital.   "Operatives'
savings are usually in savings banks and cottage property."[3]
But most writers agreed that loan capital was easier to
raise than shares, as a wider field of investors was
covered, and that there was "no dearth of loan capital."[4]
     A second factor that led to the widespread use of

---

1) "Cotton", Journal of the Cotton Trade, Vol. 1, 1877, p.430.
2) C. P. Brooks, op.cit., 1889, p.9.
3) "R. C. on the Depression", 1886, Qu. 5136.

loan capital alongside share capital was its effect on the
dividends.   It tended to increase these considerably in
times of prosperity.   "There is no denying that loan
capital has been an important factor in the making of
dividends."[1] If 20% profit were made on the capital
of £100,000, of which £50,000 was loan capital at 5%, the
direct benefit to the shareholder of such a financial
structure is obvious.   Mills declaring $32\frac{1}{2}$% dividend as
did the Sun Mill in 1871[2] through the existence of large
loan capital were an encouragement to others.   The instability of loans and the drag of increased interest
charges in a period of depression were not thought of in
the boom period.   But in the depression of 1877 to 1879
attempts were made to cut down this loan structure.
Calls were made, and mortgages established to pay off the
loans, but the next boom in the 'eighties saw a return to
the old system.   As one contemporary said, "10% on shares
and 5% on loans proved irresistible."[3]

The uncalled share capital acted to a certain extent
as the security against which loans were raised, as also
did the property of the company, but the loans legally

1) "Cotton", ibid., p.430.
2) T. Ellison, "The Cotton Trade of Great Britain", 1886,
p.134.
3) Statement by Mr. Simpson, "R. C. on the Depression",
1886, p.379.

were not secured against anything.   They were payable
at call and dependant purely on the company's promise to
pay.   The figures for 90 mills in and around Oldham
given by Mr. J. M. Kidger before the Royal Commission on
the Depression in 1886 show that only 20% of the loan
capital specifically was mortgaged:

> Share capital (paid up) £3,455,676
> Uncalled capital £2,807,859
> Loan capital £3,435,427

This latter figure includes the £710,000 raised in 35
companies on mortgage.   From these figures, the security
for the loan holders would appear to be partly, the unpaid
shares and partly the property erected with the paid up
capital.

To sum up, then, the position in the cotton industry;
the shares of the limited liability companies in Oldham,
the chief centre of this development, were of a
comparatively low denomination because the middle class,
merchants, and upper working class formed a big section of
the investors in those areas.   They were not fully called
up because once the shares were allotted, loan capital
was an easier and more profitable method of raising capital.
Only in times of difficulty when loan capital was "expensive",
e.g. 7 or 8 per cent., was it necessary to raise capital

by calling in the unpaid calls.[1]

The major reason for the high and uncalled shares of the financial companies, banks, investment, insurance, etc., was the need of this type of company, more than any other, for good credit and high standing in the eyes of the public and in the opinions of their creditors.[2] They had little or no tangible security to which the public or creditors could look, in the shape of land, machinery or factories, so the security took the form of large nominal capitals and uncalled shares. Further to make this uncalled capital absolutely safe, the shares were high, as it was still maintained that high shares appealed to wealthy investors.

With the changes in the types of investor and the spirit of investment, the shares of these companies began to be issued in smaller units. Bank shares in the 'eighties were often at £10 and £25 each and some insurance shares were as low as £1, but the uncalled character was maintained. The insurance companies with £1 shares would only have five

1) "The Co-Operative Wholesale Society Annual", 1883, p.166.
2) Some of these companies had raised debentures under the Mortgage Debenture Act of 1865 which as pointed out above required shares of £50 or over with 50% unpaid. However this clause was repealed in 1872 and the shares of finance and land companies tended to be more fully paid up by the 'eighties.

to ten shillings called up, and the Bank Act of 1879
established a reserve liability on bank shares.

In the bank and insurance companies the unpaid share
played the role of keeping up the credit of the organisation.
In the trust, loan and investment companies, the unpaid
portion of the shares was used directly as a means of
obtaining loans. Mr. G. A. Jamieson in a paper read
before the British Association in September 1887 referred
to "a certain class of company, the main purpose of whose
existence is to borrow on the faith of their uncalled
capital and to employ the money so borrowed in trade or
in making loans in the Colonies and elsewhere."[1] This
latter use of the unpaid shares fell into disfavour later
and was superceded by the issue of debentures, but in the
former case, banks and insurance companies, as we shall
see later, continued with unpaid shares in the twentieth
century.

In the shipping industry the habit of investment had
been developed to some extent before the introduction of
limited liability. The high risk factor had tended to
a dispersion of ownership through the 64ths system. This
prepared the way for the shipping companies to react

1) Reported in "The Accountant", 1888, p.405.

quickly to the changes in the type of investor willing to
invest in the industry.   As early as 1864 the British
Ship Owners Company Limited can say in their prospectus,
"Shipping has always been a favourable investment in this
country, notwithstanding the difficulties necessarily
incident to the present system of ownership."   In the
'sixties and 'seventies the investing public appealed to
were merchants and ship brokers in the large sea-ports;
the fairly high shares corresponding to this class were
typical of the industry.   The increase in the cost of
ships through technical changes and the building up of
fleets or "lines" also tended to keep shares high.
Between 50% and 75% was usually paid up, the remainder
being kept as reserve against liabilities through accidents.
With the improvement in underwriting and insurance this
reserve became less necessary.

The smaller lines or companies with just one ship
had already in the 'sixties found a wider public than the
capitalists in the ports, with their smaller shares.   The
"single ships" of the 'eighties appealed very successfully
to these investors.   From working seamen to servant girls,
all are said to have been attracted by the £1 shares fully

paid of this type of company.[1] The bigger lines, mainly
passenger, tended to remain at the "sixty-fourths" stage
of semi-private companies with a few wealthy shareholders,
but the cargo and tramp companies, increasing as the
Empire and world trade grew, with small paid up shares
became investments for the general public.

The iron, steel and coal industries had, as shown
above, a different tradition from the shipping industry
in the middle of the nineteenth century.   Private fortunes
of iron masters or coal owners were more conspicuous than
any development such as the 64ths system towards
co-partnership and investment.   The prospectuses of the
iron and coal companies in contrast to those of shipping
start off, "... all the collieries being in the hands of
wealthy capitalists"[2] or "a trade which has hitherto been
within the reach of large capitalists only".[3] But although
these prospectuses go on to hold out hopes of the smaller
capitalists now being able to invest in these companies,
in fact the biggest and most important iron, steel and coal

1) "R. C. on the Depression", 1886, Qu. 11,217, "... the
   fact is notorious that even servant girls and small
   greengrocers all round the country have been induced
   to put their small savings into tonnage."
2) Prospectus of the Aberdare Colliery Company Limited (1861).
3) Prospectus of the East Rosedale Iron Company Limited,
   (1866).

companies that were formed, appealed only to this same rich
capitalist who had made or inherited a fortune from private
furnaces or mines.   Nearly all the companies were
conversions and the basis was widened to some extent, but
not very much.   The Ebbw Vale Coal and Iron Company with
a capital (nominal) of £4,000,000 had only about 500
shareholders in 1875 and this number was much greater than
in most of these companies.   Vickers Sons & Company,
for example, at the same date with £500,000 capital had
only twenty-five shareholders.   With this type of shareholder and this capitalisation naturally the shares were
high.

In 1870 to 1875 the profits that were being made in
these industries attracted investors.   New companies were
established with lower shares to cater for them.   But the
general features of investment in these companies remained,
that is, long term investment rather than easy marketability.
The shares remained comparatively high until the turn of
the century.

The other feature about the shares of these companies,
that of a large proportion uncalled, was partly due in the
early period of company formation to mistakes of valuation
when the company was established.   Very great pressure

came from the directors of these companies in the 1867
committee for power to reduce the nominal value of the
shares so that they corresponded more with their paid up
value.   David Chadwick said that in the case of companies
like Bolcow Vaughan, Palmer's Shipbuilding, Ebbw Vale,
the company had to be registered with nominal capital and
share denomination before the final report of the valuers
was available.   It was found that the valuation was less
than the nominal capital, consequently the shares were
largely unpaid.[1]

But in the 'seventies some of the smaller companies
deliberately refused to call up all their capital in order
to be able to borrow on the security of the unpaid portions.
In the case of a company like Bolcow Vaughan, which
according to Chadwick did not need credit in 1867,[2]
additional capital was not difficult to raise, but smaller
companies which worked only a part of a process were not
in this fortunate position.   Various kinds of devices were
used to obtain the additional capital and credit and the
security of uncalled capital was a very useful basis for
loans of debentures.

1) 1867 Report, Qu. 857.
2) Ibid., Qu. 862.

By the decade of the 'eighties, then, the changes in
the denomination of the shares and in the character of the
shares had already begun to cause a breach between the
ideas of the promoters of limited liability and the actual
course taken. The Chairman of the Institute of Bankers
referred in 1884 to the disappointment of the originators
of limited liability because they hoped that "limited
liability would be adopted with shares of some hundreds
or thousands of pounds each instead of in shares of a
shilling or a pound, not for the purpose of creating capital
for speculative purposes but to enable persons to put their
money into well established businesses in considerable
sums without being involved in unlimited liability."[1]
The thousands compared with the shillings is rather
exaggerated, but the main point is sound.

The reasons for this disappointment, the lowering of
share denominations and the increase in the proportion
paid up, were firstly the increasing desire of the investors
for greater security through the spread of investments and
removing the "unlimited liability in fact" by paying up
more per share, and secondly the introduction into the
investment market of a new type of investor who was interested

1) "Journal of the Institute of Bankers", Vol. V, 1884, p.13.

almost solely in dividends and security of capital. In
order to attract these investors the denomination and
character of the shares were changed. But the change
was not speedy, the use which high uncalled shares could
be in encouraging creditors, in raising loans, or in
securing the wealthy type of investor prevented a rapid
transition to small paid up shares. In the 'eighties
in most trades and industries the £100 share had gone,
but the £1 share was not yet prevalent; the high proportion
unpaid had gone but the average was still about 25% of
issued capital uncalled.[1] In banking and insurance only
a quarter of each share was paid up. For a new company
the denomination and character of the shares to be issued
were still important matters to be considered; but they
had lost some of their key importance of the 'sixties.[2]
Other factors were appearing which were removing from the
share the function of differentiating between different
types of investors: uniformity in share denomination was
appearing on the one hand, and at the same time

---

1) See Appendix D - for proportion uncalled in other than
   banking and insurance.
2) e.g. A. Packer, "How the Public are Plundered", 1878,
   p.18, was still referring to the use of different
   denominations of shares to attract "the monied" and
   "the industrial classes", £20 to £50 for the former,
   £1 for the latter.

differentiation in the types of share, preference or
founders, and in the use of loans and debentures, on the
other.

In the second main period, from 1885 to 1914, the
share denominations of companies pursuing different types
of enterprise tended to become settled around a common
figure.   As variation was the feature of the first period,
1856 to 1885, so similarity was the feature of the second.
The small fully paid share had first been introduced to
companies other than speculative mining in the beginning
of the 'eighties.   Burdett had written in his 1882
"Official Intelligence" of "this new departure",[1]
referring to £1 shares.   By 1889 the "Law Quarterly
Journal" could say "Shares are now rarely more than £10
and are frequently paid up within a few months of allotment."[2]
By 1914 low shares fully paid up were typical of new and
old industries alike.   In 1915 of 5,337 companies given in
Burdett that year, 88% of the capital issued was paid up.
If banking and insurance companies are excepted, the percent-
age would be nearer 96%.[3]

In the iron, steel and coal industries advantage was

---

1) "Burdett's Official Intelligence" 1882, Preface.
2) "Law Quarterly Journal", No. XVII Jan. 1889, article by
   E. Manson.
3) See Appendix D.

taken of the 1867 Act in the 'nineties and the first decade of the twentieth century, to subdivide their shares. An interesting illustration of this is the Powell Duffryn Steam Coal Colliery Company (1864). In 1864 it issued shares of £5,000 each fully paid. Its next issue of ordinary was in 1877 with shares of £1,250 each fully paid. In 1882 it divided both sets of Ordinary into shares of £25 each fully paid. And in 1907 these shares were further subdivided into shares of £1 each fully paid. Other examples of subdivision of shares of £50 to £100 into shares of £1 are Vickers in 1897, John Brown's in 1899, Armstrong Whitworth's in 1900, Bolcow Vaughan in 1900, and Stavely Coal and Iron in 1907.

New companies or amalgamations in these industries were generally formed with £1 or £5 shares. For example Dorman Long's £1, Bell Brothers £5 in 1899, Guest Keen and Nettlefold's £1 in 1900, William Beardmore's and Baldwin's £1 in 1902, and Cammell Laird £5 in 1903.

The shipping industry did not show such a complete adoption of the low share. By the turn of the century 'single ship" companies were no longer being formed in quite large numbers and the bigger lines were still to some extent in private hands. The new companies had shares of

£10 rather than any lower figure.   Subdivision of larger
shares took place as in the iron and steel companies but
the division was rarely into units of less than £10 each.[1]

New industries and old ones adopting the company form,
generally for the first time reflect this tendency.   Of
104 electricity companies listed in the "Stock Exchange
Official Intelligence" for the year 1910, 101 had shares
that were fully paid up.   None of the shares were over
£10 each and 82 of the companies had shares of £5 and under.
The ordinary shares of brewery companies are not such a
valid example as they were very frequently held privately
and not offered to the public.   A selection of 110 companies
in 1910 shows that 107 of these had fully paid up shares.
Six companies had shares of £100 fully paid up but these
were all held privately.   The usual denomination of shares
that were offered to the public was £10.

There were four exceptions to this general tendency of
low shares fully paid up.   Private companies often had
very high shares in the hands of very few people.   The

---

1) For example, in 190⁰ the amalgamation of the "Union"
and "Castle" lines to form the "Union Castle Mail
Steamship Company Limited" subdivided the £20 shares of
the "Union" company into two £10 shares of the new
company.   Also in 190⁰ the Clan Line divided its £50
shares into five £10 shares.

"one man" private company on the other hand had small
shares, and six "dummies" were rarely down on the share
register for more than a £1 share each.

The banking and insurance companies form the second
exception. Only 26.2% of the issued capital of 80 banking
companies and 32.3% of the capital of 102 insurance companies
was paid up in 1915.[1] In 1894 it was remarked, "A
feature peculiar to companies of this class ... is that of
calling up an installment only of say, one-fifth part of
a share."[2] The necessity for this reserve has been discussed
above; the change in the type of investor brought a smaller
share denomination but did not affect the importance of
the uncalled capital.

In industry, the cotton companies were a noticeable
exception. The cotton boom of 1900 to 1907 did not show
any great change from the practice adopted in the "Oldham
Limited's" boom of the 'seventies, that of £5 shares only
partly paid up.

The speculative mining companies constituted the fourth
exception. As in the 'sixties when this group had been the
first to use the £1 fully paid share, so in the later

---

1) See Appendix D.
2) J. D. Walker and Watson, op.cit., p.137.

period when other companies were adopting this denomination,
mining concerns went still lower. The South African
Mining and the Klondyke booms saw shares of five shillings
fully paid up. These companies wanted capital quickly
from a large number of speculative investors. With the
improvement of advertising and other means of reaching the
investor, the lower the share, within limits, the easier was
this done. The rubber boom of 1910 went even lower.
Two shilling shares became a popular denomination.[1]
But there was no fundamental reason for stopping at two
shillings. With the education of a wider public into the
mysteries of investment through the War Loan issues, the
post-war speculative companies introduced the one shilling
and the one shilling deferred share.[2.]

In discussing the causes of the high shares used by
companies in the period 1856 to 1885 we dealt with four
factors. Two of these, namely the tradition in business
organisation and the type of investor, had undergone changes
before the 'eighties which led to a tendency to use smaller
shares. These changes continued in the period 1885 to
1914. The other two factors that gave rise to the uneven

---

1) Rubber commpanies had very small capitals, usually
   developing one estate only. Two shilling shares
   permitted mixed investments in several companies.
2) Cf. Colin Brook, "Theory and Practice of Finance", 1934,
   p.247.

character of the evolution of the share denomination,
namely, the uses to which the uncalled shares could be
put and the differing needs of different industries,
became less important in the period 1885 to 1914 as the
extent of the company system was enormously increased and
alternate methods were developed of raising additional
capital for industry.

The "tradition" that low shares with no additional
liability would lead to insecurity and fraud was still
voiced in the 'eighties and 'nineties. In 1883, "Jaycee"
remarked, "The £1 share is very popular nowadays especially
in companies whose motives are not the purest because it
attracts the savings of the poor investor."[1] In 1893
A. J. Wilson attacked small shares and wrote "... shares
of this class, whether in mining companies or not, have
lately been a more general source of loss to the moneyed
classes than those in companies whose shares are for
larger amounts and perhaps saddled with further uncalled
liabilities."[2] "The Statist" on the other hand was
horrified at the danger and insecurity of uncalled capital.

---

1) "Jaycee", "Public Companies from the Cradle to the
   Grave", 1883, p.18.
2) A. J. Wilson, "Practical Hints to Small Investors",
   1893, p.14.

"No bankrupt railway, no exploded mining company has ever
caused a tenth part of suffering which invariably attends
the liquidation of a bank or any large institution which
has traded on the credit of its uncalled capital."[1]
Both these types of argument, however, tended to view
matters from the winding-up angle; they did not discuss
which type of share was best suited to a going concern.
The force behind these "security" doctrines weakened
considerably when faced with the factors of the demand for
capital and the sources of supply.

We have discussed above the beginnings of the change
of attitude of the wealthy investor towards investment.
The change became marked in this second period.   He
discovered other ways of satisfying his desires for power,
income, or excitement, than by investing heavily in one
or two concerns.   The multiplication of companies meant
multiplication of directorates, and a man of wealth and
reputation had no difficulty in obtaining a seat on the
board of a company and at the same time was not expected
to invest extensively in the company.   Directors share
qualifications tended to fall.   If he wanted income, then
distribution of investments was a sounder basis for this

1) "The Statist", Vol. XVI, 1885, p.147.

than concentration and a prerequisite of distribution was marketability of shares. If he wanted excitement, the stock exchange was steadily growing in importance, and in speculation, small subdivisions with no liabilities were absolutely necessary.[1]

To strengthen these tendencies the new class of investor whose emergence we had noted in the first period was increasing in numbers and importance. He was the middle class and rentier type who was interested chiefly in security and income. He was urged by myriads of circulars and investment journals to make "no permanent investment",[2] never to invest unless the shares were fully paid up and quoted or easily saleable. He was not expected to be interested in the company in which he invested but rather to spread his investments over twenty companies in

---

1) In addition it should be mentioned that other avenues of investment were now available for the wealthy investor desiring a regular income that were not present in the 'sixties. Preference and debenture issues were now used by this investor and ordinary shares were regarded as slightly speculative. Mr. Boulter expressed this common attitude towards ordinary shares in 1897 before the House of Lords Select Committee. "There is the ordinary shareholder who says 'I will put a small amount into the company in the hope of getting a high return'". "Report of the House of Lords Select Committee to Report on Companies Bill" X, 1892, Qu. 824. (later referred to as 1897 Report). This "small amount" made a small share fully paid imperative.
2) e.g. "Duncan on Investment and Speculation", 1894.

ten different countries. The small share was the only
one that would appeal to this type of investor.

The importance of unpaid capital as a source of raising
additional capital remained in some industries. The
banking and insurance group and the cotton companies have
been mentioned above as still using this method up to 1914,
but for most of the other industries the development of
preference and debenture issued provided them with an easier
method of raising further capital.[1] This method also
enabled them to differentiate between types of investor
in the market as the different share denominations had
done in the first period. The varying needs of different
types of industry were met. by these "new" issues of
preference shares and debentures. The problem of
overcapitalisation that confronted the converted iron and
steel companies of the 'sixties did not disappear. But
there was no longer any necessity to rely on "calls" for
additional capital as it was needed. The mechanism of the
investment market had so far been perfected that, except

1) We discuss debenture and preference issues later, but
it should be noted that sometimes their very existence
in a company meant the continuance of unpaid shares,
e.g. 1897 Report, "often the case that a certain quantity
of ordinary shares is kept uncalled in order to attract
debenture holders", Qu. 200.

in periods of intense depression, capital was always available in one form or another. The problem for the company had changed from that of deciding "which is the best possible share denomination to use at this particular time to which is the best and 'cheapest' type of share or loan to issue."

In the 'sixties the industries that required capital had found /the safest and easiest way to raise it was by placing the shares in a "few good hands", with variations from industry to industry as /the amount paid up and as to the purposes to which the unpaid reserve was put. By the twentieth century both the amount of capital required and the investors had changed. Then it was most suitable to issue small shares with additional preference and debenture issues to cover all the types of investor in the market and to raise the capital quickly.

CHAPTER V.

The Development of the Preference and
Founders Shares : the Extent and Reasons
for their use, 1856-1914.

I. PREFERENCE SHARES.

When the Companies Acts of 1855, 1856, and 1862
were passed the framers of the legislation were under
the influence of the ideas associated with the
partnership form of business organisation.   The Acts
were in effect, as has been pointed out above, nothing
more in content than giving legal permission and form
to a contract between various partners in an undertaking
which laid down that, in case of bankruptcy the partners
were liable only to the extent of their investment.   In
spite of /the influence of the big joint stock associations,
which had at that time permission by special Act of
Parliament to limit likewise the responsibility of the
shareholders, their experiences and examples appeared to
play little part in guiding the legislation of Companies
Acts.   A case in point was the use of the preference share.
By the 1850's the use of this particular device was in
great favour in Railway companies .   J.S. Jeans suggests
that it was only the use of this instrument that made

possible the increase in mileage in English railways in
the period 1850-1858.[1]   And a Parliamentary return
published in 1858 shows that nearly a quarter of the total
share capital of £225,805,058 of the railway companies in the
United Kingdom was raised by preference shares.[2]   But
there was not a word about preference shares either in
the Companies Acts or in the innumerable books, pamphlets
or journals which were discussing the application of the
very same principle that obtained in railways, to general
trading, commercial and manufacturing concerns.

The reason for this omission was not solely the
spirit of laisser faire. The opponents of the Bill would
have used any argument if it occurred to them, and the
suggestion that limited liability would lead to a widespread use of the preference share, that is investing
money in a concern but with very little control over the
methods of spending the money, would have been an effective
and well-used weapon in the hands of the opposers of the
Bill. But neither they nor the supporters thought that
such a development would occur. Both were agreed in
considering the experience of railways, canals, water and
gas companies as something entirely apart from ordinary
commercial practice and history. The methods of raising

1)   J.S. Jeans, "Railway Problems", 1887, p.22.
2)   "Return giving share capital of railways and
        canal companies for year 1857", 1857-8, Ll.

capital for commerce and industry up to the 'fifties
were through the partners' investments and through loans,
short term, though sometimes long, from the banks or
individuals.[1]   It was assumed that these two methods
would continue to be the only two, although through the
Act the number of partners and the attractiveness of
investment would increase.

We will deal later with the changes that took place
in the loan capital coming into industry; the development
from short term loans to perpetual debenture stock, and
from being used for temporary measures or variable capital
to becoming part and parcel of the fixed capital of the
company.   These changes were, however, comparatively
logical compared with the development of the preference
share.   The briefest of glances at railway company finance
would have shown the legislators on limited liability that
there was in existence a class of investor who was interested
almost solely in the regular return on his capital and not
in the conduct of the particular company in which he had
invested, yet they assumed, so far as ordinary trading
and industrial organisations were concerned, that the
investor would be of the adventurous type who desired the
interest and sport of a fluctuating return and wished only

---

1) The position of individuals lending to a partnership
was severely handicapped by the Usury Acts until
their repeal in 1854.

to be safeguarded from losing his all.[1] For about
twenty five years they were right, but at the end of
fifty years the "adventurous" gentlemen were in the
minority and the "safe" investors in a large majority.

From 1856 to the decade of the 'eighties, there
were few issues of preference shares by the "new" limited
liability companies. But in railway companies and in
a number of chartered/incorporated gas, dock, canal and
telegraph companies this method was pursued with greater
and greater success. In railway companies 24.8% of the
total share capital was raised by preference shares in
1857-8, and had risen to 61% of the whole in 1884.[2]
The legal position of preference shares was regarded as
watertight as early as 1862,[3] and there was no Lord
Cairns to frighten the investors in this type of security.
Discussed later are the character of these preference shares
and the uses to which they were put.

In companies, other than railway and incorporated, the
preference share was most widely used in the sixties and
seventies by Rolling Stock and Wagon concerns, followed by
iron, coal and steel concerns. The North Central Wagon
Company, the Birmingham Wagon Company, and the North of

1) cf. W.S. Lindsay, M.P., and Richard Cobden, M.P. op.cit.p.4.
2) J.S. Jeans, op.cit. table p.24.
3) "Herepath's Journal", 1862, May 3rd. "We now understand
   it (preference share) to be a security occupying a
   given legal position which nothing can shake or alter".

England Railway Car and Iron Company issued preference shares in 1867 within two years of their formation. By 1875 these three had been joined by five other Wagon companies of those listed in the Joint Stock Company Directory. The Powell Duffryn Company was the first important iron and steel concern to issue a preference share, which it did in 1864. But until the seventies with the boom in steel production, this type of issue was rare in these companies. By 1875 however, Bolckow Vaughan's, Shott's Iron Company, John Brown and Company, Hempstead Iron, Nantyglo Iron, and the Patent Shaft Company all had preference issues.

But it cannot be said that there was a general trend towards the issues of preference shares up to the eighties. This is shown by the figures for the year 1885. Out of the 661 companies listed in Burdett's Official Intelligence for that year which came under the headings of Commercial and Industrial, Shipping, and Iron Coal and Steel, of the total share and loan capital of £114,558,000 only 8.8% was raised through preference issues.[1] Not only this but over one-third of the companies issuing preference shares had been formed in the five years previous to 1885.

The position was not very different in other types of enterprise. In the Financial, Land and Investment subdivision for example, of the total capital of £72,149,000

---

1) see appendix E.

of 226 companies, only 10.3% was raised through preference
issues.[1]   In the cotton companies only 29 of whom were
listed in the London Burdett's, a similar position prevailed.
Of the 93 Cotton companies listed in the Liverpool paper
"Investments", only 7 had other than ordinary shares.   Of
these, only two were called "preference shares", the others
going under names such as, "B" as opposed to the first issue
of "A" shares, and "new" as opposed to "old".[2]

To sum up the position of the use of preference issues
in 1885 the figures of the total companies listed in
Burdett's can be taken.   For while the selection only numbers
1,585 out of a total number in existence in England and
Scotland of 8,924 or only 17.7%, they were the largest
companies and the companies whose shares were most available
to the investor, both of which attributes, as we will show
later, were present or necessary when preference shares were
issued.   Of the £419,240,000 of capital raised by these
1,585 companies, 9.7% was raised by preference.[3]   And it
was estimated that only about 14% of the total number of
companies had more than one type of share.[4]

---

1) see appendix E.
2) "Investments", Liverpool, 1885, January 10th.
3) see appendix E. It should be pointed out that this total
      number of companies, excluded all the incorporated
      railways, but included overseas railways and financial
      companies.
4) an unpublished M.Com., Thesis by A. Essex-Crosby, "Joint
      Stock Companies in Great Britain 1890-1930". 1937. p.31.

The character of these preference issues was very
much influenced by railway practice. G.H. Evans has shown
in his study of Railway Preference shares, that they were
invariably issued to raise additional capital once the line
had been started. "Difficulties" in the continuance of
the company and in the building of lines and stations were
reasons for their introductions[1]; difficulties resulting
from an incorrect estimate of the total cost of the undertaking, and difficulties resulting from the inability to
secure further subscriptions from ordinary shareholders at
par, when no dividends were paid and from the legal inability
to issue shares below par and the inability to pay interest
on ordinary shares out of capital[2].

The preference shares of the new limited liability
companies in this period had almost the same character.
One of the few mining companies that issued preference shares
wrote in their annual report for 1875 .. "all the money
difficulties have been surmounted by the issue of preference
shares"[3]. J.A. Temple reported the same features of
preference shares in 1880 though his reason for the "difficulty"
was deceit or fraud by the company. "Many companies have

---

1) G.H. Evans, "British Corporation Finance, a study
in Preference Shares", 1936, Baltimore. p. 81.
2) G.H. Evans, op.cit. p.2. and "Herepath's Journal", 1867.
p. 769.
3) Report of "Boy Mining Company" in Stock Exchange Year
Book, 1875.

mislead the public relative to the amount of capital
required to complete an undertaking ... the company is
compelled to borrow giving the lenders a "preferential"
claim".[1] It is interesting to note the word "borrow"
being used for preference shares as early as 1880.

In some companies the preference capital was used for
extension of the business and not only to relieve difficult
financial pressure. This was the case in a number of the
wagon and iron and steel companies where it was not possible
or desirable to call up any more capital on the ordinary
shares, so preference were used, for example, in the Bristol
Wagon Company,[2] and in Bolcow Vaughan and Company.[3]

Another similarity with railway preferences was the
method of offering the new issue to the existing ordinary
shareholders first.[4] In the sixties it was generally
accepted that they should have first option on any such
issue.[5] Though already in the eighties, there was a
tendency to offer them to a wider field of investors, who
would be attracted by the security". The analysis of the
shareholding in railway companies in 1887 showed

---

1) J.A. Temple, "Hints upon Finance" 1880, p.31.
2) "Bowyers Investment Circular", Jan:29th,1870, "£30 -
   £40,000 are needed to invest in wagon leaves". p.203.
3) Chadwicks Investment Circular", 1871, p.91, "additional
   capital is needed to buy some properties".
4) G.H. Evans, op.cit. Ch. VII.
5) There are many references to this "first option" or
   "pro rata" to old or existing shareholders, e.g.,
   in the articles of Association of these companies,
   e.g., Bolckow and Vaughan Art.42, and this right
   is usually mentioned in the paragraphs about
   companies in the Company Directories and Journals,
   e.g. "The Investors and Stock Exchange Magazine"
   1863.

hat the average holdings per head of preference shares
ere by this date usually larger than those in ordinary
hares, implying a different group of shareholders,[1]
nd as early as 1875 the "Economist" had noted that some
reference issues from the start were deliberately appealing
o a wider and different section of investors.[2]

The denomination of preference shares was, in this
eriod usually lower than that of the ordinary shares.
his was partly the result of the practice of calling up
ll the capital on preference shares, whereas ordinary shares
s shown above, were not fully called up, and, partly, when
he denomination of the preference shares was as low as
5 or £10 when the ordinary shares were £100, it was the
esult of a desire to appeal to a different section of
nvestors for the additional capital, to the class of investor
ho wanted a steady return with no "unpaid" liabilities.
his happened in some of the Iron and Steel companies. For
xample in connection with the issue of preference shares
f Bolckow Vaughan's at a lower denomination than the ordinary
hares, Chadwick writes "We have confidence in recommending
hese to those who are seeking a severely safe and remunerative
nvestment without risk or fluctuation"[3]

What was the position then up to 1885 of the preference
hare? First, it was not at all widely used in the

1) "The Economist" 1887, p.107.
2) ibid. 1875. p.245.
3) "Chadwick's Investment Circular", 1872, p.91.

companies formed under the 1856 and 1862, limited
liability acts. For additional capital, these companies
still used the resources of the ordinary shareholders,
and were beginning to raise long term loans in the form
of debentures. Second, in cases where the preference shares
were used, the company was in some difficulty and could not
raise money /any other way. There was no attempt to "trade
on the equity", both the amount issued and the practice of
offering them first to old shareholders ruled out this
device.[1] Thirdly, there were however, one or two signs
indicating a tendency in a different direction. These are
seen in the rush to issue preference shares soon after formation,
by the companies in the 1880's,[2] and in the use of
the "wider" appeal to investors other than the present
shareholders, which it was found preference issues possessed.

The period 1885-1914 saw quite a dramatic rise in the
importance of the preference share as a means of raising
capital for industry, and at the same time an almost complete
transformation in it's character and the uses to which it
was put.

---

1) Where the issue was not offered to ordinary shareholders
   first, far from them benefiting, it was claimed "that
   their interests were sacrificed". "Shareholders Guardian"
   1865, p.409.
2) We mentioned above that over 1/3rd of the companies
   issuing preference shares in 1885 in the industrial
   group had been formed in the previous five years.

The most spectacular rise in the percentage of the total capital that was raised by preference issues was in the commercial and industrial companies. In this group, which consists of these companies under the headings of Commercial and Industrial, Shipping and Iron Coal and Steel in Burdett, we have shown above that in 1885 the percentage of the total share and loan capital raised by preference was 8.8%. By 1915 with a selection of 2,367 companies with a total share and loan capital of £898,456,000, the percentage had risen to 29.7. The significance of this increase is seen even more clearly when put alongside the changes in the percentages raised by ordinary and debenture issues. The former fell from 74.4% of the total in 1885 to 47.6% in 1915; the latter rose from 16.8% in 1885 to 22.7% in 1915.[1]

It was in these industries, the "old" rather than in the "new", that there was the most widespread increase in the use of the preference share. For example, in the Electric Light Supply group the proportion of capital raised by preference issues remained almost stable between 1895 and 1915. In the former year 21.2% of a total share and loan capital of £7,201,000 was raised in this way, in the latter year 21.8% of a capital of £40,594,000.[2] A wider selection

1) see appendix E

over slightly fewer years taken from Garcke's Manual of
Electrical Undertakings, covering Supply, Traction, Manufacturing and Miscellaneous, gives a very similar result.
In 1899-1900 for 357 companies with a total capital of
£54,263,000, 20% was raised by preference issues. In 1915-6,
with 980 companies and a capital of £298,760,000, 22.5% was
raised by preference.[1] In the shipping and Iron Coal and
Steel industries on the other hand, the percentages of the
total capital raised by preference issues had increased
between 1885 and 1915 from 3.8% - 25.4% and 8.0% - 24.4%
respectively.[2] Finally, the figures for the total number
of companies listed in Burdett, (excluding as before home
railways etc.) show that in 1885 for 1.585 companies with a
total capital of £419,240,000, 9.7% of this was raised by
preference, and in 1915 for 5,337 companies with a capital of
£2,433,398,000, 21.2% was raised by preference.

The character and reason for use of preference shares
underwent a similar change in this period.

The rights and privileges of the holder of preference
shares became more regularised and defined. Their ability
to vote at shareholders meetings was now in most cases
confined solely to the cases where the company was behind-hand

---

1) "Garcke's Manual of Electrical Undertakings", 1897-1916,
      their lists comprise of the great majority of the
      electrical undertakings in the country.
2) "See appendix E.

in paying the dividends. Before,the position had varied considerably from company to company, in a number of cases the preference shareholders had equal rights to vote along-side the ordinary shareholders.[1] With this clearer definition of voting rights, though there was no mention of this question in the companies Acts, and with the greater use of preference issues, new types of preference shares became popular. In the 'eighties and 'nineties the companies favoured the Cumulative Preference share. It carried a guarantee, not present in the ordinary preference share, that if the interest were foregone one year, the following year would pay the "cumulative" amount; a more attractive proposition than the earlier issues where, although offering a "preferential" dividend, the actual payment depended on the necessary profit being made by the concern during the year in question.[2]

In the twentieth century an even more seemingly "attractive" preference share was being used: the Participating Preference share, "which in addition to a fixed dividend shared in the surplus profits after the ordinary shares had received a certain amount".[3] This type of share became increasingly popular after the war.[4]

1) cf. "The Economist" 1875 p.245, and Essex-Crosby op.cit. p.131.
2) J. Whitehead, "Guaranteed Securities, Their merits as Investments Considered" 1859, p.vii.
3) J.F. Wheeler, "Stock Exchange" 1913. p.34.
4) E. Burns, "Modern Finance" 1922, p.16.

But while on the surface the preference share-holders
were having everything their own way, their privileges were
apparently increasing, this was not necessarily a true guide
to their position. Special inducements have to be judged in
two ways before it is possible to discover the reasons underlying their purpose. First, to what extent are the promises
of cumulative and participating preference rights carried
out, and what power have the holders to enforce these rights?
Secondly, why does the company offer these inducements? Was
it purely a question of obtaining capital, or was it affected
by either a serious financial position which would lead
ordinary shareholders to make sacrifices, or were these
privileges made necessary by the refusal of investors to take
up ordinary preference issues?

It is only possible to judge the extent to which
promises were carried out to the preference holders by the
amount of outcry that the contrary was occurring. Until
1900 it can be said that there was no serious dissatisfaction.
Attention was concentrated on debenture issues and these
were being used more extensively than preference. But in
the period 1900-1915 this was no longer the case. Debentures
for a variety of reasons were no longer so popular, the
amount of preference issues rapidly increased and at the
same time an outcry against unfair treatment of the preference
holders increased in volume.

Guy Ellis in his address to provincial solicitors had

hinted in 1895 that although at that date preference shareholders were apparently carrying all before them, there might
come a time when the ordinary shareholders would, by means of
their voting control, turn round on the "preferred" holders
and deprive them of some of their security.[1] This was
happening in a number of cases, 1900-1906. In Brewing companies
e.g., Allsopps, some iron companies, Barrow Hematite, and
large combines like the Salt Union, attempts were made,
successful in some cases, to reduce the rights of preference
shareholders to income while leaving the equity untouched.[2]
These attacks did not have a serious effect on the investors'
faith in preference issues, but they did tend to show that
the additional privileges granted to preference holders
carried, at the same time, an almost complete lack of power
to enforce these privileges.

The reasons for issuing preference shares, our second
criteria, had changed considerably from those dominant in the
period 1856-1885. The clearest illustration of this is the
method of issuing at the formation of the company, one-third
of the capital in ordinary shares, one-third in preference
and one-third in debentures; a practice claimed to be
"almost universal" in the City.[3] In the new public companies

---

1) Guy Ellis "Appreciation of Gold and it's effects on
   Investments, 1895, p.18. It was a paper read before
   the Provincial Meeting of the Incorporated Law Society.
2) Details of these cases are given in A. Essex Crosby op.cit.
   p. 155 ff.
3) 1898 Report, Qu. 789 et.seq. We will deal with this
   method later when discussing debentures.

of any size that were being formed, preference capital was
now regarded just as much a part of the necessary capital
of the company as were ordinary issues.   All talk of
"difficulties" and "urgent methods" had gone. This applied
equally to the big amalgamated companies that were appealing
to the public for capital. The driving force behind the
issue of preference shares in these companies had passed
from the necessity of raising additional capital to avoid
difficulties, and which capital could not, through the in-
secure position of the company, be raised by ordinary shares,
to the necessity of appealing to different sections of the
investing public, due to the size of the capital required.

In the established industrial companies a somewhat
similar position prevailed.   Here the necessity was not
the initial capital but additional capital to increase and
extend the business.   The reasons for not issuing only
ordinary shares to provide for these extensions were twofold.
Firstly, the great difficulty there was in securing investors
for home industrial ordinary issues.   The resources of the
wealthy industrialists in the North could no longer be
tapped so easily.   They already had full committments.
And outside this group, the self-appointed advisers and
stockbrokers were advising investors through myriads of
books, journals, circulars, and interviews, to leave ordinary
shares alone, and particularly anything connected with iron,

steel, coal or shipping.[1] Secondly provided the company
was well established it was proving advantageous to issue
pre-ordinary stocks and shares: advantageous from the
aspect of increasing the possible dividends of the ordinary
shares, and advantageous in keeping the company under the
control of the original, or descendants of the original,
shareholders. These two factors led to additional capital
usually being raised either by preference issues or
debentures. We have shown above that in 1885 16.8% of the
capital of a selection of commercial and industrial companies
was raised by the latter method. But the extent to which
debentures could be used, even with the use of the floating
charge, in any company was limited. Both trade creditors
and possible debenture holders would refuse to deal further
with the company after the assets had been completely
mortgaged. On the other hand a preference share was purely
a guarantee of a certain fixed income, and until the fixed
charges were too great, had fair security and certainty of
dividend. Apart from this there were several economic and
social factors operating which lead to a relative decline in the
amount of capital raised by debenture compared with
preference. These are discussed later.

In the private and semi-private company which in this
period was rapidly becoming the most frequent   type of company

---

1)   e.g. E.R.Cabbott: "How to Invest Money" 1905.p.36. "The
average investor should leave ordinary shares in our
mineral undertakings alone".

registered, the attempt to retain control in a few hands
was even stronger. The private companies were very often
"converted" into a company from a private firm, and it was
the practice both in the very large conversions, e.g.
breweries, and in the small companies with capitals
under £50,000, for the vendor to take in return for the
property all the ordinary shares, and then the company would
issue debenture and preference in order to raise the working
capital. Anything further from the spirit of the 1856 and
1862 Acts is difficult to imagine. But preference shares
were not so popular with small private companies as were
debentures. For the preference shareholder in these
companies had little or no security, no control,[1] and the
turnover was often insufficient to allow for large fixed
charges. "Unless there is some special temptation such as
a high fixed dividend, preference shares of small trading
companies are not found easy to place".[2]

The use of preference issues on a large scale to
raise capital for the public company, and a similar though
limited use in the private company, had brought about a
change in the character of preference shares.

---

1) e.g. H.W.Jordan, "Private Companies", 1915.p.33. "The
holders of preference shares of private companies need not
be given the same right of receiving and inspecting balance
sheets and reports as is possessed by the holders of
Ordinary Shares."

2).C.W.Turner, "Treatise on the Conversion of a Business into
a Private Limited Company", 1907. p.18.

> The original idea in the creation of
> preference shares was to provide a readier
> and more attractive means of supplementing the
> ordinary capital in the too frequent case of
> it proving insufficient. But now it is quite
> common to issue both classes at the outset in
> order to appeal to a wider circle of investors
> as well as to leave a larger margin of possible
> profit to the ordinary shareholder."(1)

It is now possible to answer some of the questions
asked above as to the nature of the increased privileges
granted to the holders of preference shares. For the
company the issue of preference shares was a means of
obtaining capital from the type of investor who was not
interested in ordinary shares. In addition, the extent of
the issue meant the control by the holders of equity over
a capital almost equal in size to their own, and the
possibility of increased returns on the ordinary shares.
In order to persuade the investor to take preference
shares giving these advantages to the ordinary shareholder,
it was necessary, as the pressure on the savings market
increased, to offer additional inducements in the shape
of cumulative and participating shares. But the chief
test of the validity of these rights, was the power to
enforce them in "bad" times, and to see that in "good"
times sufficient capital was allocated to reserve, to provide
for payment of the dividends later. This power was not

1) J.D.Walker and Watson, op.cit. p.167.

possessed by the holders of preference shares. Almost
their only weapon was a legal injunction against the
Company, which might involve for them not only loss of
dividend but capital as well. Up to 1914 the rights
of preference holders had not been extensively tested,
but the reorganisations that took place had already
revealed some of the real weaknesses of this "privileged"
position.

The changing composition of the investing classes,
their changed attitude towards investment, the total
greater need for fixed capital consequent on the different
methods of production and the adoption of the company system,
and the necessity or possibility of concentration of control,
had interacted to produce in the company structure by 1914
an instrument, namely the preference share, that was
completely foreign to the framers of the Limited Company
Acts in the fifties and sixties. To say that this was an
inevitable outcome of the necessities of company finance is
a commonplace: but the suggestion that this development
entails a completely new re-orientation of the legislation
concerning the company and the attitude of the state towards
the company, is not so generally accepted.

II. FOUNDERS SHARES.

Founders shares, if they had kept their original purpose, would have appealed greatly to many of the enthusiastic supporters of limited liability of the fifties. They were always conjuring up pictures in their minds' eye of full many a poor inventor who through lack of contact with/a rich patron was born to blush unseen, and then appeared the company waving the flag of "limited" and both inventor and investor were happily united. It was in order that both the subscribers of the capital and the inventor should be equally rewarded, the device of the founders share was used.

However as shown above not very many companies were formed to work new inventions and when inventors did suggest that a company should be formed they took little part in it; the usual process being to buy up the rights of the inventor on behalf of the company. But there was another group of hardworking souls, the promoters and managers of the company, who did not possess much capital but who in view of their work for the company, were considered worthy of a handsome remuneration but in a fashion that would not harm the ordinary investor and would keep the managers hard at work. When the company was formed they were given, or officially bought, a small number of founders shares which

were always very low in denomination. Once the company
was in operation and paying dividends, the ordinary
shareholders received up to a certain fixed per cent
dividend on their capital, and all the remaining profit
after that was either to go wholly to the owners of the
founders shares, or more frequently, was to be divided
equally between the ordinary shareholders and the founder
shareholders.

Up to 1885 the cases of the use of founders shares
were not very frequent and they were adopted in the spirit
of either of the two cases outlined above. "When the founder
worked hard to put the company together and to run it,
but he puts little capital in himself, he should have a
share in the company but it should only be realisable
and tangible in the event of success."[1]

In the iron, coal and steel conversions of the
seventies there appeared however another type of share
which had the same features as the founders share. This was
called either the "vendor's deferred share" or just the
"Vendor's share". In these cases the vendor had agreed,
in part exchange for his property, to take shares which
would not rank for dividend until a certain percentage had
been paid on the ordinary shares that were subscribed by
the public. In the Brynmawr Coal and Iron Company for

1) J.D. Walker and Watson, op. cit. p.92.

example, the total capital was £200,000 in £10 shares.
The vendors took 10,000 shares in payment for
the property but these shares were only to rank for
dividend after 6% had been paid on the other 10,000[1]
But while these shares had the same financial effect on
the company as did founders shares, their purpose was
entirely different. They were usually well boosted on
the prospectus as showing the confidence the vendor had
in the company, but since the vendor naturally would not
take shares just for the fun of the thing, the silence
on the question of how long this agreement lasted or how
the profits were divided, if at all, after the 6% was
reached, seems to indicate that these shares were not
wholly free of the atmosphere of a "confidence trick".

In the ten years following 1886 there was a very
big boom in the issue of founders shares. The companies
making most use of this instrument were usually of the
rather speculative type. In particular mining companies,[2]
investment and trust companies were prominent.[3]

But its character had undergone a big change from its
use in the sixties and seventies. With the increase

---

1) From the prospectus of this company, 1873.
2) "The Accountant" 1890. p.42.
3) "The Statist", 1889 Vol.II. p.473.

in the size of the companies that appealed to the public,
a small number of founders shares which shared the profits
equally with the rest of the capital after a certain rate
had been paid, rapidly became a source of untold wealth
for the owners.[1] To increase further these profits, in
some companies where it was possible, only a small portion
of the ordinary shares were called up, say £2 or £3 per £10
share, and on the basis of the uncalled portions debentures
were raised. This had the double effect of increasing the
total amount of profits and the proportion going to the
holders of the founders shares.[2]

The publications for intending investors were most
scathing in their denunciation of this "one of the most
objectionable of the devices of modern finance".[3] The
Investors Monthly Manual published an article in 1890 on
"The Danger to Investors in Companies with Founders Shares"[4]
and A.J. Wilson, a Scotchman, became quite eloquent on the
subject and invoked the Englishman's Old School Tie. "This
mighty wealth creating tool has been known abroad for many
years and casually one has met with it in the City, but it

---

1) Founders shares were used with particularly spectacular
results in big retail companies like Harrods and D.H.Evans.
In both cases the shares were so remunerative that
companies were formed specially to hold them, in the former
case in 1895 in the latter case in 1900. The value of the
founders shares in Harrods had increased from £1400 in the
1890's to £1,470,000 in 1911. (J.H.Clapham, op.cit, Vol.
III. p.243.).
2) "Investors Monthly Manual", 1890, p.156.
3) J.D. Walker and Watson, op.cit. p.92.
4) see note (2).

had an un-English look." (1)

Not only was this instrument now a source of an
unnatural amount of profit for the holders, and very
unpopular, but also it was no longer in the hands of the
inventor or the manager.   With the growth in professional
promoting and the inability to pay promoters any commission
out of the capital of the company, the founders share was
now being used for their remuneration.(2) Now was this
all, for with the growth of professional promoting there
also grew up underwriting, and the founders share could be
used "as a powerful auxiliary to underwriting".   In the
first place founders shares could be given to the underwriters in payment for services rendered.   This was done
quite extensively up to the legalisation of underwriting in
the 1900 and 1907 Acts.(3) Secondly they could be used as
an inducement to the public to take up shares, either by
giving them away freely prior to public issue, or by the
promise to the investor of one founders share with every
allotment of a specified minimum of ordinary shares.(4)This latter

1) "Financial Review of Reviews" Vol. 1. 1892. p.28.
2) CF.&H.Hurrell and C. Hyde. "Joint Stock Companies practical
   Guide", 3rd Edition, 1889, p.7. "The old system of Founders
   shares has recently been revived - to reimburse the
   promoters for the expenses incurred by them," and J.D. Walker
   and Watson, op. cit. p.92.   More than this, they were used
   by "promoting octopuses" like the British Electric Traction
   Company to obtain with little expense a large proportion of
   the profits of their subsidiaries.
3) D. Finnie, "Capital Underwriting", 1934. p.44.
4) J.D. Walker and Watson, op cit. p. 93.

method led eventually to the decline of founders shares, for the more that were issued the less value they possessed. In 1896 founders shares were declared to be "nearly played out, happily for investors."[1]

This view of their decease was supported by E Manson in an article on them in the Encyclopaedia Brittanica for 1902. But in 1906 they are reported as reappearing again in "numerous motor bus companies ... all of which are issuing founders shares under the name of deferred capital.[2] In 1914 deferred shares were quite common in speculative companies, but they were no longer issued to reimburse promoters or to place ordinary shares. Their denomination was still small but they were issued in large numbers in each company and were issued generally to the public. The investor purchasing these shares did not expect a regular high return as had happened in the founders shares in the nineties but regarded them frankly as "gamblers counters". The legalisation of underwriting in the 1900 and 1907 Acts had removed some of the attraction which these shares had for the promoter and underwriter.

Throughout this period in the private companies, founders shares were from time to time being used,[3]

1) W.H.S.Aubrey. "Stock Exchange Investments", 1896, p.68.
2) "Investors Monthly Manual", 1906, p.58.
3) F.D.Head, "Formation and Management of a Private Company , 1932,p.15.

but their character was different from both the Vendors
shares that were issued in the big public companies and
from the founders and deferred shares that we have just been
discussing. As there was no public appeal the fact that
the vendors /taking "founders shares" could not have any
power in attracting the investor. The cases where they
were used were much closer in character to the position
of the manager or inventor who had little capital but a great deal
of energy that needed repayment in some fashion, advantageous
to both the individual and his friends who were assisting
him with their capital.

Founders shares, like preference shares were, except
for the purely speculative cases, the outcome of the
necessities of companies. In the case of preference issues,
the main force for their use came from the need to attract
certain sections of investors to put their capital in the
company: in the case of founders shares, they were used, not
to recruit capital but to solve the internal problem facing
the company of how to remunerate promoters, underwriters and
managers who, owing to the size to which the public companies
had grown, could not hold any substantial proportion of
equity. In practice, their roles overlapped to a certain
extent, the preference share assisting in control and
remuneration to the "founders" and the founders shares

assisting sometimes in recruiting capital, but in general
the main distinction holds good. Neither of these
developments were to any real degree anticipated by the
legislation of the fifties and sixties, and growing as
they did out of company practice without legislative control,
both tended to develop certain obviously unattractive
features. With the preference shares the chief trouble was
their very weak position in relation to maintaining their
rights: with the founders shares, it became clear that the
dividends on these were out of all proportion to the work
done by the owners, and in fact they tended to be bought and
sold as "little gold mines" by small groups of people who
had nothing to do with the foundation of the company. To
counteract the opposition of investors and investors journals
to these glaring weaknesses, new devices were introduced. In
the case of preference shares the cumulative and participating
shares were developed which won to some extent the confidence
of investors: but founders shares could not be so successfully
disguised. They disappeared into two separate schemes.
On the one hand the gambling element remained with the
"deferred shares", but these were issued generally and did
not often prove gold mines. On the other hand, the
remuneration of promoters managers and underwriters left the
dividend sheet and became immersed in the depths of the
expenses side of the balance sheet.

CHAPTER VI.

The introduction and use of debenture issues as
a method of raising capital, and the change in the character of debentures between 1856 and 1914.

────────────

We have seen that the changed needs of the limited liability
company consequent on its spread to all types of undertakings
and its growth in size, and the changed composition and
characteristics of the investing classes, brought about two
important developments in the financial structure of companies.
The share denomination fell and the unpaid portion disappeared,
and new types of shares, founders and preference, were introduced.
There was a third development brought about by the same forces,
the use of debentures and loans, and the transformation of these
"loans" from a short term financial expedient to a widespread
method of raising working capital.

Up to the decade of the 'eighties the most familiar type of
debenture was the railway debenture. As the practice and
experience of railway companies not only influenced the limited
liability joint stock companies in their adoption of debentures,
but also familiarised the investing classes with this type of
stock, we will discuss the railway debenture in some detail.

Borrowing powers were part and parcel of railway finance.
In commercial and manufacturing firms it was expected that the
fixed capital would be provided by the partners and part of the
working capital through credits and bank advances, so it was
assumed that railways would be financed in a similar way.

However, since both the scale of the railway undertakings was
greater and the source of loans not so much financially informed
banks and discount houses, as financially ignorant investors,
the ratio between loan and share capital was made definite.
"In 1836 ..... the House of Commons adopted a Standing Order
which provided that no railway company should be allowed to
raise by loan or mortgage a larger sum than one-third of its
share capital, and this amount only after one-half of the
latter had been paid up."[1]   The effect of this limitation was
two-fold.   Firstly, it was a legal encouragement both for
companies to raise part of their capital in loan form and for
the investors to subscribe with some feeling of security.
And arising out of this it tended to transform what was first
purely a "borrowing power", conceived in terms of short term
loans and advances, into a well recognised and universally
adopted method of obtaining roughly one-third of the capital
sunk in the railway.   The second effect was to force railway
companies when they needed further capital, over and above that
raised by shares and borrowing powers, to use other expedients
such as preference shares and depreciated ordinary shares (to
increase borrowing powers) for their fixed capital and loan
notes and Lloyd's Bonds for their working capital.

Of these developments, the two most important in their
influence on limited liability companies were the change in the
character of the borrowing powers from temporary loans to

1) G.H. Evans, op cit, 1936, p.63.

debenture stock and the expedient of preference shares. Depreciated shares were not necessary in this particular context for companies, as their borrowing powers were not limited. Lloyd's Bonds, which were "simply an agreement between a company and any person to whom they may owe money whether for land or goods or services performed, that instead of paying at once, they are to pay in three or four years time with interest. Thus the company cannot borrow money, but they borrow money's worth, which comes to the same thing,"[1] were only used occasionally in company finance and even in railways, were said to be "extinct" by 1880.[2]

We have dealt above with the influence of railway preference shares on their subsequent use in limited company finance: here we will deal with the transition from short term loans to debenture stock in railway companies and trace its influence on the use of loans by limited companies.

The first development was the employment of these loans by railway companies for construction purposes, and not only as working capital, and their regular renewal as they fell due rather than their repayment.

> "In the earliest times it was supposed that these debts would only be incurred for temporary purposes, namely for the completion of the undertaking and for providing it with rolling stock, etc., and that they would then be paid off. This idea was soon shown to be a fallacy: all companies have renewed their debentures from time to time as they came due and have no intention whatever of paying them off." (3)

1) "Quarterly Review", 1867, April, art. on "Railway Finance, p.495.
2) "Journal of the Inst. of Bankers," vol.I, 1879-80, p.440.
3) "Quarterly Review", loc cit. p. 501.

A year later "Herepath's Journal" summed up the position
when it wrote "as things are, debentures really form a part of
the capital of a company as much as ordinary share capital.
They are only another means of raising the required capital."[1]

But this widespread use of debenture loans as part of the
fixed capital of the company, led to insecurity. "It is
impossible to examine the financial position of railway companies
without seeing that the Debenture Loan System is the most
vulnerable part",[2] wrote Henry Ayres in 1868, and he went on to
point out that when these loans became renewable they were renewable at the current rate of interest, and, with a total of
£105,000,000 in debenture loans in 1866 and over one hundred
changes in the Bank Rate between 1857-1867 fluctuating from
2% to 10%, it is easy to see how unstable this system was.

The second development, arising out of this instability,
was the transformation of debenture loans into debenture stocks
bearing a fixed rate of interest. "Loans" had ceased to be
loans; they had become part of the capital of the company, so
it was thought that their position should be regularised.
"Herepath's Journal" argued on these lines when advocating the
change from loan to stock. "The raised capital of a railway
company is not floating and available for paying off loans. It
is spent and fixed in the construction of lines, stations,

1) "Herepath's Journal", 1867, p.1150.
2) H. Ayres, "The Financial Position of Railways", 1868,
p. XVIII.

rolling stock, etc. Therefore the capital should also be fixed."[1]

The advantages of this system of debenture stock were "generally admitted in the 'sixties[2] but only a few companies had turned their debentures into stock at that date. In 1865 it was estimated that only 3.24% of the total capital raised in the United Kingdom for railways was in this form.[3] But twelve years later "Herepath's" reports that "The transformation of 'loans' into 'debenture stock' which has been going on for some years is approaching its completion, and the danger to railway finance from the existence of a large floating debt has to all intents and purposes disappeared."[4] By 1889 "debentures", by which was meant "loans", were said to be non-existent.[5]

By the decade of the eighties, then, the influence of railway finance in connection with debentures had two main aspects. First railway companies by the extent to which they used debentures[6], had popularised them as a method of raising capital. Secondly, by their use of them alongside share capital in construction, etc., and not solely as working

1) "Herepath's Journal", 1866, p. 1041.
2) H. Ayres, op cit. p. XXI.
3) ibid. p. XXII.
4) "Herepath's Journal", 1877, p. 958.
5) G. Bartrick-Baker, "Sound Investments for Small Savings, 1899, p.23.
6) In 1884, 25% of the total share or loan capital of the railways of the United Kingdom was raised by loan and debenture stock. 3. Van Oss, "Stock Exchange Values, 1885-1895", 1895, p.LXXXVI.

capital, and by the change from debenture loans to debenture
stock, this use and form was encouraged in the limited liability companies.

From the 1880's to 1914 there were no major changes in the
character of railway debentures. Some companies converted
Debenture stock carrying high rates on interest into new stocks
with low rates; the effect of this was to increase the nominal
capital of the railways but not to change the uses to which the
debentures were put.[1] While the influences of railway
debentures outlined above continued to affect company finance
in this second period, the companies themselves carried the idea
of using debentures as part of the fixed capital to its logical
conclusion of issuing them simultaneously with share capital
at the formation of the company and also evolved new uses for
debentures.

We will make a closer study of both the influence of
railway debentures on company finance and the independent
developments of the company in the sphere of debentures at a
later stage, but first there is one other important influence
which railway debentures exerted, to be considered: namely,
on the investor. The familiarisation of the investor with
debenture issues by the railway companies was just as important
a factor in the later use of debentures by limited companies as
were the lessons in financial method and expediency.

The attractiveness of debentures lay, of course, in their
security. Railway companies established in the minds of the

1) W.R. Lawson, "British Railways", 1913, p.1.

investing public the idea that debenture and security were one
and the same thing: but not without a struggle. Up to 1867
it had been assumed that the debenture and loan holders had a
legal right to the property of the railway company, the rails,
stations, rolling stock, etc., if the intereat was overdue.
But in that year "a legal flaw brought down debentures ... and
dealt a blow at railway securities in public estimation, of
which the effect will not be removed for years".[1] This blow
was the judgment by Lord Cairns that debenture holders were only
entitled to the first surplus over and above the cost of working,
and therefore not to the property of the company.

However, Goschen in his estimate of several years before
the investors would recover from this shock, was making a
mistake. He was thinking more in terms of the legal and
technical aspects of the question rather than in terms of the
average investor in railway debentures. The fact that after
1867 they could no longer claim the right to occupy railway
stations if the line failed to pay their interest, was not of
great importance to them. What use was a railway station anyway?
Provided they obtained an income regularly, and could, when
necessary, market their holdings easily, they were content to go
on investing, and go on they did. Purely legal decisions on
security should not and cannot be considered, as Goschen

1) G.J. Goschen, "Essays and Addresses", published 1905, p.63.

attempted, in the abstract: the background of habit and alternative investment must be considered.   In the eighteen sixties
and seventies the investors in railway debentures had already
formed the habit of looking to the income and the possibility
of easy selling rather than looking to the ultimate security of
their loans, and   alternative investments with as high a
standing as railway debentures were almost non-existent.   Consequently while Lord Cairnes finds a place in legal text books,
he is rarely mentioned in "Guides of Investors".

The problem of marketability of debentures, which increased
in importance after the Cairns' decision, was solved in part by
the transformation of debenture loans into debenture stock.
For while this meant a lower rate of interest in most cases, the
loans were always for very large amounts whereas the stock could
be subdivided and therefore more easily saleable.   A "debenture
holder" in a letter in"Herepath's Journal" in 1867 explained
this:

> "A chief reason for the very high rates paid by
> railway companies for the renewal of their debentures
> is that the greater part of these bonds are issued in
> sums of £500, £1,000 and upwards and are therefore not
> readily marketable.   The security of the debenture
> stocks of the large companies, North Western and Great
> Western, is little if at all inferior to Government funds
> and they have the great advantage of being readily saleable
> or purchaseable in large or small quantities."   (1)

At the same time the increase in the amount of capital raised
by debenture stocks and the smaller units tended to increase the
number of investors holding this type of security.

---

1) "Herepath's Journal", 1867, p.889.

In 1886 in a Parliamentary Return the number of debenture
holders in all the Railway Companies in the United Kingdom was
given as 118,545;   a smaller number than the holders of
ordinary or preference shares, for they were investors mainly
interested in a regular income and safety of capital and who
invested heavily.   Goschen in a well-known passage gave a vivid
picture of the debenture holder.   He described railway
debentures as:

> "the favourite investment of couples about to marry;
> the last resort of trustees distracted on the one hand
> by their own anxiety to avoid responsibility and on the
> other by the importunities of their wards not to be
> sacrificed to Consols - railway debentures the cynosure
> of the old-fashioned school of investors, in whose
> nostrils every other form of join-stock credit savoured
> of abomination ...." (1)

Goschen was not misled in this description by abstract legal
points.

We have suggested above that the holders of Consols formed
the base of the Victorian investment market.   If this is so,
then the holders of railway debenture stock formed the strata
immediately above them, and after experience of investment
some of them moved out of the ranks to more risky but more
lucrative investments higher up.   The "couples about to marry"
when they were married and had children and property found the
financial position eased when investing in the debentures of a
land company at six or seven percent rather than railway
debentures at four percent.   Further, other investors who
desired the security of railway debentures but were unable to

---

1) G.J. Goschen, op cit., p. 62.

purchase any at par, tended to invest in the debentures of other companies because they had the same safe sound about the name. [1

One type of investor not mentioned by Goschen who was quite important both in railway and limited company debenture finance was the institutional investor. Banks, insurance companies, trusts, public bodies, etc., all invested quite heavily in Railway Debentures. In 1869, the Railway Almanak wrote "If railway companies are as a body, the largest borrowers of the age, the life assurance offices as a body are the largest lenders. A very considerable proportion of the funds of life offices is invested in railway securities, chiefly in the form of debenture bonds." [2] With the increase in wealth of these institutions their importance as investors increased, they spread out beyond railway debentures into other types of debenture.

The debentures of railway companies influenced limited liability company finance in two ways: they showed the utility of these issues to the company, and they familiarised them with the investors. We will now trace the extent to which debentures were used by companies in the period 1856-1914, the changes in the character of these debentures, and the reasons for these changes. The example of railway companies outlined above was one powerful factor in the acceptance of debentures by the

1) cf. 1877 Report, Qu. 1699.
2) "The Railway, Banking, Mining and Insurance Almanak" 1869, p.48.

limited companies, but there were other independent forces to
be discussed.

The Companies Acts of 1855, 1856 and 1862 did not mention
debentures directly.   Loans and mortgages were expected, for
under Section 43 of the 1862 Act "a register of charges affecting the property of the company must be kept", but long term
debenture stock was not expected.   Companies found it easy
enough to raise all the necessary capital by the issue of shares,
or additional capital by calls on shares.   Some companies,
however, chiefly land companies, were specifically allowed to
raise mortgage debentures on their property by the Mortgage
Debenture Act of 1865.

Generally speaking, debentures were rare in the sixties.
The Committee on the Limited Liability Act in 1867 discussed
debentures with reference to their position if the nominal
capital and shares of a company were reduced.   Most of the
witnesses declared that debentures were not important in
companies other than land companies.   William Newmarch said
"Parenthically I may state that the number of cases where any
large amount of money has been raised upon debentures is
exceedingly few". [1]   Another witness reported that out of
"some thirty companies for which I act, I should think there
would not be above three who issue debentures", and, asked if
the sums were large in proportion to the share capital, he
replied "very small". [2]

1)   1867 Report, Qu. 574.
2)   ibid. Qu. 641.

The boom in converting iron and coal firms and partnerships into limited companies in 1870-5 saw a new use for
debentures. Several of the companies, e.g. Darlington Iron
Company, 1872, Llynvi Tondu and Ogmore Coal Company, 1872,
Bonville's Court Coal and Iron Company, 1873, John Bagnall
and Sons, 1873, and Andrew Knowles and Sons, 1873, issued
debenture to the vendors in part payment for the property.
Though the number of these companies issuing debentures in
this way was few compared with the total number of limited
liability companies in existence, this new use for debentures
which had not arisen in the case of railway companies was a
development which was later to play a very significant part in
company finance.

In the same years there was also the use of debentures by
iron and steel companies to raise additional capital. By 1874
five big iron, coal and steel firms, with which David Chadwick
was associated had issued debenture bonds that were available
to the public and quoted in his circular. The five were
Stavely Coal and Iron Company, Ltd., Sheepbridge Coal and Iron
Company, Ltd., Charles and Cammell Company, Ltd., Vickers Sons
and Company, Ltd., and Llynvi Tondu and Ogmore Coal Company Ltd. [1]

The practice of issuing debentures in order to obtain
additional capital, though it was most noticeable in the iron
industry spread to other miscellaneous companies. The

1) Chadwick's "Investment Circular", 1874, p. 228.

Bessemer Ship Saloon Company used this method, as did some
trading companies of which Laurie and Marner Limited, 1873, is
an example. The practice, however, was in the main confined to
those companies which had some extensive property on which to
secure the debentures.

By the eighties borrowing through debentures was popular
with all types of companies. Of the 661 companies listed under
the headings of "Commercial and Industrial", "Shipping" and
"Iron, Coal and Steel" in Burdett's Official Intelligence for
1885, 16.8% of a total capital of £114.5 million was raised by
debentures.[1]   Put in another way between 30-40% of these
companies at this date had debentures issues of one kind or
another besides their share issues.

But this important use of debentures took place only in
the late seventies and eighties. A smaller selection for
1872 and 1875 shows this. The "Investors' Guardian Guide to
Investments" lists 320 limited liability companies in 1872.
Of these only 3 had debenture issues.   In 1875 the "Financial
Register" lists under the headings of "Miscellaneous, Mining,
Telegraph, Water and Gas, and Shipping", 227 companies.
Eighteen had debenture issues or c.8%. While these selections
do not give the debentures to vendor, which are included in the
"Burdetts" list, they do cover roughly the same types of
company, that is the large   important on es which were relying
to some extent on the general public for their capital. A

1) See Appendix E.

large number of small companies which did not appeal to the public and whose shares were not quoted on either the London or provincial Stock Exchanges, are not included in either list.

As is to be expected the "Financial, Land and Investment" group in 1885 had a very high proportion of it's capital in debentures.   Of 226 companies under this heading listed in Burdett for 1885, 43.5% of a total capital, share and loan, of £72.2 million was raied by debentures.[1]   And here the use was not altogether recent but had been a regular practice since the Mortgage Debenture Act of 1865.

These figures give us some indication, though not complete, ofthe extent to which debentures were used in company finance up to 1885:   the next considerations are the form and character of these debentures and the reasons for their use.

The form and character of the debentures of limited liability companies in the period 1856-1885, were strongly influenced by railway debentures.   They were used in the same way in the seventies as part of the fixed capital and not necessarily only for working capital.   For example Charles Cammell and Company, Ltd., in 1874 needed a source of fuel for their steel works; they bought the Oaks Colliery near Barnsley and paid for it by issuing £200,000 debentures.[2]   Again the loan capital in cotton companies, although it was renewed at different rates of interest, was used in the same way as share capital in building

1) Appendix E.
2) "Chadwicks Investment Circular", 1874, p.222.

mill.[1]

After the Cairns judgment in 1867 the security of debentures
imited liability companies was slightly different from that
ailway companies.   They were usually secured "by a general
ge upon the assets of the company", but these assets were
cted to be tangible property, etc. not book debts.[2]   The
tice of securing them against uncalled capital has been
ussed above.

Debentures in limited companies as with railways were
ed to obtain additional capital and not capital at the
ation of the company.   Cotton companies were a major
ption to this general rule in this period.   The development
ron, coal and steel companies noted above of issuing debent-
to vendor was not raising capital by debentures at the
ation of the company, but vendors taking their payment for
property in a different form than hitherto.   No new capital
brought into the company through this method.   A third
larity with railway practice was the transition from loans
ebenture bonds.   This occurred both in relation to the
vidual company and in company finance as a whole.   With the
ption of the land companies under the 1865 Act and some of the
tered and incorporated companies, the limited liability
anies using debentures in the sixties raised them in loan

Co-operative Wholesale Society Annual", 1884, p.189.
hese are the words used in Cammell's debentures, see above.

form and expected to pay them off.[1]   In the seventies and
eighties the debentures had become long term and it was not
expected to pay them off.   And some companies floated issues
of debenture stock in order to buy up their loans and put their
interest charges on a more stable basis.[2]

In the late seventies and early eighties however the
character of limited liability company's debentures was beginning to differ from those in railway companies.   With the
increase in the number of conversions of private firms the
practice of issuing debentures to vendor became popular.   And
as a method of securing debentures the much discussed "floating
charge" began to be used generally.   It cannot be said that
the majority of debentures were secured in this fashion, but
it was widespread enough in 1881 for the Annual Meeting of the
Associated Chambers of Commerce to pass the following resolution
"That the Joint Stock Companies Acts require amendment to make
it illegal to defraud their ordinary creditors for the benefit of
debenture holders as they may now do by mortgaging their future
property and book debts".[3]

This divergence in the form and use of debentures of
limited liability companies away from their use in railway
companies was intimately linked in the minds of contemporaries

---

1) Bolckow Vaughan in 1869 raised money by debentures on the
    security of uncalled capital - £20,000 - and they stated
    that they intended to buy them off in 1871. "Chadwick's
    Investment Circular," 1871, p.91.
2) e.g. the Ebbw Vale Company raised debentures to pay off
    mortgages in 1878-9.
3) Reported in "Journal of the Institute of Bankers", vol.III,
                                                        p. 247

with the whole question of the legal position and control of
debentures in trading companies.   We pointed out above that
railway debentures had been legalised and controlled by Acts
of Parliament, but limited liability company debentures were not
so much as mentioned in the Companies Acts (except for Land
Companies) and provided the investor would accept them and the
Courts legalise them, they could be to any amount and of any
type.

As early as the sixties there was a campaign started to end
this "undefined" position of company debentures and bring them
into line with the "legal" railway debentures.

> "The importance of holding in perfect check and controlling
> thoroughly by force of law, the borrowing powers of
> public companies, cannot well be exaggerated ... It
> should be remembered that the holders of the particular
> securities of which we are treating have no voting or
> restraining power in the affairs of the undertakings
> which they have aided with their capital." (1)

This was written in a pamphlet by Effingham Wilson, published
in 1866.   Before the 1867 Committee on the Companies Acts,

the lawyer, Latham Browne, pointed out that, of a selection
of 35 companies, in 22 cases the directors had unlimited borrowing powers, and only in one case had they no power.(2)   But
at the time neither of these statements were very startling,
'or they were forecasts of what might happen rather than what
was happening.   However, with the divergence between the
practice in trading companies and that in railway companies

) Quoted in the "Shareholders Guardian", 1866, March 14th,
 p.204.
) 1867 Report, Appendix V.

which we noted as appearing in the late seventies and eighties, the attack on debentures began in real earnest. The details of the attack need not concern us here, it is sufficient to note that there was a united front ranging from private traders and ordinary creditors at one end to the Anti-Usury Association at the other. Every type of argument was used from quoting the bible to holding up the railway companies as examples of "just trading". But they had little or no success. The necessities of the companies and the persistence of the investors in regarding debentures as "safe" were too strong for them; And had there been some success in the legal field, in practice the companies,if necessary, would have adopted the same roundabout means as did the railways when issuing Lloyd's Bonds, and depreciated shares, etc.

Apart from this use of debentures as a part payment to vendors, their form and use was dominated by railway experience up to the eighties. We now go on to discuss the reasons underlying their use in trading companies.

The forces that brought about the introduction of debentures into company finance and that changed their character between 1856 and 1885 can be most easily discussed under three heads. First, the necessities of the company, second, the type of invest or available, third, the particular economic conditions, prosperity, crises, etc. that reacted on the capital market.

In this period the necessity of the company that led to debentures was simply that of wishing to increase the size and

scope of the concern.   This advice was given in the 1877
Commission, "if a company wishes to increase and extend business
then call up money or issue debentures".[1]

The need was for additional capital, and was felt particularly by iron and steel firms who wished to enlarge their
operations as steel grew in greater demand, and also, as in the
case of Cammell's given above, wished to integrate their operations.   Shipping companies also, with the development of iron
ships and the beginnings of steel, and the transition from single
to compound engines around 1870-5 were faced with new demands
for capital.   With commercial companies the need for extra
capital was due more to the increased market demand than to
technological changes.

The advantages of raising this extra capital by debentures
were many.   First they could be raised whether the company was
prosperous or no.   They could be issued below par if necessary,
and if the security were good, the investors would accept them.
Secondly, in prosperous times they had a beneficial effect on
the dividends of ordinary shares.   Thirdly, an important consideration in the beginning of company finance, they were more
secure and cheaper than advances from a bank in the long run,
and they could, if desired, be paid off.   The advantages of the
"floating charge" debentures will be discussed later.

The payment of vendors in debentures arose in the iron and
steel and coal companies through the desire of the vendors to

---

1) 1877 Report, Qu. 1690.

retire from active participation in the concern and the inability
of the company to raise sufficient capital to pay them off in
cash and the inadvisability of such a course if it were possible,
as the investors looked before investing at the extent to which
the vendor was still "in" the company.   An example is
Bonville's Court Coal and Iron Company (1873).   The Vendor
"in consequence of deaths and family arrangements ... determined
to dispose of his property", but "as a proof of his confidence
in the undertaking, he has consented to allow the sum of
£95,000 to stand as a deferred payment for five years taking
Mortgage Debentures bearing interest at 6% per annum for such
sum" (he took the balance £115,000 in cash).[1]

The preparedness of investors to accept this type of
security was an important factor governing the amount that
could be issued.   The role of railway debentures in paving the
way by familiarising the investing classes with the ideas of
debentur meaning security of capital and a fixed income, has
been discussed above.   Debentures of limited companies were
directed towards the same class of investor which had taken
railway debentures.   Chadwick when he was issuing the iron,
coal and steel companies debentures in the seventies addressed
himself to "professional gentlemen and others who do not invest
in the ordinary shares of trading companies" and to "ladies
and persons not possessed of separate sources of revenue".

---

1) Quotations from the Prospectus of this company.

By 1874 he can write, partly truthfully and partly by way of encouragement, "we observe an increasing degree of confidence deservedly reposed in this class of security".[1] By 1885 this "degree of confidence" had, according to "The Statist" increased to a dangerous extent. "Solicitors and investors have got it into their head that mortgage debentures have a charm about them possessed by no other security."[2] Warnings against debentures were frequently given in the eighties to

investors: "There is a common impression that by giving a particular instrument the name Debenture - it confers on the holder a right in case of insolvency to rank prior to ordinary creditors. Not so unless the assets of the company or part thereof are specifically charged as security for payment of the debentures." [3]

But the confidence of investors in debentures was growing rather than weakening[4] in the eighties, and the legal support of the "floating charge" secured this confidence.

In the seventies and eighties the demand for debentures as investments was increasing outside the circle of "safe" investors. Banking and insurance institutions were extending

---

1) From "Chadwick's Investment Circular", 1872, p.152; 1874, p.214 and 1874, p.228.
2) "The Statist", 1885, Vol. XVI, p.147.
3) "Journal of Institute of Bankers", "Questions of practical interest" 1880-1, Vol. 2, p.437-8.
4) The increase in the number of companies issuing ordinary shares had at the same time increased the attraction of debentures. The investment market was becoming bewildering in it's variety, whereas debentures appeared the same whatever company issued them. H.S. Foxwell remarked in 1886 that if debentures were made illegal, "everyone would in a small way, no matter how occupied, have to make for himself the difficult examination of investments which now taxes the skill of bankers", "Journal of the Institute of Bankers", Vol. VII, 1886, p. 73. This same difficulty led, as we shall see later, to the boom in investment trusts in the late eighties.

their investments beyond railway debentures and the growth of
Trust companies increased this demand.   Trust companies, the first
of which for buying Stock Exchange securities was formed in
1869, were at this stage mainly interested in the securities of
Foreign and Colonial Governments and the debentures of railway
and other incorporated companies.   The "Foreign and Colonial
Government Trust", 1868, "The Submarine Cables Trust", 1871,
"Mortgage Debenture and Government Security Trust", 1873, "The
Railway Debenture Trust", 1873, and "the Gas and Water Debenture
Trust", 1873, illustrate this tendency.   In 1875 it was calculated that 18 were still in existence.[1]   These companies
affected the demand for debentures in two ways.   In the first
place they issued debentures themselves.   The "Gas and Water
Debenture Trust Company" was one of the first companies to issue
debentures to the public at the same time as ordinary shares.
Secondly they invested the proceeds of the share and debenture
issues in debentures.   They did not, as shown above, invest to
any great extent in the debentures of trading companies, but
they increased the demand for the "safer" type of debenture.

In the eighties both "The Statist" and "The Economist" refer
to the advance in securities other than first rate.   "The rise
in stocks having somewhat less than first rate rank in the
market is phenomenal"[2] and "The Economist" refers first to
the "gradual but distinct appreciation in the value of first

1) A. Scratchley, "Average Investment Trusts", 1875, p.13.
2) "The Statist", 1884, Vol. XII, p.525.

class fixed interest bearing securities" in 1885 and a year later to the "advancement of second rate securities".[1]

Part of this advancement was due to the economic conditions prevailing which will be dealt with later, but part was due to increased demand. Institutional investments and Trust companies were one source of this extra demand. "Trust money has continually accumulated with a steadying effect on stocks previously unsteady and the same with banking money."[2] Individual investors were driven to other securities. The increase in trustee investments had the same effect. "The better class of securities are snapped up by trustees".[3] The practice of primogeniture continually increased the amount of capital seeking "trustee" investments, although the actual scope of these were widened very slowly under the Trustee Acts. But the trustee legally had no alternative and the institutional investors, the banks, insurance companies and trusts would not take any alternative investments, so it was the individual investor who was driven to second and third rate securities and as the demand increased, so these securities appreciated.

These two factors, the necessities of the company for additional capital and the growth in numbers and wealth of the investors and institutions demanding debenture investments, were present throughout the period 1856-1885 and in the subsequent

1) "The Economist", 1885, p.1350, and 1886, p.983.
2) "The Statist", 1884, Vol. XII, p. 526.
3) "The Economist", 1886, p. 1046.

period.   The reason for the outburst of debenture issues in 1879-1885 was a combination of the influence of these factors with the economic character of that period.

The much discussed depression in trade and industry starting in the middle seventies had curbed the adventurous tendencies of both investor and promoter.   "A loss of faith in speculative industry" was the description given by "The Economist".[1] Ordinary shares were about this time building up a reputation of being unsafe and speculative so the only alternative was debenture investment.   This was the first depression period in which it had been possible for investors to switch over from the ordinary shares bought in prosperity to fixed interest bearing securities.[2]   This periodical turn towards 'better' class securities became a feature of company finance both pre-war and post war.   An illustration of the tendency in the post war period is that in the 1921-2 depression investors were said to be "queuing up to buy preference and debenture stock".[3]

A second feature of the conditions 1879-1885 was the "cheapness of money".   Skinner wrote in his "Stock Exchange

---

1) "The Economist", 1885, p.1350.
2) It was not only a question of a switch from relatively less secure investments to more secure ones, but also as W.W. Rostow has shown, a switch from foreign to home investment, increasing the pressure in the home market for "safe" investments. "Economic History Review", 1938, May, p.136 ff.
3) "Finance and Collections," 1923, p.46.

Year Book" for 1885, "High class borrowers never borrowed so
cheaply as they have of late".[1] The average bank rate for the
long stretch 1873-1887 was barely 3 per cent.[2] With a
"depression in prices and a depression in interest" it was
advantageous for the investor to have fixed interest bearing
stock and for the company to borrow money at low rates.

Not only this, the fall in prices and the cheapness of
money had led to discussions of the advisability of converting
the "Funds" to a lower rate of interest.   This was not carried
through until 1889, but the threat had driven many investors
to company debentures which were not in such a strong position
to force conversion.[3]

Debentures by the eighties were recognised as a fairly
normal method of raising additional capital for the company.
There was still an element of "necessity" about them, that is,
calls on shares or additional issues of share capital were
considered by some experts on company finance as the sound and
proper method, while debentures savoured of "financial difficulty" and "unsoundness".[4]   But this viewpoint was rapidly
losing ground.   The character of debentures followed closely
railway experience.   They were usually issued after some share

1) W.R. Skinner, "Stock Exchange Year Book and Directory"1885,
    Preface, and"Herepath" 1880, p. 1050.
    "One of the most remarkable features of the times ... is the
    extreme cheapness of money.
2) J.H. Clapham, op cit. Vol. II, p. 384-5.
3) cf. "The Statist", 1884, Vol. XII, p. 526.
4) e.g. "Herepath's Journal" 1873, p. 537, had a leading article
on "How to raise new capital" which stressed strongly use of
ordinary shares rather than Preference and Debentures on the
grounds of "fairness to present shareholders" and "general
soundness".

capital had been raised and were regarded with highest favour
when secured against existing property.   Debentures to vendor
and the "floating charge" were not very extensively used up to
this decade.   The chief reason for the use of debentures,
apart from economic conditions, was "to lighten the capital
charge on the undertaking"[1] not for "gearing"or "control",
nor for raising initial capital. The next thirty years saw a
rapid change in the form, character and use of debentures,
a change which had most fundamental effects on the finance of
companies and the relations of the investor to the company.

In the period 1885-1914 the issue of debentures became
a normal step in the finance of the company.   In 1897 it was
said to be a "universal" practice for all new companies and
private businesses converted into companies.[2]   In 1906
"every industrial company issues debentures as a matter of
course."[3]   By 1914, with certain conspicuous exceptions all
types of companies had debentures, whether they were newly
established, or conversions, or old companies dating back to the
dixties.   E. Manson, a legal authority on debentures in 1910,
described these facts of increase very eloquently.   "The

1) "Journal of Institute of Bankers", 1886, Vol. VII, Article
     by H.S. Foxwell, p. 73.
2) 1897 Report, Qu. s.400, 938, 1223, inter alia.
3) "Financial Review of Reviews", Vol. II, 1906, p.32.

history of debentures - almost untouched by legislation - springing out of mercantile usage, this branch has grown with the marvellous growth of the company and strengthened with its strength."[1]   The adjective "marvellous" was not so generally accepted as he wished to believe, but there was no doubt concerning the widespread adoption of the method.

The actual amount of capital raised by debentures is a further illustration of the extent and use of the method. Estimates of the total amount of the debentures of trading companies (not including railway and incorporated companies) rose from c. £250,000,000 in 1893[2] to c. £400,000,000 in 1905[3] to c. £750,000,000 in 1918.[4]   These estimates were obtained by calculating the normal ratio that debentures bore to paid up share capital, ranging from 1/5th to 1/3rd, and taking that proportion of the total paid up share capital of all the companies in existence.

The percentage of the total share and loan capital raised by debentures increased for the companies given in "Burdetts Official Intelligence" from 20.7% for 1,585 companies with a capital of £419 million in 1885, to 28.7% for 5,337 companies with a capital of £2,433 million in 1915.[5]   This figure tends to show that the estimates given above were, if anything, underestimates.

1) E. Manson, "Debentures of Trading Companies", 2nd Ed. 1910, pref.
2) J.D. Walker and Watson, "Investors and Shareholders Guide" 1894, p. 53.
3) F.B. Palmer, 1905, quoted in "Chamber of Commerce Journal" April supplement, 1910.
4) P.F. Simonsen, "Debenture Holders Legal Handbook" 1920 pref.
5) Appendix E.

There were, of course, variations from industry to
industry in the extent to which this method of raising capital
was used. Details of the different percentages of the total
capital raised by debentures in different industries are given
in Appendix E, but here we wish to contrast three different
types of industry.

First, the "old" established industries: in, shipping there
was the biggest advance in this period; the percentage of
capital raised by debentures compared with the total share and
loan capital of the companies given in Burdett rising from
15.4% in 1885, to 28.4% in 1915. In iron, steel and coal
the rise was smaller, from 17.0% in 1885 to 21.6% in 1915.

Secondly, in the "new" industries, for example/electricity,
there was a very extensive use of debentures. The percentage
of debentures to the total share and loan capital of 31 electric
supply companies in 1895 was 19.7. In 1915 this figure had
risen to 39.5%. A much larger selection in 1914-15, given in
Garcke Manual of Electrical Undertakings, of 269 supply companies with a total share and loan capital of £58 million,
shows 40% raised by debentures.

Thirdly in the "conversion" industries, e.g. breweries,
there was the greatest use of the debenture issue. The
percentage rose from 34.6% for 189 companies in 1895 to 42.9%
for 348 companies in 1915. The use of debentures in these
companies naturally attracted the greatest attention of
contemporaries.[1]

1) e.g.A.J. Wilson "Practical Hints to Investors" 1897, p.56-7,
and the "Investors' Review" 1896. Vol.I. p.212 ff.

We have mentioned above the relatively greater increase in the use of preference issues compared with debentures in this period, especially after the turn of the century. Some of the reasons for this will be discussed later. But it is interesting to note that in the "old" established industries and the general commercial and industrial companies this tendency towards preference issues was most marked. In the "new" industries and the "converted" companies, the generalisation does not hold good. The tendency was the reverse.[1]

In the period 1885-1914 there was a general acceptance of debentures as a method of raising about one-third of the capital of most public companies. There were variations of the amount raised in each industry; mines and insurance and banking companies for example did not use this method; electricity and brewery companies used it extensively, and in shipping, coal, iron and steel, and general commercial and industrial companies the proportion was about 20%.[2]

This increase in the use of debentures as a method for raising capital, was paralleled by a change in the character of "this hybrid creation"[3]. Legally, however, there was little development from the indefinite position of the previous period. The power to issue debentures still rested on the terms of the

1) Full details of this contrary tendency are shown in App. E.
2) The use of debentures in "private" companies will be dealt with separately.
3) J.D. Walker and Watson, op. cit. p. 168.

Memorandum of Association, as did the amount to which they could be issued. Further, if the Memorandum were silent on the question of borrowing, yet such powers to borrow were considered "properly incident to the course and conduct of the business for its proper purpose", then the right was implied. "Properly incident" was found to embrace "a shipping company, omnibus company, colliery company, and generally any trading company".(1) So that, in practice, either by the nature of the company, or by altering the Memorandum of Association, all companies had the power to issue debentures to almost any extent. The Companies Act of 1900 made the registration of all company debentures and mortgages after that date a condition of their legality, but it did not interfere in any way with the amount or character of the debentures issued.

The changes in the character of debentures in this period were two in number. First, the time, method and use of issue, and second, the type of assets against which they were secured. There was a third development which was a continuation on a much larger scale of the practice, mentioned above, of using debentures as payment to vendors.

Debentures were, for new companies, no longer issued at the time and to the extent that new capital became necessary, but they were issued alongside preference and ordinary capital at the formation of the company. They were not regarded as a special method of raising capital, but as normal as was ordinary

1) F. Gore Brown, "Handbook of Joint Stock Companies" 1919, p.209.

share method in the first period.

Mr. Henry Cosmo Bonsor before the 1896 Select Committee, claimed to have been the first promoter to have used this method. "I was, I believe, one of the first to promote an industrial company under the modern ideas of debenture, preference and ordinary stock".[1] The company in question which used "this novel idea", was not mentioned but apparently it was one of the brewery companies in the eighties. In the nineties, for London promoters, this simultaneous issue was recognised as the usual method. "Every large and successful company that has come out in the City within the last two years has had its capital raised substantially in that way more or less - one-third debentures, one-third preference shares, and one-third ordinary, and they have all been raised on the same prospectus."[2] At the 1897 Committee "the practice of the present day, i.e. for the capital to be divided into three parts, that is almost the universal case now".[3] Existing companies when they were reconstructed or amalgamated, usually followed the same course of one-third of their capital to each type.

An attempt was made by a Bill which was discussed by the House of Lords Select Committee in 1896, to break down this practice of issuing all three "lines" of capital together. The Bill was to make the issue of debentures only possible when

---

1) "Report of House of Lords Select Cttee. on Companies Bills 1896", IX, Qu. 866 (later referred to as 1896 Report).
2) 1896 Report, Qu. 132.
3) 1897 Report, Qu. 938.

a certain proportion of the share capital had been called up:
an attempt to make debentures once more an exceptional or
emergency method of raising capital, as they had been when they
originated with railway companies.   But this legal distinction
between shares and loans was already foreign to company practice
and the measure was defeated.   It was pointed out that in the
case of a purchase of an undertaking, all the capital had to be
raised at once; there could be no waiting.   "If you wanted
to raise the money to buy a business, say £1,000,000, you must
raise the whole capital at once."[1]   In other companies this
tripartite issue was necessary

> "because the shareholders on the one hand want to know
> that the debentures are subscribed, and the debenture
> holders on the other hand want to know that the shares are
> subscribed.   The capital of the company would be in-
> sufficient without either the one or the other and unless
> they can be both subscribed contemporaneously, it cannot
> commence business". (2)

Neither the vendor nor the contractor would move or publish
anything unless they knew that the whole capital was going to
be subscribed.[3]   These reasons were put forward by the few
men with commercial experience attending the Committees, and
it is noticeable that they were completely blind to the real
point of the Bill, which was to make a "fine" legal distinction
between shares and debts.   The business men saw no difference;
to them both were methods of raising the necessary capital for
the company.

1) 1897 Report, Qu. 959.
2) ibid. Qu. 341.
3) 1896 Report, Qu. 136 ff. and Qu. 161.

This proportion of one-third and the time of issue, determined the amount of debenture capital and the use to which it was put.   It was used alongside the share capital for the purchase of construction of the fixed capital of the company. In some cases, where a fair proportion of the share capital remained uncalled as security for the debentures,[1] there arose the paradoxical position of debentures being used to a greater extent than share capital as the real foundation of the company. This was more usual in financial companies than in industrial ones.

The use of the "floating charge" as the method of securing debentures, made possible the issue of debentures "simultaneously", and the widespread use of debentures in all types of companies.

The "validity of floating charges was finally established by the Court of Appeal in 1870"[2] but it's use was not common until the eighties and nineties.   In 1905 it was "almost universally used by companies for raising money, and experience has shown that it meets in an eminent degree the wants both of borrowers and lenders and of the business world generally".[3]

The characteristic of a floating charge debenture and its advantages over other types was that it could be issued by almost any company.   Its advantages over a mortgage were that, whereas a mortgage had to be specially drawn up and issued in favour of one or more persons and was not easily transferable,

1) 1897 Report, Qu. 200.
2) Report of the Company Law Amendment Committee, 1906,XCVII,
    paragraph 14 (later referred to as 1906 Report).
3) ibid. paragraph 39.

a debenture was readily marketable and anyone could invest
in them. And whereas a mortgage was a specific charge on some
piece of property which could not be sold, a floating charge was
on the property generally, all assets, book debts included, both
at the time of issue and in the future, and this stock, property
and debts could be bought, sold, or discharged.[1]

This applied to companies whose property was such that they
could choose between a mortgage and a debenture. For other
companies that were not in a position to issue a mortgage on
any specific property, the advantages of a floating charge were
more marked. Money could be raised by a floating charge on
future assets without the company possessing any tangible
property at all. In this way, said F.B. Palmer, "a floating
charge enables hundreds of concerns that could not otherwise
raise funds when they want them urgently, to raise money promptly
and easily and with very satisfactory security."[2]

In most companies which issued debentures, the specific
and floating charge were combined. An example of this is given
in Lindley's description of the working of a "series" of
debentures. These series were the natural development from the
success of a single debenture issue for a large company, and
were becoming common in the late nineties and early twentieth
century. "It is not uncommon for a company to issue two or
more series of debentures or debenture stock of which the first

1) cf. H.W. Jordan "Debentures" 1919, p. 11.
2) Report of Select Committee of the House of Lords on the
Companies Bills Report, 1898, Qu. 650 (later known as 1898
Report).

series is secured by a first fixed mortgage on certain specific
property and a first floating charge on the remainder of its
property; and the second series is secured by a first fixed
mortgage on other specific property, and a floating charge,
subject to the charge of the first series, on the remainder
of its property and so on with any subsequent series."[1]

As a result of this widespread use of debentures, the practice of issuing them alongside share capital and the use of the
floating charge, their character had changed. For the company
they were no longer considered as a debt, but as part of the
capital. When issuing debentures the problem was not so much
the question of when will it be possible to redeem them, but are
the profits of the company sufficiently stable to bear a fixed
interest charge? This was the chief tendency; it was not universal. F.B. Palmer, for example, in his evidence, of which part
is quoted above, still considered debentures as "urgent" and
emergency measures; he refers to cases where they are "payable or
demand" and there were many companies where this was the case.
But the most important development was in the opposite direction
Debentures were being issued as a calculated step to raise the
initial capital of the company, and they were secured on a floating charge which usually made them "perpetual", only realisable
from the company in certain eventualities which never happened
unless the company went into liquidation.

---

1) Justice Lindley, "A Treatise on the Laws of Companies", 6th
   Edition, 1902, p. 320-1.

Mr. Smith, the Inspector General of Bankruptcy, whose annual reports under the Companies Winding Up Act are such a valuable source of information on the "company limited", expressed this change in the character of debentures concisely before the 1898 Committee. "Debentures really form a kind of variety of capital of the company ... they are liable to the same incidents of deception, misrepresentation and fraud as the issue of capital .. they are underwritten in the same way. It is really a form of raising the capital of the company although technically it is not share capital, it is a debt."(1)

This is the first major change in the character of debentures of trading companies which had taken place by 1914 compared with their character in the first period. The debenture had been transformed by the practice of issuing them alongside capital at the start of the company and by the consequent use of the capital raised in construction, from a short term expediant to a long term method of raising capital.

The second change was a function of their widespread use. The extent to which they were issued by a company and their permanent character now made it possible for them to be used for purposes of "gearing" and control. With one third of the capital in preference shares and one third in debentures, it was possible for the owners of a proportion of the ordinary shares to gain a large degree of control over the direction of the company. Further, if the enterprise could bear the fixed interest charges

1)
   1898 Report, Qu. 1950.

arising from these pre-ordinary issues, there was the possibility
of enhanced returns on ordinary shares. We will reserve a discussion on the extent to which these possibilities were put into
practice to a later stage when discussing the relation between the
investor and the company. Here it is sufficient to note these
possibilities as arising out of the changed character of the
debenture.

We have discussed both the extent to which debentures were
used by public companies in the period 1885 to 1914,   the
changes in their character and use and the advantages these
changes offered to the company. There remains to be considered
the chief forces which led to their use by companies and to their
change of character.

The promoter in drawing up a prospectus of a public company
in this period 1885-1914 was governed by two considerations when
deciding the number of "lines" of capital he was to issue and the
types of "lines". The first was how much capital does the company need and what is the cheapest way of raising it. The
second was what will the investors in the market take and what do
the vendors (if any) want. These considerations applied equally
to the "new" company, whether converted or entirely new, and to
the "old" company desiring to raise additional capital. The use
of underwriting which was present, though not to any great extent
in home issues up to 1914, removed part of these considerations
from the sphere of the promoter proper, but they had still to be
faced by the underwriting syndicate.

The "more roundabout" methods of production which we discussed above as a feature of this period of capitalism, steadily

increased the amount of fixed capital necessary in an undertaking.
The amount of work ng capital increased as well but not in proportion and while the banks with increased efficiency through
amalgamations were able to supply this, a much wider appeal was
necessary for the fixed capital.   And given different sections
of investors it was impossible to raise the huge capitals made
necessary by these technological changes and by the tendency towards amalgamation and combination, by an issue of equity alone.
Further, in the rapidly increasing cases of amalgamation and
conversion it was necessary to safeguard the interests of the
old shareholders or the vendors and this could only be done by a
differentiation in the terms on which the new shareholders came
into the company.

These factors made the issue of stocks and shares other than
equity a necessity, and transformed these pre-ordinary issues from
an emergency measure to a normal method of raising capital.
They transformed debentures from loans on short term to long
term or "perpetual" debenture stock, used for fixed capital
equipment.   But the specific reason for the use of debentures by
a company was their "cheapness" compared with other types of
capital.   Provided the company was able to stand the fixed
interest charges, then "it is the most economical way of raising
money because you can raise money at a much lower rate of interest
on debentures than upon preference stock".   (1)   The actual rate
of interest varied of course with the economic conditions of the

1)
1897 Report, Qu. 403.

country and the standing of the individual firm; But provided
the investors were prepared to take the stock, the generalisation
about "more economical" held true throughout the period.

A second specific reason for the use by company promoters
of debentures was the power to issue them below par. All share
issues, on the other hand, had to be issued either at or above
par. This power gave the debenture issue two advantages.
First, they could be issued in depressed as well as prosperous
times. Secondly, direct allowances could be made for underwriting and other commissions, in all cases, whereas with shares
this was only possible when the issue was above par. It is
suggested that the legal ban on the underwriting of shares which
was effective until the 1900 Companies Act, and which did not
apply to debentures, was one of the sources of their popularity.[1]
After the 1900 Act and particularly after the 1907 Companies Act,
debentures lost this particular advantage.

From the point of view of the public company, then, a "line"
of debentures was necessary and advantageous for three main
reasons. First, the size of the capital to be obtained from the
public entailed differentiation between different sections in the
market. Secondly, the change in character of debentures from
loans to debenture stock had made them an economical way of
raising part of the fixed capital, and the use of the floating
charge had made this a possible method for most companies.

---

1) Cf. D. Finnie, "Capital Underwriting", 1934, pp. 45 ff.

Thirdly, there were particular reasons for their use by
individual companies. If the connections of the company with
the investment market were weak, the underwriting of the debenture issue was allowed which was not possible with share issues,
and if, in a particular company, it was desired to keep the
control in particular hands, or to increase the returns on
equity, debentures were an effective way of doing this.

The second main determinant of the use of debentures was
the demand from the investor and the wishes of the vendor.
While the reasons foruse of debentures on the part of the
company remained of equal force throughout this period, there
were some fluctuations in the demand from investors and vendors.
It was these fluctuations that were a major cause of the decrease
in the total use of debentures compared with preferemce after
c. 1896. We will deal first with the general long run demand
for debentures and then with the reasons for the fluctuations
that took place.

Debentures owed their popularity with the investor to
their almost legendary security. The capital was safe, though
it might depreciate in themarket, and more important still, so
was the interest. The debenture holders had power to appoint
a Receiver if this were not forthcoming. "The real advantage of
the debenture is the certainty of interest - if you throw any
doubt on this you cut at the whole root of the matter"; this
was the opinion of Mr. Stanley Boulter, who as Chairman of the
Law Debenture Corporation amongst others, was a fair authority on
the debenture investor. He described the considerations that

influenced this investor; he was "the man who says 'I am satisfied with 3½% or 3¾% so long as you give me a first charge on the whole business and I come in for my profits before any-body else gets anything".[1] The importance of this type of investor in company finance as a whole was defined as follows: "When you are touching debenture money you are touching the real capital of the country. The person who takes 3½% and the person who does not want more than 3½% to 4% is the person who has got the real capital of this country at his control".[2]

He was not quite so explicit on the identity of these powerful people, but he emphatically denied that debenture holders were solely or mainly "country clergymen, widows and orphans".[3] While we can agree that the "widow and orphans" myth could be dropped by the nineties, he was unfair on the country clergyman. The professional classes and the rentier were the people who invested in debentures either directly, or as Mr. Boulter hinted later, through institutions like invest-ment trusts and insurance companies. The books and journals appealing to this class of investor advised them to invest in debentures and none other. G. Bartrick Baker in his book "Sound Investments for Small Savings" in 1889 says that ordinary shares are "Exposed to most violent fluctuations" and can only recommend the secure pre-ordinary stock. Twenty years

1) 1897 Report, Qu. 824.
2) ibid   Qu. 880.
3) ibid   Qu. 923 and 1090.

later Henry Lowenfeld repeated the same advice, "investors
who desire a safe and regular income must eschew ordinary and
deferred stock entirely".[1] The rich investor who had earli*er*
lent money to railways on debentures still existed, but he had
been powerfully supplemented in the debenture market by the
rentier and professional classes.

The existence of these classes of investors is further
shown by the popularity of investment trusts which issued
their capital partly in debentures and re-invested their total
capital raised in other debentures. They had a double effect
on the market. On the one hand, by their issue of debentures
they increased the amount of debentures available for investors
and on the other hand they constituted a powerful demand for
debentures.

We mentioned above a boom in trusts in the seventies.
This was easily outdone in the three years 1888-1890. In the
year 1888 there were 23 trusts of various descriptions offered
to the public; in 1889, 60. And the total nominal capital
for the three years was £67,000,000.[2] Moreover these trusts
were formed specifically to deal, not only in particular public
utility debentures but in all types of company debenture. For
example, one of the leading and most successful was Mr.Boulter's
"Law Debenture Corporation". One-third of its capital was
issued to the public in the form of debentures and its objects

1) H. Lowenfeld, "Investment an Exact Science", 1909, p.16.
2) Figures from "The Statist", 1889, II, p. 656, and
    "Fairplay", 1891, p.355.

were "to deal in debentures and to facilitate to some extent
the formation of joint stock companies by arranging to take
their debentures when they are formed".[1]   We deal later with
the element of underwriting which is implicit in this statement.

The attraction of these trusts, when successful, for the
small investor was most marked.   They provided him with income
and some security without the trouble and difficulty of deciding
between different investments.   And by combining the savings
of a number of small investors[2] they brought into the
debenture market a new demand which before had been kept out by
the usually high denominations of debenture stock.

A second and steadier demand for debentures from institutional investors was that coming from banks and insurance companies.
The increase in the "Fund" of the latter and consequently the
amount available for investment was a marked feature of the last
quarter of the nineteenth century and the first decade of the
twentieth.[3]   The United Kingdom Life Insurance Statistics
between 1888 and 1913 give some idea of this increase:

| Year | Sums Assured and Bonuses. £.Mn. | | Assets. |
	Ordinary	Industrial	
1888	442	86	195
1913	855	429	530 [4]

Their investments were not "risky"; they "started from a point
on the security scale marked by railway and the best industrial

1) 1897 Report, Qu. 786.
2) The figures given of the number of shareholders in Trust
companies in the "Investors Blue Book" for 1912 show that
only rarely did such a company have less than 5,000 shareholders.
3) H. Levy and A. Wilson, "Industrial Assurance", p. 30.
4) G.L. Schwartz and F.W. Paish, "Insurance Funds" 1934,p.79.

debentures upwards"[1] but the size of their investments was so
great that they drove the individual investors into ordinary
company debentures.   An illustration of the size of their
investments is shown by the gigantic Prudential, which in 1915
was said to be "the biggest shareholder in the Bank of England ...
the most extensive owner of railway securities ... and of late
years one of the most important "underwriters" of all the higher
class securities that are placed on the London market."[2]

There was a third source of demand for debentures and high
class securities which, although coming from individuals and not
institutions, had the same effect on the debenture market as did
these institutions.   This was the demand from Trustees.   The
scope of Trustee investments had been widened by the Trustee Acts
of 1889, 1893 and the Colonial Stock Act of 1900.   Industrial
debentures were still barred (except of course in the case of
specific instructions), but it was again a case of driving other
investors into company debentures rather than Government Stocks.
"The best securities are snapped up by Trustees".

These two main classes, the individual investor and the
institutional and trustee investors, constituted one of the chief
sources of demand in   the   debenture   market.   The   long
run tendency between 1885 and 1914 was for the wealth and number
of these classes to increase.   There was, however, after the
nineties a relative falling-off in the use of and demand for

1) J.H. Clapham, op.cit. Vol. III, p.298.
2) H. Levy and A. Wilson, op. cit. p. 380, quoted from the
   Passfield Report on Industrial Insurance, 1915, p.9.

debentures.   This was due, it is suggested, to two factors.
First the fact, mentioned above, that in spite of the increased
security afforded to the investor by the floating charge, there
was a definite limit to the extent to which a company could issue
debentures with hope of success with the investor.   The issue
was not regarded safe when the amount of debentures exceeded the
nominal share capital,   On the other hand, for the alternative
"safe" pre-ordinary investment, namely preference shares, the
factor to be considered was not assets but earning capacity.
In the period when the greater the capital the more certain the
earning power was the rule, this was the position in the beginnings of the trend towards amalgamation and combination, the
preference share was naturally popular.

The second chief reason for the relative decline in the use
of and demand for debentures compared with preference,was the
reversal of the downward fall of prices after the nineties.
The enterprising type of investor, the business man, the engineer,
etc. had been affected more by the depression and the low prices
than the "safe" investor, the salaried classes, landlords, etc.
Wesley Mitchell estimated that about 50% of the savings of the
United Kingdom before the war came from the "business" type.
Consequently, with the rising prices and profits in the first
decade and-a-half of the twentieth century, there was an increase
in the effectiveness of the demand of this type of investor who
desired enterprising rather than "safe" investments.[1]   This is

1) C. Wesley Mitchell, "Business Cycles", 1913, p. 387 ff.

particularly clear in the case of the home industrials, the basic
industries, in which, as we showed above, there was a big increase
in the use and demand for preference issues between 1895 and 1915
compared with debentures.

In the "converted" industries this was not the case.   There
was an increase, for example, in the case of brewery companies,
given in Burdett's, of the proportion of the total share and loan
capital which was raised by debentures.   But this was due not
so much to new issues to the public of debentures, but to an
increase in the number of companies considered in the sample which
issued debentures to vendor.   It was this issue of debentures to
vendor that constituted the second main reason on the demand side
for their use by companies in this period.

The issuing of debentures to vendor which bulked largely in
the discussions on company law in the nineties, was not a new practice.   We drew attention to its use in the iron and steel trades
in the seventies.   But general public opinion on the method had
changed.   No longer did companies splash on the prospectus that
the vendor was still with them in the form of debenture stock.
That statement was no longer universally popular.   To a number of
investors and certainly to most of the writers on investment such
a statement was an indication that finances of the company were
not in too sound a condition.   But the method was not only
popular with unsound companies, though these naturally attracted
the greatest attention.

There were roughly three cases when this method of issuing
debentures to vendor was used.   "Sometimes it was done in good

faith by people retiring and wishing to leave capital in".[1]
In this case the vendor was still interested in the concern
but not sufficiently to take the risks and advantages of
equity.   But it was in its very nature an exceptional case.
Vendors did not all realise their age in the nineties and decide
to retire;   only a minority of the debentures to vendor cases
can come under this heading.

The second case is that of a going concern bought up by
a promoter, to float as a company.   This was the usual process
in large firms when debentures went to vendor.   The only cause
for suspicion here was the assessment of the property and the
goodwill, and the question of whether the business had had
profits such as would allow for a large fixed interest charge.

The third case was the obvious fraud.   Justice Lindley
said in 1897 "at the present time the vendors get paid in
debentures: the company is formed and they are masters of the
whole situation.   Those debentures are brought in the moment
the company comes into trouble and all the unsecured creditors
are left out in the cold."[2]   Put in another way, more con-
cretely: "Somerset House, since the advent of the practice
of issuing debentures to members of a company on its conversion
to the joint stock form, is fast becoming a veritable haven from
hungry creditors."[3]

The use of the debenture in public companies between 1885
and 1914 was the result then of the two main forces of the

1) "Report of Departmental Committee of Board of Trade on amendments necessary in Acts relating to joint stock companies" 1895,
LXXXVIII, Paragraph 12 (later referred to as 1895 Report).
2) 1897 Report, Qu. 32.
3) Gregory's "Hints to Speculators", 1895, p. 125.

necessity and advantage to the company, and the demand from different types of investor and from the vendor. There remains to be considered the use of the debenture in the private company.

In the spate of conversions of small concerns into unofficially "private" and after 1907, officially Private Limited Liability Companies, the "superior borrowing facilities" of the company over the private firm was prominent in the reasons given for conversion.[1] Lord Macnaghten once said "that among the principle reasons which induce persons to form private companies are ... the desire to avoid the risk of bankrupcy and the increased facilities afforded for borrowing money."[2] Not only could they give a floating charge, which was prohibited to a private firm by the Bills of Sale Act, but also up to 1900 at least they avoided publicity about their borrowings. Further, although under the 1907 Companies Act which legalised Private Companies, they were not allowed to issue shares or debentures to the public, the holders of debentures could "re-sell to the general public, thus creating a marketable security".[3]

The extent to which private companies practised this method of raising capital by debentures can be judged to some extent by the outcry against it. The Chamber of Commerce Journal, which was notable in the nineties for its "creditor" rather than

---

1) C.W. Turner, "Treatise on the Conversion of a Business into a Private Limited Company", 1907, p. 9, and cf. H.W. Jordan, "Private Companies", 3rd ed. 1915, p.
2) Quoted in "Accountants Journal", Vol. 41, 1923-4, p.312.
3) ibid. loc. cit.

"producer" attitude, was continually decrying this practice of
small companies. "The difficulty has occurred not so much with
public as with private limited liability companies" was part of
a resolution passed at the 33rd Annual Conference of the
Associated Chambers of Commerce in 1893.[1]   A year later the
Journal reports,"frequent complaints of traders as to the
injustice which is perpetrated through the conversion of private
trading concerns into limited liability companies with
debentures".[2]   They go on protesting every year in the
Journal or at the Conferences until 1900.   The same tale was
repeated before the Committees on the Companies Acts in 1896,
1897 and 1898, and although the majority of the 1906 committee
recognised debentures as a normal feature of any company, the
Minority Report on the subject of Floating Charges kept up the
protest.[3]

The issue of debentures to the vendors of these small
companies was the outcome of the same forces that led to their
similar issues in larger public ones.   Contemporaries, especially the Associated Chambers of Commerce, were convinced that the
purely fraudulent cases of this type of issue were more prevalent
in the small private companies than in the large ones.   But the
winding-up returns, while showing a high mortality among small
companies in general, do not give any conclusive proof that the

1) Reported in "Chamber of Commerce Journal", 1893, Vol. XII,
     No. 131, Jan.
2) ibid. 1894, p. 15.
3) 1906 Report, p. 27.

method was widespread in companies of under £10,000 capital.

The reasons for the issue of debentures by private companies was, just as much in the case of public companies, the result of the necessities and advantages of the company and the demand from the investor. We have discussed above "the superior borrowing powers of the private company over the partnership". There is no doubt on this point. From the investors side, while the debentures were not directly issued to the public, the proprietor of the concern going limited, usually had a number of friends who were willing to assist him; but no longer as adventurers, but as cautious lenders. Loans from individuals to a small partnership had always been possible under the common law. The repeal of the Usury Acts had made these more attractive from the point of view of interest. But the limited company made the security of the capital of the "creditors" greater, the appeal wider, and the position of the "debtor" less risky.

Given these conditions, debentures in private companies were inevitable. And the answer to the Chambers of Commerce's "maiden in distress" - the "ordinary creditor" - was given by the majority of the 1906 Committee, who replied for large and small companies alike, "caveat creditor".[1]

---

1) 1906 Report.
   A very necessary rebuke, for men like Harold Brown of the London Chamber of Commerce were never tired of telling the investor "caveat emptor" (see his evidence before the House of Lords Committees).

Had more people been prepared to reason about debentures
on the lines suggested both by Edwin Field in the fifties who
remarked "there are dishonest creditors as well as dishonest
debtors" and of Lord Loreburn, an analysis of the role of
debentures would have passed at a much earlier date from the
immediate short term criticism of "bandits of the company limit-
d" ; for given the willingness of different sections of
nvestors to accept interest, security and marketability, with
o control or direction, and given the need on the part of
ompanies to increase the amount of their fixed capital and to
oncentrate their control of this larger capital, the transition
f debentures from short term loan to part "of the capital of the
ompany though technically a debt" was the natural "outcome of
he necessities of the company".[1]   Neither vehemence nor
egislation could have effectively stopped this development.
he criticism should have passed on to the question of whether
he enormous increase in the amount of fixed interest bearing
                was
ecurities /leading to rigidity in the economic structure.   In
rosperous times it meant increased proportional returns on
quity, but trade cycles had come to stay, and the dead weight
f this interest in depression times was assuming serious pro-

---

[1] H. Hurrell and C. Hyde, "Joint Stock Companies Practical Guide"
rd edition, 1889, p.77.   It should be noted, however, that
hough debentures can now be seen as a fairly logical develop-
nt, according to men like W.S. Lindsay, M.P., in the fifties,
he very reason for introducing Limited Liability in the fifties
as to allow men to lend not at a fixed, but at a fluctuating
ate of interest, cf. W.S. Lindsay and R. Cobden, op. cit p.4.

portions. Demand and technique were continually changing,
but the problem was not quite so much that the holders of
securities might, as a result of these changes, be left "with
a depreciated or even valueless security",[1] but that because
of the huge inarticulate rather than articulate pressure of
this growing amount of fixed interest capital, these changes
would not be adopted for a period for fear of "confidence
collapse". This huge debenture capital might tend to
handicap adjustments and consequently intensify any depression,
and the real question which the inquiries and journals of the
early twentieth century should have been asking was "Have these
agencies which have been established in order to obtain security for savings now reached a point where they tend to
cause insecurity?"[2] But it was neither asked nor answered.

---

1) G.L. Schwartz and F.W. Paish, op cit, p. 80.
2) cf. "Explorations in Economics", 1936, p. 499 ff., M.T.
   Copeland on "The Social Significance of Debt".

PART III

THE RELATIONS BETWEEN THE INVESTORS AND THE
LIMITED LIABILITY COMPANY, 1856 - 1914 ; THE
CHANGES IN THE METHODS OF PROMOTION, IN THE
METHODS OF ATTRACTING INVESTORS, AND IN THE
RELATIONS BETWEEN THE SHAREHOLDER AND THE
COMPANY.

CHAPTER VII.

Changes in the Technique of the Promotion
of Limited Liability Companies, 1856-1914.

The emergence of "the company promoter" as an
individual almost completely independent of the company
or companies that he promoted was another of the many
developments that the framers and sponsors of the Company
legislation in the middle of the nineteenth century did
not foresee.

In spite of the railway experience, the legislature
assumed in the framing of the acts that a company would
be formed by a group of capitalists coming together and,
with the legal help of a solicitor that they would draw up
the Articles and Memorandum of Association and register
the company. It was assumed that the memorandum would
be signed by all those taking a large part in the company
and that the capital of the company would be great enough
to necessitate that number being more than seven. There
were no provisions in the act for expenses in connection
with promotion, advertising etc.

The fifty years after the passing of the company Acts
saw the field of joint stock organisation pass beyond the
stage where this "round the table" promotion was possible.
Increased numbers of investors and increased demand for

capital necessitated a "professional" intermediary, and schemes had to be devised to assure his remuneration.

Between 1856 and the eighteen 'eighties the professional promoter can be said to be unimportant in company promotion. In some cases his services were not needed; in others he can be seen in a crysallis stage in the form of credit associations and financial agents, but with none of the splendour and fraud that attached to his emergence in the last decades of the nineteenth and early twentieth century.

Companies tended to be formed, in the sixties, more or less on the lines expected by the framers of the 1862 Act. This is shown by the large numbers of shares taken out by the people signing the memorandum of association, and to a lesser degree by the number of people signing the memorandum. Of the 1759 companies formed between 1st June, 1864 and 31st May, 1866, over fifteen hundred of them had more than seven shares taken out by those signing the Memorandum. Only 11 % of the companies, or 208, were cases where those signing only took one share each, or seven altogether. The average number of shares taken out by those signing was between 200 and 500.[1] This figure must be considered in the light of the usual share denomination of companies at that date, and the

---

1) From "Return Relating to Joint Stock Companies", 1866.

figure of 11 % is swollen probably, by the number of
speculative concerns established prior to the 1866 crash.
Most companies did not need the intermediary services
of a promoter of a financial association to obtain the
capital required from the public. The contacts of the
group of capitalists or the "group of gentlemen"[1]
forming the concern were sufficient to provide any
capital necessary after the original group had subscribed
heavily.

In the seventies this practice of forming companies
without the help of intermediaries was continued, though
except for small companies it was a provincial and
industrial, rather than London and commercial method.
For example the cotton companies in Lancashire in the
seventies with capitals of up to £100,000 very often
did not have an agent or promoter. J. Kidger before the
1886 Commission on the Depression in Trade and Industry,
reports that the cotton companies are brought into
existence "without the aid of profession floaters, in
many cases shares were subscribed for without even a
prospectus being issued."[2] That this was not always
so is shown by the remarks of J. Mawdsley before the same

---

1) These are the words used in the prospectus of Bolckow
   Vaughan - in 1864.
2) "R.C. on the Depression" 1886. Appendix A. p.308. Vol.111.

Commission about people promoting companies from the
big centres of population, meaning Manchester and Liverpool,
purely for sale and profit![1]   Some of these Manchester
men stayed in cotton once they had promoted a company but
by 1886 Albert Simpson, a Preston authority on cotton
spinning could ask ask a question which implied that the
professional promoter had in some cases appeared in the
cotton industry by this date. Writing in the Accountant's
Journal, "Take the Oldham Limited Mills for example. How
many of the original promoters of each mill can there now
be found on the directorate?"[2]   And the question remained
unanswered. The method was beginning to change.

The cases where the embryo professional promoter
appeared, were confined to those companies whose capital
was so large that a general appeal for capital was to some
extent necessary, and to those companies which were formed,
more as a result of pressure from investors, than of demand
from industry.   There was a third type of company, the
"new" concern, where trade connections were completely
lacking and a full time agent was engaged to make these
contacts and raise the capital.

In the sixties and seventies the most conspicuous
industry of the first type in which the embryo promoter
or agent appeared, was iron and steel. The companies in

---

1) - ibid. Qu. 5043.

2) "The Accountant", Oct. 9th, 1886. p. 571.

this industry depended largely on the assistance of a
firm like Chadwick, Adamson and Collier for their formation.
This firm did not at any time regard itself as the "promoter"
of these companies. It was the agent to assist in the
technical problems of conversion, valuation, the drawing up
of the Memorandum etc., and   in the attraction of
a certain percentage of the capital from the general
investing public. By 1877, Chadwick could claim to have
helped to form 50-60 companies with a total share capital
of over £40 mn.[1] This shows the size of the companies,
and Chadwick said that the smallest company with which they were
associated had a capital of £100,000.[2] This firm was
the most important financial agent for industrial companies
in the first twenty five years of the Limited Liability Act,
but they never resembled in any great degree the "professional
Promoters" of the late nineteenth and early twentieth century.

In the first place their assistance was technical
in the formation of the company. They did not urge
firms to be converted but were prepared to give assistance
to concerns that came to them. The amount of capital they
assisted to raise from the public was small compared with
the amount left in by the vendors or invested by the
subscribers to the Memorandum.[3] And once the company
had been officially formed they did not then collect their

---

1) 1877 Report, Qu. 1993.
2) ibid Qu. 2002.
3) as quoted above Chadwick estimated that amount of "new
   blood was only 25-30%". 1877 Report, Qu. 2075-6.

commission and pass on to another company, but   stayed
with the company as auditors and felt to a certain degree
responsible to their clients whom they had persuaded to
invest.[1]

The role of Chadwick, Adamson and Collier, and similar
firms like, Richardson Chadbourn and Co., Alfred Whitworth,
Clemesha and Co., and Joshua Hutchinson and Co., was
primarily to assist those companies which, through the
technical difficulties of conversion and the size of capital,
needed professional guidance both in forming the company
and securing part of their capital. But the increase in the
amount of capital needed from the public for these "old"
firms, both in event of conversion or extension, was
steadily increasing the reliance of such firms and companies
on an agent who had contacts to secure the capital.

The second type of company mentioned above for which
there was some form of "professional promoter" was
the company formed mainly as a result of the demand by the
investors for a lucrative outlet with limited liability for
their savings. The financial and credit associations played
the role of forming such companies for these investors.
These credit associations were mainly interested in overseas
developments, because the home industrial companies that

---

1) This responsibility is shown in their Monthly Circular
     to all their clients.

were formed usually had sufficient personal contacts to raise most of the capital required. But their influence at home was not altogether negligible.

"The Mercantile Credit Association" for example was chiefly interested in companies inside the United Kingdom,[1] and this association usually worked with the "Credit Mobilier". Second in importance for home companies was the "Financial Corporation Ltd." The companies that these organisations promoted were not insignificant, the capital was usually very large between £100,000 and £500,000, but their term of existence was not very long. The "Mercantile Credit Association" promoted amongst others the "Millwall Iron Shipbuilding Company", "The Merchant Shipping Company", and "The Humber Iron-works and Ship-building Company". Other companies promoted by similar organisations included "the London Engineering and Iron Ship-building Company", "The Plymouth Ship-building Dock and Iron-works Company", and "the Tyne Iron Ship-building Company". All of these were promoted in the year 1864 and the interest in Ship-building is a reflection of the change taking place from wood to iron and sail to steam, and the traditions of general investment in shipping. A second feature is that, although these associations advertised the prospectus of these companies extensively through news-papers and circulars, the shares were never less than £25 each.

---

1) "The Shareholders Guardian", 1863, November, p.12.

Even the most widespread advertising was still only
directed to the wealthy investor who would invest deeply
in a company.

The instability of the Company promoted by these
associations compared with those assisted by, for example,
Chadwicks, Collier and Co., is seen from the position ten
to fifteen years later. In 1877 Chadwick could claim only
about one failure out of every ten companies with which
his firm was associated.[1] Whereas, of the firms mentioned
above as promoted by the Associations, not one existed in
their original form in 1882.

We have dealt above with the general reason for the
emergence of these credit associations, namely the greater
demand for investment by the investing classes compared
with the need for extra capital by industry. Savings had
outrun demand to some extent and all types of
speculative ventures had sprung up to cater for the investors.

A further cause of the instability of the companies
which they promoted was their adverse position at the very
start compared with companies formed without a promoting
agency and private concerns. For although the capital of
these "promoted" companies was great, a large part of this
capital had been eaten away by the promotion expenses.
Referring to the Humber Iron-works and Shipbuilding Company,
the "Shareholder's Guardian" wrote, "The Mercantile Credit

1) 1877 Report. Qu.1993

Association and the Credit Mobilier are the sponsors for the project : and as they are not in the habit of doing much gratuitously, we may take it for granted that a considerable portion of the proposed capital will find its way into their coffers."[1]   This "almost unlimited amount of preliminary expenses before a shilling was earned"[2] coupled with the rather doubtful character of the business at the start, due to the lack of demand by sound industrial concerns for conversion by agencies at this date, was sufficient to give this type of company promotion an unstable existence.

The individual company promoter did exist in some small companies which were either lacking in business contacts, or were frankly speculative ventures. "The promoter manager" was a fairly well known figure in the sixties[3] and he reappears again in the discussions on the "single-ships" of the eighties.   But this is clearly, in effect, another name for the role of the entrepreneur or "captain of industry" and not an entirely new type of person. In some entirely new companies the "promoter" did appear. The "Limited Liability Joint Stock Companies List" for 1866 had an article on the formation of companies. In most cases, as suggested above, the writer regards the vendor as the promoter who employs professional assistance for valuation,

1)   "Shareholders Guardian" May 2nd, 1864. p.208.
2)   "Journal of the Royal Society of Arts", loc.cit. p.23.
3)   cf.Wm.Hawes "Journal of the Royal Society of Arts", 1866, loc.cit.

advertising etc., but he gives one exception. That is
the case of a company being formed to work out a new invention.
In such a case the Financial Joint Stock Agent stands ever
ready, and it is rarely that he cannot quickly obtain funds
for every reasonable undertaking.[1] But as shown above, the
number of "new invention" companies was small. In the purely
speculative field the figure of Albert (Baron) Grant, stands
out as the most conspicuous individual promoter. But though
he was described as the "Prince of Promoters" this title was
more a comment on the flatness of the country around, rather
than on the ability and success of Grant. Although he could
erect a monument to himself in Leicester Square, his hey-day
was short, and compared with either Hudson before, or Hooley
to follow, he was quite small fry.

This was the general position of company promotion up
to the 'eighties; most of the promotion was done by the vendors
themselves, and, the minority of   larger or more speculative
companies the technical agent like Chadwick,   the financial
agent,   the Credit Association of the individual promoter
like Grant, stood ever ready to assist.

Chronologically however, there were certain differences
of emphasis.   In the seventies, while the technical agent was
increasing in importance, and the individual Financial Agent
still pursuing his unsteady path, the Credit Associations

---

1) The Limited Liability Joint Stock Companies List", 1866,
      page 14.

were no longer so conspicuous in home promotion.[1]
"Overend Friday" had injured their reputation and the
demand for savings was slowly levelling up to supply.

The prospectuses of industrial companies no longer
had headings in red type "The Mercantile Credit Association
invites subscriptions for .... " In fact they now often
advertised as an additional reason for subscribing "No
promotion money will be paid".[2] But very few were as
explicit as the "West Dronfield Colliery Company" 1873,
which wrote, "No promotion money to be paid. All expenses,
including registration law charges, advertisement and every
other expense to be allotment of shares being covered by a
commission of $2\frac{1}{2}\%$ on the nominal capital of the company".[3]
This indicates that although the initiative for the formation
of the company still came from the vendor, whereas in the
'nineties and early twentieth century, it came from the
promoter, already the business of forming a company meant
a handsome $2\frac{1}{2}\%$ commission on the capital to somebody,

1) Under other names they were still conspicuous in foreign
   enterprise. Arthur Crump gives a pleasant description of
   their work in "the Theory of Speculation", 1874, p.114.
   "Individual Promoters worked at the business of building
   up joint stock schemes, then it grew into syndicates and
   we now have wealthy firms, with large machinery, whose
   whole time and staff is devoted to hunting about the
   world for powers to bring out foreign loans, for concessions
   for making railways, docks, harbours, gas-works and the
   like; when they have procured one or the other, they fix
   the amount of capital, cut it up into shares and administer
   them to the public, by much the same process as the
   Strasburgers enlarge the livers of their geese".
2) For example "Welsh Freehold Iron and Coal Company, 1873.
3) From the Prospectus of this Company.

(Chadwick only got 1%); And as yet the commission was usually distributed to different people, the solicitors, valuers, advertisers etc., and did not all go through the bottle-neck of the promoter.

The eighties were the transition period between the methods described above and the emergence of the professional promoter. In the sixties and seventies the home industrial companies did not need the services of the professional promoter. The extra capital they required was not great and it could be supplied either through the individual contacts of the capitalist forming the company or with the help of a firm like Chadwicks who were in contact with a few thousand wealthy capitalists. Foreign investment had of necessity to be done through intermediary organisations. But even after these two fields had absorbed a large part of the spare capital of the investors, the "plethora of money" was sufficiently great in the sixties to allow for the formation of promoting companies like the financial associations.

By the eighties the position was changing. The demand for capital by industry was greater than could be supplied by a few contacts. A wider appeal had to be made. Secondly the financial agents who were present in the first period had discovered the lucrative profession of company promoting, and they now made more direct offers to firms to turn them into companies and were no longer content to act merely as the servants of the vendors. Thirdly, the number and diversity of investors had grown and alongside the

advantages of limited liability were more generally realised
by the business community,   there now arose the necessity
of some professional intermediary between the two.   The
rise of the promoter was not, as, so many contemporaries
believed an excrescence on joint stock development : it
was the natural consequence of the increase in investors
and their changed habits of investment on the one hand,
and the widespread adoption by industry and commerce of
the joint stock system on the other.   It can be argued
that he surpassed his role when he urged the formation
of companies purely in order to obtain his commission, or
that his function could very well have been performed by
the state through some form of National Investment Board,
but neither of these arguments detracts from the fact that
his was a necessary role.

        Some of the changes that led to the rise of the
professional promoter can be seen in the 'eighties. By
1885, the method laid down implicitly though not explicitly
by the Companies Act of 1862, as to the formation of the
company, had been outmoded. No longer were the signers of
that important document the "Memorandum of Association" the
real owners or founders of the company. They were "dummies"
or promoters who took only the legal number necessary to
form the company. 'In the 1886 Return relating to Joint
Stock Companies referring to 1885, of the 1,305 companies
formed, in nearly 900 cases, or 69%, those signing the

memorandum of association took only seven shares between
them, i.e., one each.   The figure given above for such
cases in 1865 was 11 %.   ¨The shares moreover were no
longer of a high denomination of £25 - £100 but were nearer
£5 or £1.   It was apparently becoming the promoter's
business to get the company formed, and afterwards the
Directors might hold a large number of shares, but they
were no longer the original founders.

The date of the emergence of the full time company
promoter can be judged to some extent by the outcry against
him.   In 1878 a book was issued entitled "How the Public
are Plundered by Promoters of Companies" by Axford Packer,
which had on the title page the following definition :
"HARPY : a swindler, an extortioner, a ravenous wretch."
This appeared to be the signal for a campaign against
promoters which lasted until the downfall of Hooley and
the passing of the Companies Act of 1900. Part of the
campaign was conducted with no other weapon than that of
colourful language. The titles of these pamphlets will
indicate the contents. "Joint Stock Company Fraud, the
Exposure of a Long Firm Gang of Bogus Company Promoters",
"How to swindle the Public, by those who have done it",
"Sham Detectives, by a reformed pickpocket, or the
Adventures of a Solicitor's Clerk".   This instructive
trilogy was issued in 1888 and almost every year brought
out a fresh batch.   The more important part of the campaign
was conducted with facts and figures. "The Statist" led

the way by starting a series of articles on particular
groups and syndicates of promoters in 1887. A.J. Wilson in
his "Investors Review" in the nineties followed these
articles up, and at the turn of the century "The Critic
Black Book" was produced, such a detailed exposure of some
of the company promoters, that in the second issue the author,
Henry Hess, could proudly announce four libel actions.

Apart from the charge of "promoting companies with
profit to the promoters whatever may be the result to the
public"[1], the attack on promoters was still concentrated
on the harm that promotion expenses did to the company".
"Out of say a capital of £100,000 actually allotted to the
general public not more than £40,000 to £50,000 in hard
cash finds its way into the companies coffers"[2]. Chadwick's
1% looked very small beside this figure.

The changed character of promotion compared with the
sixties is shown in the general recognition of the promoter
and the promoters syndicate as a distinct feature of joint
stock finance and the changed attitude of the promoter
towards the company. In 1887 "an entirely new class of
Financier, known as Promoters"[3] was generally admitted as
being important in the capital market. And it was not long
before these promoters banded themselves together

---

1) "The Statist" 1887, Vol.I. p. 307.

2) ibid ..   .. 1888, Vol.I. p.504.

3) "Phillips Investors Annual", 1887, p.30.

in syndicates or companies and so-called "Trust" or
"Investment" Companies to become even more powerful as a
"company promoting spider" or alternatively, "company
promoting octopus".[1]   In new industries, conditions were
particularly favourable to such animals. In Electricity, for
example, it was claimed in 1903 that "The British Electric
Traction Company Ltd.," had promoted no less than between
67 and 80 other electric companies.[2]   At the same time,
the promoters no longer continued with the company after its
formation, as its "promoter-manager" or auditor. Hooley
explained the attitude of promoters towards the companies that
they promoted with great clarity in his evidence before the
Bankruptcy Court in 1898. "You have to buy the business and
then you have to sell it, and then you are done".[3]   This was
the opinion of the man who had promoted 26 large companies in
the five years 1894-1898, before he was arrested. O'Hagan,
who, from some points of view was a more successful promoter
than Hooley, expressed this attitude, "the company is there to
be promoted, not to be run", all through his book.[4]   When an
exception occurred, for example in the case of the Associated
Portland Cement Company, where owing partly to the very bad
reception the issue had in the capital market, he stayed with
the company as advisor and manager in chief, (no salary
apparently); this company presents a glaring contrast to the

1)   "The Statist" 1887, Vol.I, pp. 149 and 257.
2)   "The Electric Trust", 1903, p.11.ff.
3)   Quoted from "The Hooley Book", 1904, p.38.
4)   "Leaves from my Life", H.O. O'Hagan, 1929. Two Volumes.

                which
many others /he casually referred to as the result of his
promotion. O'Hagen himself regarded it as an exception and
is never tired of impressing on the reader "the sacrifices"
he made in staying with the company.

A factor which assisted this "in and out" practice of
the promoter was the growth of underwriting of shares. We will
discuss later underwriting from the point of view of the
investor, for the promoter, it meant certainty instead of
doubt. His commission had always depended on the success with
which he induced the public to take the shares of the company
he was promoting, and his success had been fairly high. An
estimation of the failure of the public to subscribe to
advertised issues was put as low as 10% for the years 1885-
1895.[1]   This was before underwriting had become either
general or legal for public issues.   For the individual
promoter the use of underwriting from the decade of the 'nineties
on, meant the removal of this element of 10% doubt, and they
could leave companies to their fate whether successful or
not almost as soon as it was registered and the commission paid.
O'Hagen, who claimed to have introduced underwriting into
company finance wrote on its effect on promoters, "It enabled
me to greatly increase my business and engage in taking up
matters three or four at a time as with underwriting I could
cast the responsibility of taking up capital on others. I had
not to clear away the financial responsibility of one undertaking before I could safely take upon myself that of two or

---

1) S.F. Van Oss, "Stock Exchange Values", 1895. This
    estimate does not include issues partly offered abroad.
    p.LIX.

three others"[1]

The completely distinct and independent part played by
the company promoter, whether an individual,   a syndicate
or a trust company, and the role of these promoters, assisted
by underwriting to "promote" a company and then pass on, are
the first two main characteristics of company promoting in
this period. A third, was the passing of the initiative for
the formation of the company from the vendor, or entrepreneur,
to the promoter.

This was occurring, of course, only in those cases
where the promoter played an important part in the flotation
of the company, and these were a small proportion of the total
number of "home" companies formed, but there is evidence that
it was a quite important development. F.W. Pixley, who had a
good knowledge of company practice besides a knowledge of company
law, suggested that in the conversion of some private concerns
into companies the initiative from the promoter, again either
individual or company, was most marked[2]   And this is
borne out to some considerable degree by O'Hagen's numerous
instances of the need for him to use "persuasion" in order to
obtain permission to convert a company[3]   In extreme cases,
this question of initiative had gone further than persuasion
of an existing entrepreneur. The Committees', journals and
pamphlets on Company law and practice are full of examples
where the promoter draws around him a number of Directors

1)   H.O. O'Hagen, "Leaves" p.155. Vol.I.
2)   "The Accountant" 1890, p.120.ff.
3)   H.O. O'Hagen, op.cit. various cases throughout the books.

with high sounding names to form a company and not only
did the promoter himself draw commission for his work but
he rewarded the Directors for their services by "presenting
them with shares sufficient to qualify"[1].

But while these characteristics of company promotion were
a marked contrast to the embryonic forms of promotion noted
in the sixties and seventies, it cannot be claimed that even
by 1914 "the professional company promoter" was the central
figure in all home company promotion.   For foreign enterprises
and for companies with very little local contact he was
important. The financial centres like London were of course
his happy hunting ground. But outside London, the formation
of companies were still effected in some degree by arrangements
with a group of capitalists and with the assistance of a
solicitor, and although the firm of Chadwicks had disappeared,
others like George White's of Bristol, were taking their place.
The key importance that firms like Chadwicks had had in the
sixties and seventies in the iron and steel, and general
industrial fields had disappeared, but their successors still
played an effective role and on much the same lines as had
Chadwick. Outside the large firms, the figures of the number
of private companies in 1914 which were usually too small to
be worth while "promoting", are sufficient indication that the
rise of the professional promoter, while of great significance
in the general trend of joint stock finance, must not be

1)W.Peek, "Prospectus Makers and the Public", 1890, p.iii.

considered as a factor in each and every company.

The methods of promotion had changed between 1856
and 1914 in accordance with the needs of the investors and
the needs of the company. The size of the companies and the
ignorance of investors on the relative merits of different
concerns, made a full time intermediary necessary for
promotion.   But starting the company, in the sense of getting
together the leading spirits of the new enterprise was only
a half of the work necessary before the company was a going
concern. The other problem was to secure part of the capital
from the public. These two functions tended always to be
intermixed, in the sense that Chadwick's firm was patronised
for his contact with investors as well as his technical
ability in forming the company, likewise with O'Hagen for
his contact with underwriters. And as promotion developed
from a "round the table" agreement to a profession, so did
the methods of recruiting capital develop from an unorganised
appeal at large to a carefully calculated certainty. But
this increase in efficiency was not without the drawbacks
of increased rigidity and increased opportunity for fraud.
We will now go on to deal with the methods used by promotors
and others to attract the investor into taking shares in the
company.

CHAPTER VIII

The Mechanism of Investment in Limited Liability

Companies, 1856 - 1914.

"Capital can either be secured in advance or issued
to the public without precautions".   This was written by
an expert on the promotion and financing of limited
liability companies in 1894.[1]   And the choice between
these two methods was the problem that faced every promoter,

agent or vendor of joint stock companies from 1856 to
1914.   The actual decision as to which one was to be used
depended on the type of company being floated.   The
mechanism of "securing in advance" or "issuing without
precautions" varied similarly with the type of investor in
the market and the degree of organisation of the capital
market.

In the period 1856-1885, the companies that secured
their capital beforehand were chiefly those concerned with
home industry.   Through their trade and personal connections, they obtained sufficient promises of support, when
the idea of the company was first mooted, to eliminate any
necessity of appealing widely to the public either directly

---

1) "Horncastle's Manual for Investors", 1894 Preface.

through the general distribution of a prospectus or
indirectly through an agent, a credit association, or
a syndicate. A large number of these companies, as
suggested above, did not employ a promoter of any description. Of necessity they had to issue a prospectus, but
it was circulated privately, and the usual features were
lacking, e.g. promises about dividends, grandiose descriptions of the property etc. It was a business document.

These companies, which secured all their capital
by personal connections, cannot be said to constitute the
majority of the companies formed in this period. But
they did represent an important minority which must be
borne in mind to correct the balance of a picture dealing
with the more spectacular method of investment, the prospectus, advertisements, the stockbrokers, etc.

The second main group of companies were those
appealing to the public for all or part of their capital.
This appeal was made either because their capital was too
large to be raised wholly through private channels, this
applied as shown above to most of the large home industrials
in iron and steel, shipping and cotton, or because they had
weak, or in the case of "new" companies, non-existent trade
and personal connections. But there were various methods

of issuing to the public and varying degrees of certainty.

It is convenient to discuss these methods under
three heads. Firstly, there was the use of an agent like
Chadwick, who had a direct connection with a section of the
investing public. Secondly, there was the issue of a
prospectus which would be widely circulated and advertised.
This method was backed up with the use of credit associations to see to their distribution and agents throughout
the country and to encourage the purchase of shares. The third
method was by issue on the London or Provincial Stock
Exchanges. These methods overlap; a company advertising
its prospectus might also attempt to get a settlement on
the stock exchange, but this division is according to the
main direction of the efforts of the promoters to raise the
capital.

Chadwicks Adamson and Collier and similar firms
were mainly concerned with home industrial companies;
companies whose required capital was such that it could not
all be raised by trade connections and a certain percentage
had to come from outside. Through obtaining Chadwick as
the agent, the additional capital was made almost a certainty.
His firm was in touch with some of the most important
investors in the country. In 1867 the number of his

contacts was numbered in hundreds.   In 1874 he had 4,000,
(1)
and in 1878 5,000.   These investors provided about
£10,- £15,000,000 for home industrial companies up to
(2)
1877.   The companies with which he was concerned did
not issue exotic prospectuses.   But Chadwick sent round
a letter marked "private and confidential" inviting his
"friends" to subscribe.   By the seventies, the handwritten
letter used in the case of "Bolckow Vaughan's" in 1864 no
longer sufficed, and printed circulars took their place,
but the tone was still the same.   In the period 1870-1875,
when his firm was very busy in the iron and steel companies
boom, in order to organise their clients they issued an
investment circular,   Though this circular, as it only
appeared monthly, was used not so much as a means of obtaining capital for companies, as a means of linking the
clients together, quoting their shares, and giving reports
on their companies.

These private prospectuses and the "Circular" were
the only means used by Chadwicks to obtain subscriptions.
"We have no connection with the Stock Exchange, no jobbing,
and very seldom any advertising".(3)   But their reputation

---

1) 1867 Report,Q.869, "Chadwicks Investment Circular", 1874,
   p.257, 1877 Report, Qu.2079.
2) Estimated from Chadwicks statement that 20-30% of the
   capital of his companies was subscribed from "outside".
3) 1877 Report, Qu.2045.

with their clients and the efficiency of their organisation
was such,that any company formed with the help of Chadwicks
had a guarantee of their capital almost equal to that of the
companies raising their money by purely personal contact.[1]

Other firms were performing the same role as intermediary between the wealthy investors and the home industrial
companies.   Richardson, Chadbourn & Co. in Manchester for
the cotton companies, Joshua Hutchinson and Son in London,
usually for coal companies, Wilson, Clemesha and Co. Holderness
Nott and Co. and other firms of brokers and auditors,were
responsible for the capital of a number of industrial companies,
Though few of these firms had a monopoly of the issue as
almost invariably did Chadwicks, and few of them had such
an extensive clientele and such a successful experience in
raising the capital.

Taken together, these four or five firms played an
extremely important, and largely unwritten, part in the
organisation of the home industrial capital market, for the
twenty-five years after the 1862 Act.   They educated a
solid core of wealthy investors into the art of investment,
and the results of this education were not lost, as in the
more numerous cases of Credit Associations and Stock brokers,

---

1) cf. Chadwick's evidence, 1877,Report, Qu.2077-9.

by the failure of the companies in which they advised
investment. Chadwick could claim nine out of every ten
companies a success[1] at the time when the total number of
failures was being calculated at between 30 - 50%.[2]

The second, and rather more hazardous, method of
raising the capital of a company from the public was by the
general issue of a prospectus. This method was resorted
to in this period 1856-1885 by various types of companies
from the sound home industrial, to the foreign speculative
mining company. There was nothing unsound in the method
itself, but owing to the unorganised state of the capital
market it left itself open to both abuses and to failures.
The success of such a prospectus issue only partly depended
on the basic soundness of the company, for the prospects
of the company had to be communicated to the investor by
means of one or more of three intermediaries. First through
the prospectus itself, secondly through advertising and
"puffs" for the issue in financial papers, and thirdly through
local intermediaries, solicitors, stock brokers and bank
managers. In order to secure the capital which a particular
company needed in competition with other companies there

---

1) ibid. Qu.1997.
2) cf. "Journal of Royal Statistical Society" March 1870,
   article by Leone Levi, and H.A. Shannon's estimates
   quoted above.

developed a tendency to bribe, corrupt or otherwise pervert
and falsify one or all three of these channels.

The method of falsifying the prospectus and filling it
with impossible promises has received a great deal of attention from Royal Commissions and moralists.   In the 1860's
attacks on prospectuses were not very frequent.   They were
more or less honest and the inducements offered to investors
were usually capable of being carried out.   These were
mainly of a local kind.   For example, a coal company would
offer to investors cheap coal from the pithead, assuming
that the investors were local inhabitants.[1]   Again, the
"Metropolitan Lavatory Company Limited" (1863) wrote "Holders
of ten or more shares will each have a free ticket of admis-
sion to all the stations", and "each original holder of 20
or more shares" in the "London and Western Districts Cemetery
Company", "gets a free space for a vault, and each original
holder of less than 20 shares gets a free grave".

By the seventies this type of inducement had not altogether disappeared but a more effective one had taken its
place.   This was the inducement of guaranteed interest.
It was most prevalent in the iron and steel companies of the
early seventies.   The guarantee usually was by the vendors

1) This occurred in "Bath Colliery Company Limited".

who handed some of the purchase money to invest in Consols
until the time of the guarantee had expired. For example,
in the "Blochairn Iron Company" (1873), "the vendors have
agreed to leave under the control of the company one-third
of the purchase money as a positive guarantee that the net
profits for five years to come shall amount to 10% per annum
at least or 50% within a shorter period."[1]

    This attraction of guaranteed interest was most commonly
found in companies that were converted from private ownership, and only then in fairly stable companies, but it was
prevalent enough to arouse opposition. In Chadwicks
Investment Circular a shareholder wrote a letter complaining
against the system, calling it "an unsound innovation".[2]
Other writers joined in the attack[3] and the "Times" had
to produce a smoothing defence, "The idea, that there is any
inherent unsoundness in the plan of guaranteeing a minimum
dividend for a certain number of years appears erroneous.
Provided the guarantee be solid, it furnishes a good means
of redressing any original miscalculation in favour of
vendors"[4] "Miscalculation" was a   polite way of

1) Prospectus of company, in "Chadwicks Circular", 1873, p.200.
2) "Chadwicks Investment Circular" 1872, p.160.
3) e.g. A.Packer, "How the Public are Plundered" 1878, p.60-1.
4) "The Times", 27th September, 1872.

expressing the basic weakness of numbers of these converted
companies.

On the whole, however, the attraction of these guaranteed dividends was successful in raising the capital, and
except for one or two minor tricks, the promises were carried
out.   An example of the tricks played in a highly respectable company may illustrate what happened in those less
stable.   The Llynvi Tondu and Ogmore Coal and Iron Company
1872 issued a prospectus with a promise almost identical
with that quoted above from the Blochairn Iron Company.   But
in 1874 the dividend declared was less than 10%.   A shareholder protested that this was below the guaranteed figure,
and the chairman pointed out that the vendors had guaranteed
profits not dividends.   And as no balance sheet was published the shareholders were not in a position to doubt
this.[1]

These two inducements, local concessions and guaranteed
dividends,were the most frequent "special" attempts to make
investors invest through the prospectus.   The usual statements of expected dividends, and references to other companies
that had been successful in that particular industry, were
common throughout the period, but it is difficult to estimate
either their trustworthyness or effectiveness.   Perhaps

---

1) from Account in "Chadwicks Investment Circular" 1874,
   p.258.

he comparative silence about mis-statements in the pros-
ectus in Commissions and pamphlets in the sixties and
eventies, compared with the outcry in the nineties which
ed up to the 1900 Act tightening up the law, shows that
n the earlier years, the prospectus was not such a common
eans of fraud.   Also the unpaid character of the shares
nd the ability of the shareholders to escape calls by
laiming in the Courts mis-statement in the prospectus
ight have acted as a cautionary measure.

The next step to drawing up the prospectus was its
ssue and advertisement.   "Perhaps then the right first
tep is that usually taken, the writing out of a prospectus
or private circulation."   This was the advice in 1866;[1]
fter this it will be "revised, printed and privately
istributed, if the response is good then fill in the
emorandum of Association."   "The company as soon as regis-
ered should be advertised... very costly but to advertise
nly a little is to throw money away.   Therefore let this
ork be done widely and wisely under the direction of
xperienced officers and brokers."   The use of italics
or the word "printed" shows, in some degree, the still
mbryonic stage in which company financing was at this date.

The methods of sending round the prospectuses in the

) 1866 edition of "The Limited Liability Joint Stock
Companies List", p.16.

sixties were not very definite, but by 1878 some promoters
had apparently developed this to a high art.   The register
of shareholders of railway, tram, gas companies were used
for obtaining addresses and the time for sending them had
been fixed for Saturday night.   "We particularly notice and
deplore the almost universal practice ..of posting ..on
Saturday so that they can come to hand on the Sabbath morning
when it is assumed the recipients have leisure to read and
study them".[1]   And this careful preparation and labour did
not go unrewarded.

Advertising was from the beginning more organised and
more costly.   It was said in 1865 to cost £1,800 - £2,000
to advertise for ten days in the "Times", "Daily News",
"Telegraph" and "Post" for the usual time of ten days or a
fortnight.[2]   The Royal Commission on the London Stock
Exchange in 1878 showed that it had become organised.   "It
is a considerable business advertising a new company...a
matter involving a large payment of money: and that is
generally done through an advertising agent."[3]   Every
newspaper and journal from church weeklies to the "Economist"
and the "Times" was carrying its burden of advertisements.

Closely linked with advertising a company prospectus

1) A. Packer, op.cit. p.17.
2) "The Bubbles of Finance, by a City Man", 1865.
3) "Royal Commission on London Stock Exchange, 1878, XIX".
   Qu.4025. (later referred to as 1878 R.C. on Stock Exchange)

was the question of "puffs" and "write-ups" in the financial journals. Up to the 'eighties, this method of boosting a company was still in its infancy, but the very existence of the method indicates the beginning of impersonal investment, which needed outside assistance, and makes an analysis important.

There were two general types of publication; the first, books and pamphlets concerned with joint stock companies as a whole, which advised investors to invest in certain safe securities; the second, circulars and books and journals issued by firms of stockbrokers, specifically "pushing" shares that they wished to sell.

The passing of the 1862 Act brought a host of the first type of publication on to the market. One or two examples will show the type of book issued. In 1863 a book was issued "Guide to the Unprotected in matters relating to their Property and Income" by "a Banker's Daughter". The guide was a supporter of Limited Liability companies as investments. "A lady should not on any account take any shares in a joint stock Bank, Mine, Partnership, or any other joint trading concern, unless it be established under the new "Limited Liability Act".[1] The rest of the book extolled the virtues of half a dozen well known incorporated stocks. The other

---

1) op.cit. p.10.

"guides" appealed to a more sophisticated public, but their contents were usually on the same lines. Very little advice was given in these books about investments in home industrial companies; railway stocks and foreign guaranteed securities were the common recommendations. The purpose of the stock-jobbers' books was also not so much to "puff" any specific security, but to direct investments through the "right" channels. The London Stock Exchange system of brokers and jobbers in particular was attacked, and investors were advised to consult their stockbroker on all investments rather than their banker or solicitor.[1] The attack on the London Stock Exchange, which will be considered later, was a reflection of the rule that Stock and Share brokers and jobbers who were members of the Exchange were not allowed to advertise.

Not content with books and pamphlets, a number of stockbrokers edited journals and these, naturally, were more direct than the books. To give a few examples, the "Joint Stock Monthly Record" of 1866 was issued by G. Templeton and Sons, who also issued the Joint Stock Companies Directory. "Bowyers Investment Review" was issued by brokers of that name in Bristol. "The Stock Exchange

---

1) e.g. F. Playford, "Practical Hints on Investing Money" 1856, p.55. He was a stockbroker. This is one of the earliest opposing bankers as the guide for investors.

Review" in 1870 was issued by Miller and Co. "The Stock
and Share Review" in 1883-4 by E.F.Lemaire, stock and share
brokers.[1]   The method used by these journals was to give
a general list of securities quoted on the London and Provincial Stock Exchanges which gave the whole paper an air
of genuineness, and then short articles stating that such
and such a security was in great demand and held out great
promise.   The security mentioned was almost invariably
found advertised in the same issue.   Attention was drawn
to this type of advertising and boosting in the 1878
Commission on the London Stock Exchange.   Journals were
said to announce a particular stock at a premium on the
London Stock Exchange, when no dealings at all were taking
place, in order to induce investors to take up the issue.
This was done, it was suggested, because of the valuable
advertisement the company inserted in the journal.[2]

As a whole, however, compared with the later period,
this method of reaching the investor through books and
journals was of little importance.   In 1878 it could be
said that "at the present time it is the practice for stock
jobbers to write pamphlets"[3] but their circulation and

1) Some others are given in the bibliography.
2) 1878 R.C. on Stock Exchange. Qu.4025.
3) A. Packer, op.cit. p.7.

influence was small.   The personal contact was more important
for the investor.

The personal contact came through three main sets of
people;   the stockbroker, the banker, and the solicitor.
The stockbrokers, apart from their publications, were the
most active in attempting to sell shares,   Quite naturally
as it was their whole-time job and they received a commission
for having their name on the prospectus and for placing the
shares.[1]   Up to the 'eighties however, their influence was
greater in London than outside.   In the "First Stockbrokers
Directory of Great Britain and Ireland" for 1873-4, while
there were c.1400 stockbrokers "recognised" and otherwise in
London, there were only c.500 given for all the provinces.
Another comparison in 1886 of the number of "members" of the
London Stock Exchange compared with the members of provincial
stock exchanges gives roughly the same position.   There were
c.2000 in London and c.600 in the provinces.[2]

The stockbrokers were usually only in touch with the
section of investors who were interested in Stock Exchange
quotations, and temporary speculative investments.   Messrs.
Bartlett and Chapman, who were stockbrokers, remarked on
this difficulty of obtaining customers in the seventies.

---

1) "1878 R.C. on Stock Exchange", 1878, XIX" Qu.7981.
2) "Phillips Investors Annual" 1887, p.339.

Large capitalists find no difficulty in investing money,
ut thrifty tradesmen and others whose incomes are com-
aratively small...do not like to enter a stockbroker's
ffice".[1] With the growth in diversity of investments
nd the increase in investors the role of the stockbroker
s an expert intermediary became more prominent. But to
he eighties, the wealthy investors did not need much
dvice, and the small investor trusted the bank manager
nd the solicitor rather than the "new fangled stockbroker".
o the stockbroker was left handling mainly foreign and
peculative issues, and dealing mainly with the London type
f investor.

The part played by banks as an intermediary between
he investor and the company was twofold in character:
irstly that of being prepared to buy and sell shares for
ustomers, and secondly, that of giving advice to customers
hrough the manager of the bank as to which shares to buy
r sell.

Banks had little hesitation about performing the former
ask. In 1862 "The London and County Bank" inserted in
heir advertisements that they would "buy and sell stocks
nd shares for customers". This was said to be the first
ank to do this,[2] but the example was rapidly followed by

) Bartlett and Chapman, "A Handy Book for Investors"
   1869, p.1.
) "Journal of the Institute of Bankers" 1899 Oct. p.404.

others. The Prospectuses of companies also mentioned the
name of their banker and often stated that shares could be
bought from them.

The attitude of the banks on the latter question was
never so clearly defined.   The disadvantages of a bank
manager acting as a guide and counsellor to all his clients
were obvious.   As late as 1900 discussion on the question
was still taking place in the "Bankers Magazine".   Then it
was asserted that, though the usually accepted position was
that no advice should be given, there was an unwritten law
that managers should tell clients what they should not
invest in.[1]   The general opinion of contemporaries was
however that banks should and did give advice.   Those
urging less speculative investments urged all investors to
first "consult their banker".[2]   Stockbrokers, on the other
hand, desiring more clients naturally suggested that all
investments should be placed through experts and not as at
present through amateurs like bank managers.

The influence of the solicitor was probably greater
than that of either the bank or the stockbroker but the
evidence is more intangible.   In the fifties they were
already a well organised and recognised medium for bringing

1) "Bankers Magazine", 1900 Jan.-June p.731.
2) e.g. Packer, op.cit. p.13.

together partners who wanted new partners and investors
with money to invest. The growth of limited companies as
an outlet for investments presented little difficulty for
them. Some were active in selling shares of companies.
Herepath's Journal in 1867 refers to "solicitors who travel
about to get subscriptions", [1] but the role of the
majority of solicitors was rather more passive. Their
advice to investors was always heavily weighted on the side
of security, recommending gilt-edged, and railway debentures.
Up to the 'eighties this advice was not only sound but
successful, but with the Conversion and the slump in railway
securities in the nineties and the early twentieth century
the traditional "family solicitor" was hard put to find
remunerative investments. As a result of this and other
factors their influence tended to decline.

These three groups of individuals were the main means of
approaching the investor personally. The "bonds salesman"
as is known in America never existed in this country. The
nearest approach to this type of agent was in the shipping
industry at the time of the "single ship" boom. The
promoters of these companies were alleged to "have actually
been paying men to tramp the country and given them a
commission on the money which they have been able to get

---

1) "Herepath's Journal", 1867, p.420.

that class of people (servant girls and small greengrocers)
to invest in tonnage"[1]   The large credit associations,
when sponsoring home industrial issues,were content to
rely on the widespread issue of the prospectus and personal
pressure from stockbrokers to dispose of the shares.   And
the syndicates for "underwriting" that were appearing in
the eighties likewise used the channels of trust companies
and stockbrokers and the stock-exchanges to sell the shares,
rather than any independent "salesman" organisation.
Personal contact of promoters or vendors with groups who
had money to invest, or knew how to obtain that money, was
always a most important feature of the capital market.   But
the groups with money to invest were for the most part
stable and known and it was not generally necessary to tour
the countryside looking for them.

We have discussed the two chief ways of reaching the
investor, which the company not being able to raise its
capital beforehand, had to use, namely, through the prospectus and the journals, and through the personal contact
of stockbrokers, solicitors and bankers.   There remains
one further channel to discuss, that of the Stock Exchange.

There was apparently no doubt as to the use of the

---

1) R.C. on Depression, 1886, qu.11, 217.

Stock Exchange in assisting investment in railways. "The
infinity of good the Stock Exchange has done in aiding the
construction of our magnificent railway system should alone
entitle it to the favourable consideration of the nation."[1]
But the limited liability companies, as pointed out above,
not only were considered as something different from the
railway experience, but for twenty-five odd years were
governed by different considerations. "The infinity of
good" is, consequently, hardly a correct estimation of the
part played by the stock exchanges in limited company finance
down to the 'eighties.

In the 'sixties the journals interested in the new
limited liability companies were almost unanimous in damning
the London Stock Exchange. After general remarks like "the
helplessness of this body and the futility of its existence
are becoming more and more apparent,[2] and "this now effete
and obstructive institution",[3] the criticism became more
specific about the practice of "rigging the market". This
was obtaining dealings in shares before the allotment, and
attempting to drive them up to a fictitious premium. It

---

1) "Herepath's Journal" 1877, p.321.
2) "Joint Stock Monthly Record", 1867, p.53. (Limited
   Liability 1864).
3) "Shareholders Guardian" 1865, p.922, also cf. "Companies
   Journal".

was adopted according to one contemporary because:

> "The plan of allotment is of late years quite
> different...the applicant must deposit with the
> new companies bankers a deposit of one or two
> pounds per share; and to secure this condition
> being complied with the promoters of new companies
> have not only to provide a grand list of directors,
> and concoct a prospectus of great promise but have,
> moreover, to establish an artificial premium for
> the shares in the market." (1)

The effect was "to obtain shareholders for proposed associa-

tions that would have failed to attract any had they stood

on their merits and undergone the scrutiny of each intending

investor. The original shareholders became so in order to

sell their shares at a premium."$^{(2)}$ It was said of the

new companies that were quoted on the exchange "at least

7/10ths of the shares were held within a limited radius

round the Stock Exchange and.. very few get into the hands

of permanent investors."$^{(3)}$ The London Stock Exchange Committee

attempted to prevent "this killing bait" of an artificial

premium from being "manufactured" in 1864, but their ruling

on this matter broke down in 1865.

By 1866, E.W. Field, whom we quoted above as an ardent

advocate of the principle of limited liability in the fifties,

had to draw a distinction between investors entering a

---

1) Letter from a broker quoted in Hooper, "The Stock Exchange"
   in 1900, a souvenir", 1900, p.143.
2) "Joint Stock Monthly Record", 1866, p.16.
3) "Shareholders Guardian" 1863, p.30.

company to stay, and entering a company in order to get out
again.   "The fact of it being a matter of anxiety in the
promotion of the company to get it upon the stock exchange
list might be regarded as a distinctive mark of its being
merely got up for sale."[1]   He would probably have agreed
with the suggestion in the "Joint Stock Monthly Record" that
"the most profitable companies are always outside the Stock
Exchange."[2]   The experience of the London Stock Exchange
for the first ten years after the passing of the Limited
Liability Act did not encourage either companies or investors
to use it as the natural medium between them.

In 1878 a Royal Commission was set up to investigate
the working of the London Stock Exchange and to examine this
practice of quotation before allotment, and in view of the
quite successful enquiry into foreign loans four years
previously,high hopes were held out for this enquiry.   But
the hopes were not fulfilled.   For beyond airing a number
of the deficiencies of the 'Exchange and pointing out that
"an artificial market was a very common incident" in fact
"in the great majority of new companies..and it was something
the public looked for and grew up into a system",[3] beyond

---

1) "Journal of the Society of Arts"1866, p.28.
2) 1866, p.17. op.cit.
3) R.C. on London Stock Exchange, Qu.4022.

this, few sweeping reforms were suggested, and none
implemented.

Naturally there was in this period 1856-1885 a big
increase in the total volume of transactions on the stock
exchange. The general increase in savings and investment
had given the Stock Exchange, as shown in the 1878 enquiry,
an importance undreamt of fifty years earlier. But the
isolation between the industrial companies of Great Britain
and the "chief financial centre of the world" had only
slightly been broken down. The type of security offered
by these companies and the type of investor taking them
rendered London dealings unnecessary. With the result that,
while the Stock Exchange did play an important part in
developing foreign loans and enterprises, and in developing
home public utilities, it was not of great importance in
this period in either recruiting the initial capital for
home industrial companies or in recruiting the additional
capital when needed. The Home companies using the Stock
Exchange were either general trading companies or rather
speculative flotations. Nevertheless there was a growing
demand, with the widening of the basis of investment, for
quotations of securities and facilities for easy transfer.
By the 'eighties the London Stock Exchange was beginning to

perform these functions for a few larger industrial
companies, but the chief part in this was played by the
Provincial stock exchanges.

Of the eleven provincial stock exchanges in existence
in 1860, ten had been founded in either the first (1836)
or the second (1845-6) railway boom.   From 1846-1885 only
one more - Dundee, 1879 - was added to the list.   But this
insignificant growth in the actual numbers of exchanges does
not accurately reflect the increase in business done by these
bodies.   We have given the number of members of Provincial
stock exchanges in 1885 above, but it should be remembered,
when comparing the number of members with those of the London
Stock Exchange, that there was not the same high "standing"
attached to membership of provincial exchanges and consequently not so much pressure to become members.   The securities dealt on were "mainly local securities"[1] and there were
not the facilities for gambling that existed on the London
exchange.   In 1878, John Edwards of the Manchester Stock
Exchange reported "no pressure to get into the Stock Exchange
since 1845-6".[2]   The prices of local securities did not
fluctuate greatly and apart from telephone arbitrage transactions with London and other Exchanges, life in a provincial

1) "Phillips Investors Annual" 1887, p.339.
2) R.Commission on London Stock Exchange, 1878, Qu.8054.

stock exchange was very calm.[1] The investors in the
provinces were buying industrial securities to hold and
not for speculation.   But the importance for the small
investor of a regular quotation of his investments had
resulted by 1885 in seven out of the twelve provincial
stock exchanges issuing daily lists.

The importances of these exchanges as a channel for
recruiting capital to home industrial companies and encouraging investors to buy this type of security can be
immediately seen by a glance through the Stock Exchange
Year Books for 1875-1880 issued by Skinner.   Company after
company which was concerned with the iron steel and coal
trade or general manufacturing, were designated as "shares
held and dealt in locally."   The Cleveland iron and steel
companies were usually only to be found in the Manchester
list, the huge Sheffield steel companies only in the Sheffield
list, and there were rarely any cotton quotations outside
Lancashire.   The shipping industry was an exception.   The
London list was popular with shipping companies from the
start, but this was partly due to the large part financial
associations played in promoting these companies and the

---

1) cf. the descriptions of the daily reading of the
   security lists in the provinces given by witnesses
   at the above commission.   Qu.7875-8095.

tradition of investment in shipping, and partly to the fact
that the most powerful shipping firms were still in private
hands or were "private" companies.   The limited shipping
companies that were formed tended to be speculative and to
appeal to the London market.

The importance of the local stock Exchanges must not
be exaggerated - a large number of industrial firms were not
quoted at all - but it is probably correct to say that in
1885, "the provincial stock exchanges were of almost greater
importance in relation to home securities than London."[1]

Outside the Stock Exchanges proper, efforts were spora-
dically made to provide a medium of quotation and a means of
exchange of shares.   The attacks made by journals on the
London Stock Exchange in the sixties were usually followed
by some scheme or other for enabling investors to sell shares
to one another when those shares were not quoted on the
'Exchange.   Both the "Joint Stock Monthly Record" and
"Bowyers Investment Review" had a "shares for sale" column.
In the former the number of shares for sale each month was
around 60.   The "Shareholders Guardian and Circular" attempted
the same thing but it was not a great success.   In 1865 a
rival to the Stock Exchange was set up in London and received

---

1) "Phillips Investors Annual" 1887, p.339.

some support from these papers.   It was the "London Stock
and Share Company" and it held weekly auctions of shares. [1]
This idea of a rival stock exchange was always popular with
"outside" stockbrokers and it appeared again and again in one
form or another.   In 1885 one was started in Liverpool
called the "Stock and Share Agency" to help "the many persons
who found a difficulty in buying and selling shares which are
not quoted on the Stock Exchange." [2]   But of the 65 securities
quoted, 52 were mines, and the Investors Monthly Manual was
probably correct in warning investors against these "rival"
organisations as "they mainly draw together by specious
advertisements etc. a mass of low class speculative business." [3]
Besides these stock exchange competitors in the sphere of
buying and selling shares, there were also competitors in
the field of quotations and lists.   The Joint stock journals
usually concocted one, made up of some well known stocks and
some which they were interested in selling.   In Halifax in
the seventies, long before a Stock Exchange was established
there, a daily share list was published by Thackrah's, stock
and share brokers, and similar lists, though not usually so
ambitious as "daily", were published in other towns which

1) Described in "Joint Stock Monthly Record" 1866 Dec.1st.
2) "Investments", Liverpool, 1887, Vol.II. Jan1st.
3) "Investors Monthly Manual" 1886, p.1.

lacked a stock exchange. These lists, which were composed
of the well known local stocks formed a useful guide to
brokers and investors in the district. They were of
particular importance to the careful provincial investor,
for although he had been forced into industrial securities
instead of the investment his London equivalent usually held,
namely Consols,[1] he still wanted the feeling of security
which was engendered by regular quotations.

Investment in limited liability companies between 1856
and 1885 did not, as could have been expected, develop many
completely new channels or mechanisms not known or used by
either railway company or partnership financing. The
technique of the former, stock exchange quotations, advertisements, journals, stockbrokers were used to a slightly
lesser degree by the large limited companies which had little
or no business contact. The personal negotiation used in
the latter case was a feature of smaller company financing.
In practice the number of investors in each limited company
was smaller than in a railway company, correspondingly the
knowledge of the whereabouts and interests of the possible
investors was greater, so the general advertising and selling

---

1) Due to necessity of dealing in Consols through the Bank
of England. cf. "Consols are the luxury of the rich...
the only effective dealings are in London" 1878, R.C.
on Stock Exchange, Qu. 8005.

technique was less advanced. On the other hand the other
companies depended to a greater extent than did partnership
on personal negotiation and their technique in this was on
a higher level. The only important new development in
company financing was the rise of firms like Chadwick,
Adamson and Collier. Starting as technical assistant to
the company they were appearing by the eighties, with their
contact with thousands of the most important investors in
the country, as essential to both investor and company.
They were the beginning of "the more round about methods" of
investment which was such a characteristic of investment in
public companies in the twentieth century, the natural outcome of the isolation of investors from the companies in
which they wished to invest.

The period 1885-1914 was conspicuous for the increase
in efficiency of both methods of obtaining capital that were
noted in the first period, namely that of obtaining the
capital beforehand, and that of issuing without precautions.
But the balance between the two methods was not radically
changed. The increase in the number of investors, their
greater knowledge, the growth in Stock Exchange business,
the greater number of stockbrokers, all these factors tending

to a more open appeal to investors for support for a new
company, were counteracted on the other side by the growth
of the conversion of firms into private companies not
wishing, and later, not being allowed to appeal publicly,
the increase inthe certainty of underwriting and the pre-
occupation of the stock exchange with foreign business,
all of which circumstances led new industrial companies to
depend less on the general investment market and more on
private methods.   So the position in 1914 was similar to
that in the 1860's.   "The vast majority of joint stock
companies coming into being each year are either already
in possession of their capital or obtain it by private
negotiation."   This was F.E. Lavington's opinion of the
position just before the war,   (1)   and although this "vast
majority" refers to numbers and not capital, it indicates
that, if anything, the companies that secured their capital
"beforehand" had increased since the sixties.   We intend to
examine the methods used, and the factors operating in both
types of issue and to analyse some of the reasons for the
preponderance of the type of company that did not issue
publicly.

---

1) F.E. Lavington, "The English Capital Market", 1921, p.195.

The first method of securing both the initial and the
additional capital of a company without any general issue to
the public was, as in the first period, the method of private
negotiation.   The only differences were firstly, the legal one
that these companies were after 1907 officially designated as
private, and secondly, the number of such cases was greater
than the number of public issues.   From the figures given
above of the amounts considered as paid up on vendors shares,
the "new" capital brought into these companies from outside
the resources of the vendors, was small and there would appear
in most cases to be no necessity for public appeal.   If
business associates and immediate friends did not prove
adequate to supply the capital needed, the local solicitor
was usually in a position to suggest further names of
possible investors.   But the whole process of forming such
a company from the aspect of the mechanism of investment was
closer to the methods of starting a partnership than a
company.   And the fact that there were 48,492 of these
companies with under fifty shareholders registered in 1914
in England and Scotland compared with 14,270 "public"
companies, shows the basis of Lavington's statement quoted
above.

The second method of securing the capital beforehand, which came into great favour in this period for public companies, was that of underwriting. Use of this method did not necessarily, as in the case of a private company, rule out all appeal to the public, but it ensured for the company the capital necessary for commencement, whether the issue was a success or not.

Underwriting in one form had been practised by some of the Financial associations of the sixties. They "would contract to bring out a new company in the sense of undertaking to float its capital, whatever the public did not take they would take."[1] But the widespread use of this method was held up by two factors. In the first place there was not the need on the part of companies nor the organisation in the market to enable such a scheme to be widely used. In the second place the issue of shares at a discount was forbidden by law and the devices to overcome this were often too expensive to make the method a paying one.

In the eighties and nineties however the size of the capital required by those companies who could not raise the money by private subscription, and the expense of starting a large company of this description, made a guarantee of the

---

1) 1878, R.C. on Stock Exchange. Qu. 7955

capital an attractive proposition. The promoters wanted
this guarantee, the vendors wanted it, and as these two
sets of people were the most influential in the formation
of the company, underwriting gradually became recognised
as the most efficient way of floating a company in which
the reimbursement of the promoter and vendor was regarded
as the primary question.

The legal position was briefly, that up to 1900 underwriting was in a doubtful position, the Courts passing
contradictory judgments on its legality.   By the 1900
Act it was recognised "grudgingly" with the proviso that
the shares must be issued to the public.   In the 1907 Act
this and other restrictions were withdrawn provided the
underwriting commission was mentioned in the Articles of
Association.

The extent to which it was used and the methods are
more difficult to determine.   The journals and books on
investment in the 'nineties were writing about "these underwriting days" and "that most ingenious and at the same time
most pernicious of all devices of modern finance - viz.
underwriting",[1] but by about 1920 it was estimated that
60% of the home industrial companies handled their own issues
and did not resort to syndicates or investment bankers.[2]

---

1) J.D. Walker and Watson, "Investors and Shareholders
   Guide" 1894, pp.57 & 86.
2) B.D. Nash, "Investment Banking in England", 1924, p.49.

This would indicate that, important as underwriting was
as a new method of raising capital, its influence in home
industry was comparatively small.

David Finnie in his book on "Capital Underwriting"
described the method used in detail.   Before 1900 the
underwriting commission, since it was not allowed to be
paid out of capital, took the form of "Founders shares"
or a direct commission from the vendor.   The company could
not contract directly with the underwriters, this had to be
done through third parties, the promoters or vendors.   These
factors naturally increased the cost and the unsoundness of
the method.   After 1900 "issuing became organised".   The
Issuing House entered into the main underwriting agreement
with the company and distributed its risks among its following.   An issuing house was in touch with stockbrokers,
banks, trust companies, finance houses, underwriting syndicates and others who were on its books as willing to follow
its lead and to bear a share of risk of the issues it sponsored. [1]
This division of risks was not encouraged by the 1900 Act
because of its proviso that the shares must be issued to the
public, which ruled out the promoter issuing them to his
friends, but with the withdrawal of this clause in the 1907

---

1) D. Finnie, "Capital Underwriting" 1934, p.52 ff.

Act, the above outline became the usual method used.

The rise of Trust Companies, which we noted above in the late eighties, had an important effect on underwriting. In 1887-9 the Trusts were openly recognised on all sides as obtaining part of their profits directly as a result of "underwriting".   Successful trust companies, like insurance companies, began to play an important part in underwriting important home and foreign issues.   The less successful started a round of underwriting each others issues which inevitably led to the collapse and the disrepute of the system. "The Statist" was describing the latter type in 1890 as nothing but "promoters relief organisations".[1]

But apart from specific underwriting cases, the influence of Trust companies, which under that or other names were increasing, though rather unsteadily, up to 1914, and of Insurance companies, whose growth we mentioned above, on the problem of securing either the initial or additional capital of a company beforehand, was enormous.   The policy holder or the investor in these concerns had little or no interest in the question of where their money was invested, they had little control on the direction, the effective power was invested in the Board of Directors.   The actual

---

1) "The Statist" 1891, II, p.353.

investment of the capital would naturally depend, to some
degree, on the soundness and market quotations of various
alternatives, but the amount of capital these companies had
to invest, and the lack of control on the activities of the
directors, left the door wide open for pressure from promoters
and others to influence the direction of the investments. The
fact that both trusts and insurance company were engaged to
some extent in underwriting by 1914, illustrates the beginning
of this tendency, but there were other less obvious ways in
which a trust company could assist a company without the
fairly high risk of underwriting, and if assistance of this
description started, could control of the companies be far
behind?

Underwriting and other effective methods of securing
the capital beforehand were still partly a question of
private negotiation in this latter period, with the difference
that it was now well organised in scales of commission, etc.,
and in some cases the negotiations took place not with the
direct owners of the capital but with the controllers of the
centralised capital of thousands.

Up to 1914, however, as shown above, the use of
underwriting in public "home" companies was not very widespread, and for both initial capital and particularly
additional capital the methods of "securing without precautions", had to be used. These methods were the same as

suggested above but there was a difference of emphasis,
and a difference of efficiency.   We will deal with the
methods in turn with one exception.   The "financial agent"
like Chadwick, more or less disappeared as an independent
method of securing capital; he was superseded by underwriting and promoters' syndicates on the one land and by
stockbrokers on the other.   The similar organisations that
did remain in this period will not be dealt with separately
but together with the discussion on the roles of the
solicitor and stockbroker.

From 1885 to about 1900, "The high art of Prospectus
making"[1] came into its own.   The fairly sober documents
with offers of local concessions had given place to brilliant pieces of writing in which all kinds of tricks like
big and small type, red ink, headings of "private and
confidential" were fully developed.[2]   The drawing up of
a prospectus had become a full time occupation in London
at least.   "The City is overrun with professional prospectus jugglers each of whom has his special methods, and
plays as it were his own game".[3]   In the 'nineties the

---

1) "The Statist", 1887, vol.I. p.11.
2) For details, cf. R.E. Wall, "Hints to Intending Investors"
   1891, pp.84 ff. "Jaycee" op.cit. pp.18-19. and "The
   Statist" 1888, vol.I, p.736.
3) "The Statist" 1887, Vol.I, p.496.

deception practised in the prospectus made the slogan of
"clean up the prospectus" a major plank in the platform
of company reform.   Sober journals like "The Statist" and
'The Investors Review" filled their columns year after year
with attacks on this particular form of "company rascality".
These were continued in the spate of Commissions at the end
of the century.

The Companies Act of 1900 attempted in some measure to
check flagrant abuses in the "word painting" of the prospectus, and to some extent it succeeded.   There was a very
startling decrease in the number of companies issuing prospectuses.   The Inspector General of Bankruptcy wrote in
1903 that "I estimate the reduction in the number of
companies issuing a prospectus during the last two years as
compared with the two years immediately preceding the
passing of the Act at about 70%".[1]   Between 1901 and 1907
an average of 85% of the total number of companies registered each year, filed a declaration that, "the company does
not issue any invitation to the public to subscribe for
its shares".[2]   The particular reasons for this decrease
were the stringent conditions in the 1900 Act as regards
prospectuses and the general increase in the number of

1) "12th Annual Report of Board of Trade under Companies
   Winding Up Act" 1903, p.8.
2) 1906 Report, paragraph 11.

private companies, but these figures alone do not give an
accurate position of the appeals to the public.

In the first place, the numbers of those not appealing
to the public do not represent that percentage of the total
capital being subscribed by private channels.   Between 1900
and 1907 the percentage of the total number of companies
registered each year which specifically were to appeal to
the public was on the average 0.9%, but the average percentage of nominal capital represented was 25% of the total.
In the second place the declaration not to go to the public
was, until the Private Companies recognition in 1907, often
more formal than real.   The prospectus may not have been
used, but other channels, which we discuss later, were.
"The records show that within a short time after registration the names of the shareholders in many of the Companies
which did not issue any invitation to the public may be
counted in hundreds."   Thirdly, the emphasis had apparently
changed in the twentieth century, so far as devices for
attracting the investor were concerned.   In the 1895
Committee Harold Brown for the London Chamber of Commerce,
had advised investors in his evidence to look to the directors for proof of the soundness of the firm.   This practice

---

1) ibid Further Memorandum by Registrar of Joint
   Stock Companies, p.93.
2) 1895 Report, Memorandum submitted by H.Brown, p.73.

became more and more general, so that although it led to attacks on Directors as being paid fees purely to attract investors there was less outcry against the prospectus. "In practice few persons apply for shares solely on the showing of a prospectus, relying far more on the Directors and others connected with the concern."[1] To this extent the emphasis had moved in 1908.

As the writing of the prospectus had fallen more and more into professional hands, so had the question of distribution. The Companies that did make an appeal to the public relied on the wide distribution of the prospectus for the success of their appeal and they found well equipped organisations ready to assist them. "Specially prepared lists" of present shareholders who would be likely to invest further were the vogue.[2] The position in 1892 is outlined in Horncastle's Manual.

> "Until a couple of years ago when the list of
> Investors compiled by the London Share and
> Debenture Company became available to promoters,
> the business of circulating prospectuses had
> been done in a most haphazard sort of fashion.
> ...the company (London and Share Debenture
> Company) has compiled a list of all the leading
> shareholders in the United Kingdom, arranged
> according to class of undertaking each preferred,
> as shown by previous investments." (3)

---

1) Journal of the Institute of Bankers, S.E.Perry, "History of Companies Legislation in England", Nov.1908, p.500.
2) cf. R.E.Wall, op.cit. p.91, "Prospectuses marked 'private and confidential' and sent out to specially prepared lists is a serious danger now to be met."
3) "Horncastle's Manual" 1892, p.26.

The necessity for some professional organisation is seen in
the estimates that Horncastle gives for the number of prospectuses that should be sent out;   he suggests between
50,000 and 200,000.[1]

The advertising methods had not changed very much.
Avenues such as "Church weeklies" were now cited as being
regularly employed.[2]   And the actual time of advertising
had been cut down from "ten days" to nearer four.[3]   The
biggest increase in advertising, however, was not in the
direct form of greater space in the newspapers, but in the
increase of journals dealing with investments that were
used to write up particular issues.

"The Statist" in 1887 under the heading of "The Sham
Financial Press" wrote "Last year there was a terrible erup-
tion of these spurious organs of finance.   They fall over
each other in their hurry to get launched into a congenially
wicked world."[4]   Their contents were not different from those
published in the sixties and seventies, but the number of
them was four times as great.   It was in these years, the
latter half of the eighties, that the North of England was
honoured with its first "financial Journal".   Up to this

---

1) ibid. p.50.
2) "Jaycee" Public Companies from the Cradle to the Grave"
   1883, p.26.
3) "Horncastle", 1891. p.10.
4) "The Statist", 1887, Vol.I, p.389.

time the men with capital had been too close to business to
need much help in   directing   their investments.   But
with the rise of smaller share denominations and the salaried
investing class there was a market for this type of advice.
The paper claiming to be "The only financial paper published
in the Northern Counties" was the Liverpool "Investments"
which started in 1885.   This was in liquidation in 1887 but
its place was soon taken by "The Financial Guardian" of
Manchester in 1889, which in turn pointed out "That in the
wealthy and wealth-producing northern provinces there is not
a single organ devoted to the interests of the capitalist
and investor."[1]   This spread of financial papers to the North
was only symptomatic of the great outburst that took place in
London and the Home Counties.

   The purely "Bucket shop" newspapers had worked themselves
out by the nineties, and the "great advice" to the investors
took more the form of books and pamphlets dedicated to "the
Science of Investment".   These books or circulars were
issued by brokers, according to them, because of the need for
knowledge on the part of the investor.   "The necessity for
information... is admittedly so clear that a custom has arisen
for many dealers and brokers to send out circulars at frequent

---

1) "Financial Guardian", Manchester, Vol.I, No.1, p.2, 1889.

intervals."[1] The titles of these books, for example,
"Hints to Small Investors", "Profitable Investment in
Stocks and Shares", How to Operate successfully in Stocks",
"The Successful Investor", the same idea being repeated in
the titles and the books coming out in their dozens year
after year, illustrate to some degree the triumphant statement in the "Investors Blue Book" for 1905 ... "the era of
universal investment has come."[2]

The type of advice given in these volumes was similar
to that of the previous period. The most respectable
brokers advised only "gilt-edged", railways and debentures
and guaranteed loans, the less respectable urged high dividends through mining investments and such-like. In between
these two extremes there were many different shades. Particular trades now had their own "investment" paper. For
example, in Electricity, the British Electric Traction
Company which we mentioned above as being one of the leading
"promoting spiders" had branched out in the nineties into
journalism with a paper called "Electrical Investments". It
had the same air as the stock-jobbers papers,of being a
serious contribution to the new science of investment, but
in effect it was, as to be expected, a boost for the progeny

---

1) "Financial Guardian" loc.cit.
2) "Investors Blue Book", 1905, Introduction.

of the Traction Company.

But one type of advice that came clearly to the fore-
front/which had not been expressed in the first period, was
that for constant investment and re-investment, and geographical distribution of investment.   The growth in the
number of enterprises adopting the joint stock form paved
the way for the former advice: the firm establishment of
imperialism and the growth of communications paved the way
for the latter.   Some of the implications of these types
of advice have been touched on above and will be dealt with
again when we are considering the investor.   From the point
of view of the methods used to secure the investors for a
company, it is only necessary to mention that in the "Practical
Construction of an Investment Scheme", which this type of
book invariably attempted, the companies cited were, without
exception, old established companies.   New companies were
specifically stated time and time again as being doubtful
investments, (except of course in the frankly speculative
pamphlets) and, as mentioned above, the emphasis was on pre-
ordinary stock, the fluctuating character of equity being
anathema to these instructors on investment.   The conclusion

---

1) e.g. J.D. Walker & Watson, op.cit. p.110 "subscribe for
   nothing new".
2) e.g. "Capital and Investment", 1909, p.9.

reached from a study of these books is that while they were
effective as channels of information on investment to an
important section of the investing class, the professional
and salaried groups, and the growing number of rentiers, they
had no influence on investment in new companies, and the
holders of equity shares in the home industrials were
recruited from a different class by less public and more
personal means.

We pointed out above, that the mere circulation of the
prospectus and the writing up of the company in the financial
journals was usually not a sufficient attraction to secure
the investor.   Personal contact was necessary over and above
this.   In addition there were the many companies that did
not use either of the above methods yet   had to obtain
some of their capital from the public, which could only be
done by personal contact with the investor.   There were
three main groups of people performing this function in the
period 1856-1885.   These three groups, the stockbrokers,
the bankers and solicitors were still the main channels in
this period but their importance in relation to one another
had changed.   The stockbroker had easily out-distanced the
other two in importance.

The major reason for this relative increase in the
influence of the stockbroker was the increase in the number

of alternative investments that were appearing on the market,
both on the stock exchanges and outside, leading to the
necessity of expert advice.   The old-fashioned family
solicitor tended to become out of date in his suggestions
of Consols and railway debentures, and the banker was
similarly hesitant about advising clients on new and untried
investments.   By 1908 it could be claimed that "investors
are not now content as they once were to entrust their
monetary interests to, or seek for financial guidance from,
their bankers or the family solicitor." [1]

The stockbroker began by rapidly consolidating his
position as the normal channel through which investments
were bought and sold.   This can be illustrated by the
appearance of his name on the prospectus of the company.
In the period 1856-1885, a stockbroker's name only appeared
on about four or five of every ten home industrial company
prospectus issued: in the period 1885-1914 the average
was nine out of ten, and in the last ten years almost
universal.   The natural consequence was an advance to the
position of adviser and not merely go-between.   The change
that took place must not be ante-dated.   From the point of

---

1) "Financial Review of Reviews", Vol.V, 1908.

view of home industrial issues the increase of placing of
shares through stockbrokers was not so important quantitatively as it was qualitatively. The use of the stockbroker on a significant scale at all was the important
change, and not the actual amount of money that was
invested through him. On foreign issues and more speculative ventures, the stockbroker had in the eighties been
as important as the other two means; in the later period
he became quantitatively and qualitatively pre-eminent.

The importance of the stockbroker as a medium between
the investors and the company, was further enhanced by the
decline in the number of companies issuing prospectuses
after 1900 and the continued small percentage of public
companies quoted on the Stock Exchanges. Already in 1896,
before the 1900 Act had tightened up the prospectus, it was
suggested that often outside of London a company wishing to
raise capital "gets hold of brokers and spreads the shares
privately throughout the main towns in the country."[1] The
figures given above of the actual number of shareholders
in these companies "not issuing to the public" shows that
the use of the method must have been much more extensive

---

1) 1896 Report, Qu.1810.

after 1900. Stockbrokers were the only medium for this
sort of thing. Neither bankers nor solicitors were prepared to do it. In the second place the small number of
companies quoted compared with the increase in the number
of investors desiring security,drove the latter to brokers,
for brokers where in a/ better position than any other group to
quote or buy and sell these securities. "The business of
outside brokers has enormously developed and one important
reason for this has been the fact that the small investor
has not been catered for by the Stock Exchange." (1)

The position of the banker in the later period has
been mentioned above. The concentration and amalgamation
of banks that was taking place throughout this period,
involved, on the one hand, a greater extension of banking
facilities through the opening up of branches where banks
had not previously existed, and on the other hand, the sub-
stitution of an independent bank and banker by a branch
bank and a bank manager. For the investor the result was
less definite advice from the bank manager than that he had
received from the independent banker, though with the close
association of the amalgamated banks with both stockbrokers
and the capital market itself the advice was said to be more

---

1) "The Contemporary Review", March, 1907. XCI, p.415.
   an article by E.Crammond on "The Stock Exchange and
   the Public."

sound.   In a difficult case the bank manager would tend
to telephone the local stockbroker and pass on his advice
to the client.

The generalisation suggested above that solicitors
lost their influence in the capital market through not
keeping "pace with the times" so far as new fashions in
investment were concerned, is only partly true.   The fact
that Guy Ellis could give the paper he read on "The Appreciation of Gold and its Effects on Investments" before the
"Provincial Law Society" in 1895 the sub-title of "A Cracker
under the Family Solicitor's Chair", shows that some
contemporaries regarded them as falling asleep.   But their
role in the industrial towns and country areas in bringing
small groups of shareholders and entrepreneurs together
was extremely important.   F.E. Lavington, writing of the
position of solicitors just before the War said:

> "He may relieve the investor of marketing work
> by placing him in contact with a suitable borrower,
> in which case he receives an additional fee.   Other-
> wise his function is to reduce risks by investi-
> gating the security and casting the loan contract
> into its appropriate legal form .. he forms a
> local market for capital" (1)

---

1) F.E. Lavington, op.cit. p.117. and cf. "There are
many solicitors who make a speciality of bringing
together firms with debentures or mortgages to
offer and clients who have money to invest."
"202 Methods of Raising Capital and Credit to
Develop Business", p.44.   No date but c.1922.

Outside these three groups there were other channels
between the investor and the company which played the part
of influencing the investor by more or less personal
contact to take up issues advertised impersonally in the
prospectus or perhaps not advertised at all.   We have
discussed the role of Chadwicks Adamson and Company in the
home industrial field above.   It is not possible to trace
such a powerful organisation encouraging investment in
industrials in this later period.   Some observers claimed
that these firms were entirely lacking.   "Formerly any
security offered by certain firms, remarkable for intelligence no less than for honourable dealings, could be bought
with confidence that its merits had been carefully examined
and that firm itself believed it to be a safe and sound
security.   I know no firm of that class now." [1]   But it was
really a question of the functions being performed by
Chadwick being now split up among various organisations.
Powerful stockbroking concerns like George White & Sons of
Bristol assisted in promotion, [2]   others concerned themselves
with sub-underwriting and between 1890 and 1914, there was a
big increase in limited liability stockbroking concerns who
gathered round them a large clientèle of investors.

---

1) "Counsel to Ladies and Easy-Going Men on their Business
   Investments", 1892, p.42.
2) H.S. Foxwell, "Papers on Current Finance", 1919, p.126.

The "outside" brokers that organised themselves on
Chadwicks' lines differed from his firm, however, in
concentrating more on dealing in established securities
than in selling new issues.   Two prominent examples are
George Gregory and Sons, and the Investment Registry
Limited.   The firm of George Gregory was started in 1883
and by 1892 had an annual turnover of 50 million pounds,
and a clientèle numbering 20,000.   Their regular issue
of "Gregory's Hints to Speculators" was said to sell 60,000
copies a year.   To illustrate the character of their
clientèle, they reported five branches in 1892 amongst which
there was one in the West and of London, one at Brighton
and one at Hastings.   (1)   The stock they dealt in naturally
included a number of industrials but the emphasis was on
foreign issues and ordinary shares were never much in favour.
The whole organisation was, in some ways, more a rival to
the Stock Exchange than an intermediary between the company
needing money and the investor as in the case of Chadwicks.
They claimed to have introduced the "noteworthy system of
dealing direct with the operating client by means of which
commissions, brokerage and other extraneous charges are

1) All the information from "Gregory's Hints to Speculators",
   1895 Introduction.

avoided by the customer."[1]   The Investment Registry Limited,
1880, which flourished in the years just before the war was
more akin to Chadwicks firm than was Gregory's.   In 1909
it was said to have 9,500 shareholders and investors on its
books and claimed to be "The largest association of Private
Investors in the World,"[2]   with investments of £30,000,000.
But although it specialised in permanent investment rather
than speculative dealing, foreign issues were its main field.
It was one of the many organisations of the time that claimed
to be experts in "geographical investment".

Some of these numerous concerns were nothing more than
trusts, the clients taking shares;   others approached more
a stock exchange organisation;   and others were merely an
enlarged stockbroker giving advice and taking commission.
From their own literature, of which there is a large quantity,
it would appear from the numbers they give of their clients
that they were an important force in the capital market.
We are assured that their pamphlets rarely had less than a
15,000 circulation.[3]   But it is certain that most of their
activities were in connection with foreign investments, and
until their figures can be checked by less interested sources,
it will be impossible to estimate correctly their influence.

---

1) op.cit. 284.p.
2) Sir John Rolleston, "The Elements of Safe Investment", 1916.
3) cf. "Investment vs. Speculation" 1906-7, p.2.

One other factor about these bodies that should be
noted is their use to a certain extent of "salesman"; not
on the American lines of calling at door to door and
attempting to sell a particular stock, but in sending
agents round the country recommending the particular
investment agency.   An amusing example of an extreme case
of this was given in "The Statist" in 1887.   At a tempe-
rance gathering at the Three Bridges Chapel the minister
delivered a prayer and some of Sankey's hymns were sung
and in between an address was delivered from the "Provident
Association of London Limited.[1]

We have discussed the part played by the prospectus
and the intermediary agencies like banks and stockbrokers
in securing the investor for a company.   The third major
channel was the Stock Exchanges.   Of these the London one
remained the most important from the total value of the
securities quoted.   But its importance for the capital
market as a whole cannot be measured solely by the value
of the securities.   The character of the investments
resulting from stock exchange dealings and the type of
security dealt in have to be considered.

There is no doubt as the general increase of both
the business and the membership of the London Stock Exchange

1) "The Statist", 1887, Vol.II, p.652.

in this period.   A few figures illustrate this.   The
amount of business, as indicated by the value of the
securities quoted, had increased in the thirty years from
the first issue of the Daily List in 1867,   by 157%.[1]
The membership had increased in the forty years 1875 to
1905 from 1,979 to 5,567.[2]   But this increase did not
mean a similar increase in the importance of the Stock
Exchange as a method of financing home industry.   The
conclusions that were being reached in the first decades
of the twentieth century were the contrary.   "There is a
peculiar lack of contact between the greatest financial
market in the world and the industrials of the same country".[3]
"The Market for new Stock Exchange securities plays a
smaller part than one would suppose in facilitating the
movement of the annual flow of resources into home investment."[4]   And "the assistance of well organised Stock Markets
is needed to place and popularise industrial stocks as
invesments".[5]   The briefest glance at the London Stock
Exchange Daily Lists in the fifteen years preceding the
war leaves no doubts that these conclusions reached by
contemporaries were correct.

---

1) W.E. Hooper, op.cit. p.
2) figs. from Hooper and J.H. Clapham op.cit. Vol.III, p.
3) H.S. Foxwell, op.cit. p.132.
4) F.E. Lavington, op.cit. p.205.
5) L.Joseph, "Industrial Finance", 1911, p.25.

We suggested above that a similar position of little
use by home industries of the London Stock Exchange, existed
in the period 1856-1885.   But there was one important
distinction.   Whereas, in the first period those companies
which did use the Stock Exchange were usually attempting to
raise their initial capital, in the later period the chief
use was by companies which required additional capital. Before,
once   the   shareholders were obtained, they usually provided "a valuable field for future demands for capital",
in the later period, however, the appeal, particularly for
ordinary capital was invariably made to a wider field and
an established company of some size found the Stock Exchange
an efficient method of doing this.[1]

The reasons for the general lack of use of the London -
Stock Exchange had changed a little in the period 1885-
1914.   The feeling that stock exchange investors never
bought securities to hold was still present as a factor
keeping companies away.   Anthony Pulbrook, "after twenty
years' experience in Public Companies" wrote, "Nine hundred
and ninety-nine shareholders out of every thousand go into
public companies as a gamble hoping to sell at a premium".[2]
Needless to say his years of experience were almost

---

1) cf. the figures given above for the issues on London
   by "old" compared with "new" companies in years 1899-1913.
2) "Horncastle's Manual", 1892, p.44.

exclusively in and around the London Stock Exchange and
the Bankruptcy Courts.   In the twenty years after he wrote
the use of the tape machine and the telegraph increased the
excitement and efficiency of this type of investment.

But new reasons for staying away from London had
developed.   The very increase in the organisation of the
capital market, particularly in connection with overseas
issues, the rise of the professional promoter, use of underwriting, etc., while it meant increased certainty of
securing the capital, also meant increased cost.   Messrs.
Chadwicks had claimed 1% commission, but the combined
promotion and under-writing expenses often approached
10 - 25% of the capital.   The consequence was that not
only were the expenses too great to be worth while but
also "as a rule our English industries are too small in
scale to attract issue houses".   (1)   And without some sponsors
on the London money market the issue was very uncertain.
Only very large firms found a London issue worth while.

A second result of the smallness of size of home
industrials compared with the foreign loans and companies
was difficulty in obtaining quotations.

> "When they can boast of a capital of several
> millions like Allsopp or Guinness they
> have nothing to fear.   But the small companies
> with capitals varying from £100,000 to half a
> million are getting in an awkward corner.   The
> jobbers cannot keep them all to the front." (2)

1) H.S. Foxwell, op.cit. 128.
2) "The Statist", 1887, Vol.II, pp.37-8.

Without a regular demand they could not be kept on the
London List so "the smaller industrials are betaking
themselves from London to the provinces."[1]   There the
congestion was not so great, the buying and selling more
leisurely, and all were kept to the front by the method
of "daily reading through the list".

These factors combined with the ability of home
industrial companies to raise their capital by means other
than the London Stock Exchange, were the main reasons for
the much commented "isolation" of industry from the London
financial market.   It was easy enough to prove that this
isolation was a fact, but then to go on and add that this
was therefore a "weakness" as did numbers of the financial
writers, was more a compliment to the effectiveness of
German competition, where banks and industry were linked,
than an objective judgment.   Other ways and means besides
the London market existed to raise the capital.

The provincial stock exchanges increased considerably
in importance in the period 1885-1914.   We noted above
12 provincial stock exchanges in 1885;   by 1900 there were
21, and by 1914 there were 22 in existence.   Their organisation was improved and co-ordinated by the formation of
the Council of Associated Stock Exchanges in 1890.   But

---

1) ibid. loc. cit.

the actual number of Stock Exchanges do not adequately
represent the number of these types of organisations
existing in the provinces.   For example, the Lancashire
Sharebrokers Association in Oldham, which dealt mainly in
cotton spinning shares, was far more important in financing
industry than was the official Southport Stock Exchange
that was formed about the same time at the end of the nineteenth century.

At the turn of the century the most important exchanges
were those which had been founded sixty odd years ago;
the Irish and Scottish ones being the most important,
Dublin, Edinburgh and Glasgow followed by the chief centres
of English industry, Manchester, Birmingham, Sheffield and
Liverpool, (in that order).   Of the new ones that were
opened after 1885, three were Scotch or Irish, Cork, Belfast
and Greenock, one Welsh, Cardiff, and of the four English
ones opened three were in the woollen district, Halifax,
Huddersfield and Bradford, and one in a residential area,
Southport.   The new English ones tended to be formed
more to cater for the needs of investors in those cities
than to form a market for the shares of local companies.
The public limited liability company did not spread very
rapidly in these woollen areas in the fifteen years after

1885 and in that year in Bradford, Sir Jacob Behrens could report "we have none (limited companies) in our district.
(1)
I cannot remember one."

The growth of the stock exchanges in the provincial districts, which were for the greater part of the nineteenth century the centres 'par excellence' of private investment and re-investment in the family or partnership firm, shows the general change of attitude towards investment which was developing among the investors in those areas. The original shares of the big iron and steel, cotton, or coal companies might have been held in a few hands, and to some extent still were, but the additional ordinary capital issues were often directed to a wider circle of investors and pre-ordinary issues almost certainly. But this wider section of investors needed more evidence of security than the narrower group, as they did not have the advantage of being 'au fait' with the progress of the company from the inside. The provincial stock exchange quotations provided them with the security they desired.

The provincial stock exchanges were still important as centres of local industrial financing, and the growth of new industries, e.g. in Birmingham this was an important factor in making the stock exchange in that town of greater

---

1) R.C. on Depression, 1886, Qu.6791.

importance than those in either Liverpool or Sheffield.
The general increase in importance of these Stock Exchanges
however was due not so much to the growth of local industry
as to the increased number of investors, their changed habits
in using stockbrokers and their desire for security.   Quotations and easy transferability were becoming as important
to provincial investors as they had been to London investors
in the sixties and the local stock exchanges supplied these.
For the companies with private financing still raising an
important part of the capital, the local markets were
sufficient to supply the remainder at a much lower cost than
the London market.

Outside the stock exchanges proper, efforts
continued to be made to set up competitors in the field of
buying and selling stocks and shares.   These organisations
were usually centred in London, and the publicity for them
usually stressed first, the inadequacy of the London Stock
Exchange as it did not quote all the companies in which the
public invested, and secondly, the expensiveness of the system
of "brokers as middlemen".   An advocate of the "ideal stock
exchange, viz. The Universal Stock Exchange", founded in
1885, estimated that "eight millions were wasted yearly on

brokers"[1]. Others were established in rapid succession up
to the first decade of the twentieth century. The Open
Stock Exchange in 1886, the Union Stock Exchange and the
Investors Exchange both in 1893 and the Westminster Stock
Exchange in 1903 were among the largest. "Fairplay",
representing an industry, shipping, in which while the
shares of the companies were quite widely held, only the
very largest companies managed a quotation on either London
or the provincial stock exchanges, strongly supported these
"outside" exchanges. "A very admirable mode of enabling
people to buy shipping shares which they otherwise might
not hear of..."[2] But a study of the lists of shares
quoted, reveals the same tendency as noted above of speculative rather than sound companies, and the comparatively
short existence of these exchanges is perhaps a further
indication as to their character. But neither of these
tendencies should obscure the fact that these organisations were established and, taken together, assisted the
investor considerably in finding an outlet for his savings.
The desire from some investors for transferability and
marketability had outrun to some extent, the capacities
of the official stock exchanges.

---

1) W.H.S. Aubrey "Stock Exchange Investments" 1896, p.97.
2) "Fairplay" 1893, I, p.39.

The mechanism and the channels through which the savings
of the country entered limited liability companies between
1856 and 1914, showed two main lines of development.   The
first was the method of private negotiation to secure the
capital from individuals who knew both the firm and the entrepreneurs.   The second was the impersonal investment by, at
first, hundreds and then thousands of capitalists.

The first method was present in the eighteen sixties and
in the twentieth century, and there was not much change
in the technique used.   The solicitor remained important as
a go-between should immediate personal contacts fail, though
the provincial stockbroker was, through his development due
to other factors, becoming able to act as an equally efficient
intermediary.   Naturally the capital of these companies
raised by private and direct negotiation remained small and
they had usually become officially, "Private" companies
after 1907.

It was in the second method that the most important
changes took place.   The background for the changes was
the increase in the number of investors and the increase in
the size of the capital needed to develop large schemes, the
multiplicity of investments that were open to the investor
and the smallness of his individual shareholding or loan

compared with the total capital of the company.

Given these factors, some kind of intermediary organisation became necessary.   From the standpoint of the
investor, he needed advice as to which securities were
to be bought, and he needed transferability in case of
loss or necessity, since his individual investment was too
small to direct or control the firm.   The company on the
other hand needed certainty of capital and the ability to
raise additional capital with comparative ease.

For the investor there were three types of organisation willing to assist him in his choice of investment.
Firstly, there were the general financial papers and books.
These increased in number in the later period when the
number of investors had grown and their isolation from
the general industrial field was greater.   This literature
was rarely without ulterior motives and   formed the
path along which the investor went to the second organisation, the stock and share broker, the financial agent or
the investment company.   These companies or individuals,
along with bank managers and solicitors, constituted an
important intermediary organisation for the investment of
savings.   In the first period they had acted, as did
Messrs. Chadwicks, as both assistants to the company in

formation, and as guides to investors. Their functions
were more often split in the second period, but there was
the same growing reliance of the investor not on the
intrinsic merits of the company as seen from the prospectus (if possible), but on the opinion of their
"commissioned" expert. Already in the seventies
Chadwick's support of a company was a sufficient guarantee
for hundreds of capitalists, whether they had heard of the
company before or no. In the twentieth century the advice
of the stockbroker was almost supreme in determining the
choice by investors.

The third type of organisation which assisted the
investor, and was "very attractive to the small confused
investor" was the trust company. These had a rather unsteady
existence up to 1914, but the support/they did receive in
the seventies and late eighties and nineties, showed
impersonal investment at its height and gave an indication
of possible future developments. The choice of alternative
investments was left almost entirely in the hands of the
Directors. Often the companies selected for investment
were not published to the shareholders, who were content
merely to receive their dividends.

The general desire for marketability which was
naturally encouraged by stockbrokers was provided to some
extent by the growth in the business of the official and
unofficial stock

For the company, the problem of certainty of capital
tended to pass with the use by investors of "expert"
assistance in their investments, from one of a direct
appeal to investors, to one of an indirect appeal to the
sections who could influence the choice of investors.
Underwriting syndicates and groups of stockbrokers were
becoming rather more important than the general prospectus.
The change was not rapid.   Efficient distribution of the
prospectus in the 'nineties was still proving an effective
way of raising the capital,   but there were clear signs
by 1914 that "private negotiation" with Trusts, stockbrokers
and underwriters, was becoming important in public companies.
The chief difference of course with the "private negotiation"
              of private companies was that in the public
companies it was conducted not by individuals providing
their own capital, but with individuals who had control
over the capital of others.

By 1914 the use by investors who invested in home
industry of the "expert" intermediaries and the use by
home companies of stockbrokers and underwriters had not
proceeded very far.   Genuine "private negotiation" between
those owning the capital and those requiring it, was still
a very important method.   But new industries were tending

to be forced to use the new methods, and old companies
desiring additional capital very frequently used the
stock exchanges and all that entailed.   The contrary
tendencies were present. The enormous wealth and the pride
in self sufficiency of the industrial capitalists had
rendered the new methods unnecessary for a long period,
but by 1914 there could be noted both an exhaustion of
the resources of the individuals relative to the increased
demands, and a change in their attitude towards self-
sufficiency.

CHAPTER IX.

The Investor, his attitude towards Investment, and the Relations between the Investor, the Company and the Board of Directors.

The change in the methods of business organisation
from those which were adopted during the Industrial Revolution in this country to those adopted at the present day,
is probably most strikingly illustrated by the change in
the relationships between the capitalist and the firm or
company which is assisted by his capital. The major part
of the Industrial revolution was accomplished by means of
the partnership form in business units. All the partners
had a direct stimulus to be active in the running of the
concern. The most "sleeping" of them was kept partly awake
through the Common Law practice of holding as liable for the
debts of the concern all those participating in the partnership. The result was, generally speaking, that the firms
were carried on and controlled by those whose capital was
sunk in the undertaking.

The hundred odd years following the industrial revolution saw the expansion and consolidation of the methods of
machino-facture in most industrial fields: skill developed,

new inventions were continually introduced, the size of the
unit expanded, the size of the market increased. But these
changes,in contrast to those which had occurred during 'the
Industrial Revolution' were quantitative rather than qualiti-
tative in nature. In direct contrast to these were the
developments on the financial and capital side. Here, after a
series of slow changes throughout the period 1760-1830, the
next. hundred years presented a revolution in the methods of
recruitment of capital to industry, and in the methods of the
control and direction of the capital. By the twentieth
century business units and enterprises were beginning to be
carried on with other people's money. The functions of ownership of the capital and control of its use were being
separated. The right hand did not know, was losing the power
to know, and often did not want to know, what the left hand
was doing. The implications of this divorce of ownership
and control are being widely discussed at the present time.
Its existence in the United States has been the subject of
statistical enquiry and proof.[1] In this country, while such
a convincing analysis is not yet available, and the problem
is usually couched in less definite terms, articles in
Journals like the "Economist", the "Accountant", and the

---

1) e.g. A.A. Berle and G.C.Means, "The Modern Corporation
   and Private Property", New York, 1932: and Th.Veblen,
   "Absentee Ownership", New York, 1923.

"Bulletin of the Federation of British Industries", have
drawn attention to the question as being one of immediate
(1)
concern.

In the last mentioned publication, "The Bulletin of the
Federation of British Industries" in 1934, Robert Ashworth
made the following statement, using the guarded language
common to all British contributions on the subject.   "It is
now impossible for the shareholders to exercise effective
control in their corporate capacity, so that a huge amount
of capital remains in the uncontrolled hands of the management,
(2)
in which such management may itself have little at stake".
The remedies advanced both here and in America though varying
slightly according to the political opinion of the writer,
have running through them, the common denominator of control
by the State.   A far cry from the exuberant days in the
fifties and sixties of last century when "Limited liability
(3)
was Free Trade in commerce",   and "Free Trade was Jesus Christ".
(4)

Here we intend to trace the development of this tendency

---

1) e.g. "The Economist" 1926 articles on "the ownership of
   British industrial capital" Dec.18th & 25th and Jan.1st 1927.
   "The Accountant" April 1934; "The Bulletin of the F.B.I."
   July 1934: also other books e.g. "Financial Democracy",
   by M. Miller & D. Campbell, 1933.
2) "Bulletin of the F.B.I." loc.cit.
3) cf. Cobden's letter in the pamphlet written by him and
   W.S. Lindsay, "Remarks on the Law of Partnership", 1856.
4) K. Marx, "Free Trade", 1889 quoting Dr. Bowring, p.29.

from the first stages of the changeover from a partnership
form of business organisation to the Joint Stock Company form,
to the position immediately before the war. By studying the
composition of the investing class, their attitudes towards
investment and management, and the role played by the Boards
of Directors, we hope to throw some light on the course taken
by this revolution in business ownership and control.

Both the practice of Limited Liability and to some extent
the legislation on limited liability in the 'fifties and
sixties expected and encouraged only the wealthy type of shareholder. For example, by the 1855 Act it was established that
"the deed of settlement shall be executed by shareholders not
less than 25 in number, holding shares to the amount in the
aggregate of at least three-fourths of the nominal capital of
the company". [1] Those forming the company were not only all
expected to sign the deed of settlement but also to hold
between them the majority of the shares. Though this pro-
vision did not appear in the following acts, the practice
continued and it both affected and was encouraged by the high
denomination of the shares. We have given details of share
denomination above. The effects were clearly to keep out
of the investment market all those who had not a substantial

---

1) Section 9 I.(4) of 18th. and 19th. Vic. c.133. quoted from
A. Parsons, "The Limited Liability Act and its Legal Interpretation", 1855.

sum to invest for a long period. For besides the high denomination, the unpaid nature of the shares entailed a large reserve
to meet calls, and meant complete, or nearly complete, inability
to transfer the shares easily. The remark that "the middle
classes of commerce were kept out", (1) was partially true.

This was the background of the composition of the investing classes for the first two decades of limited liability
companies. But there were interesting and important differen-
tiations of types within the group of investors who were
sufficiently wealthy to take shares.

The London paper "the Shareholder's Guardian and Circular",
when discussing the differences between the shareholders of
joint stock banks which were formed in the 'thirties and
'forties and those which were formed under the 1858 and 1862
Acts, analyses two of the types in the market.

> "The former already begin to partake of the aris-
> tocratic attributes of our older private banks - the
> shareholders consisting principally of spinsters,
> widows, gentry and professionals but scarcely a shop-
> keeper and comparatively few men of business; these
> latter have long since sold out at large premiums
> and gone into newer concerns. In the newer banks
> we find the shareholders almost entirely composed
> of the commercial classes and a very large proportion
> of such shopkeepers as a quarter of a century back
> scarcely thought of even having an account at a bank".(2)

The third type of investor was the industrial capitalist

---

1) Loftus Fitz-Wygram. op.cit. p.14.
2) "Shareholders Guardian", March 17th. 1864, p.150.

,o whom the limited liability company was "only a new branch
(1)
>f the craft by which they obtain their wealth". We will
liscuss each of these types in turn and examine their rela-
:ions, as investors, with the company.

The "spinster, widow, gentry and professional" type of
investor, variously described by observers as the "rentier",
(2)
:he "safe" investor or the "steady and legitimate" investor
vas mainly interested in sound investments. We mentioned
this class above as investing in Consols and thereby forming,
what can be described as the base of the Victorian investment
market. Certain sections of them had risen above Consols
and were investing in railways, and as shown above, in other
established public utilities like banks and telegraph, dock,
water and gas companies.

While having the "aristocratic attributes" of the
partners in private banks, they differed widely from partnership investors in their numbers, in their tendency to invest
in large undertakings, and in their attitude towards investment.

The number of fundholders in the fifties and sixties
varied from between 260,000 to 270,000. In 1870 there was
a slight fall to 250,000 and a further decrease in 1885.

---

1) ibid. Jan. 4th, 1865, p.89.
2) e.g. D. Morier Evans, "Speculative Notes and Notes
on Speculation", 1864, p.175.

This decrease in actual numbers of holders had been accompanied by an increase in the number holding larger amounts. But there had been no substantial additions to the National Debt in this period.   In railways on the other hand where building had been continued, there was an increase in the number of shareholders.   The number of shareholders in the United Kingdom in 1864 was 209,126.[1]   In the return presented in 1887, the number of individual investors in the United Kingdom was given as 546,438, Ordinary - 259,234: Preference and Guaranteed - 242,556, and Debenture holders 118,438.[2]

The difference between these investors and those joining a partnership, from the point of view of the numbers of shareholders in the undertaking and their attitude towards investment, was seen particularly in joint stock banking companies.

J.W. Gilbart made an analysis of 5 London joint stock banks and 65 London partnership banks in 1845.   In the former there were 3013 shareholders, or an average of 600 per bank: in the latter there were 217 partners, or an average of 3.5 partners in each private bank.   And of the 3013 shareholders of the joint stock banks, 1106, or just over a third, resided outside   a radius of 15 miles around London.[3]   Investment at a distance usually implied impersonal

---

1) "Herepath's Journal" 1864, p.749.
2) "The Economist", Jan.22, 1887, p.107.
3) J.W. Gilbart, "The London Bankers, an analysis", 1845.

investment.

The next forty years of joint stock banking development,
saw an increase in the acceptance of banks as a secure investment, and a corresponding increase in the number of shareholders per bank, until in the 'eighties there were more
shareholders per banking unit than in any other enterprise
adopting the joint stock form except railways.   This development is shown in the following table.

English and Welsh banks listed in the Bankers' Almanack in
the following years:

Number of Shareholders	1860	1870	1880	1885
1,000 - 2,000	2	4	10	8
2,000 - 5,000	-	3	5	5
5,000 - 10,000	-	-	-	4

The rentier and "legitimate" investors were conspicuous
early in the investment market for their "impersonal" attitude
towards investment and for the large numbers in which they
invested in any particular concern.   But they were not an
enterprising force; only established undertakings could gain
their confidence.   Limited liability only affected them
indirectly; it was the more enterprising "commercial" classes
and "native trading" community which had to lead the way in
the new limited companies before the "safe" investor would
follow.

This second type of investor was concentrated in the
large commercial centres.   It was from them that pressure
had come in the fifties and sixties for the change in the
Partnership Laws.   Their capital was accumulating, but they
were insufficiently in touch with the industrial districts
of the North to make partnerships a safe venture.   Foreign
lending and Railways had provided them with temporary outlets, but in the late fifties and early sixties with "a
plethora of money" available and almost stagnation in the
home railway field, they demanded and obtained Limited Liability which allowed them to invest in, and direct companies
without too much danger to their total capital.

These investors both assisted in forming, and invested in
a number of the financial credit associations and general
wagon and hotel companies of the sixties and seventies.
"Successful traders have been leaving trade and going into
the money lending and financing business...in proof... refer
to the lists of Directors of our Banks and Finance companies
to see how largely the money lending community consists of
mercantile men."
(1)
        "The Shareholders Guardian" reported
the same thing happening and regarded it as serious.

_____

1) "Credit and its Bearings upon the Crisis of 1866",
   1866, pp.17-18.

"the London Gazette however shows that the great
body of investors in recent undertakings do not
belong to the class of simple investors, but to
the native trading community......the inadequacy
of the individual capital to meet the increasing
requirements of trade is the very motive assigned
for the formation of companies; yet we find the
whole industrial community actually denuding
themselves in order to promote schemes outside
their sphere." (1)

This investor was more enterprising than the "safe"

investor, but his attitude towards investment was still

personal. This is shown partly by the interest he took in

forming companies and by the comparatively few shareholders

per company in those enterprises in which he was concerned.

His role as promoter we have discussed above.   Some idea of

the number of investors in each company is given by analysis

of some of the most important of these companies given in

the "Joint Stock Companies Directory" between 1865-9.   For

example, of a selection of 46 finance and credit companies

formed in the four years after the 1862 Act, 27, or almost

60% had under 200 shareholders, 15 between 200 and 1,000,

and 4 between 1,000 and 5,000, and it was these companies

that were very widely advertised when formed.   In the wagon

companies,the number of shareholders was usually smaller.

None of those given in the Directory for any of these years

had over 500 shareholders.   In hotels only one had over 300

---

1) "Shareholders Guardian", April 18th, 1864, p.184.

shareholders and of a sample of 20, 11 had under 100 shareholders.[1]   The companies listed in the Directory were the
most important ones, and consequently had the largest number
of shareholders.

These three types of enterprise together with the
telegraph and transport companies mentioned above formed the
probable limits of the investments of this "commercial" class.
The telegraph companies at one end of the scale were verging
into the safe investment field, with small returns.   The
hotels at the other end were verging into the "trade connection" type of investment, where local prominence of the
promoter was an important factor in success.   The number of
shareholders as given in samples above, indicate, that with
some exceptions, the majority of the companies in this class
were still small enough to allow of a certain amount of
participation in the management, through the shareholders
meetings, by the subscribers.   The figure of almost 60% of
the most important Discount, Finance and Credit, and Contract
and Investment Companies, with the number of shareholders
below 200, would seem a confirmation of this view.

The third type of investor, was the industrial capitalist.
Before the introduction of limited liability they had

_____

1) All these figures taken from the details given each
    year in the "Joint Stock Companies Directory", issued
    by Charles Barker and Sons, 1865-9.

conducted their enterprises on a partnership basis. They
were enabled by the Acts to regularise their partnership
contract and draw in a certain amount of new capital. Here
the investment was, to a large extent, "personal", though
with the activity of a firm like Messrs. Chadwicks, the
responsibility was tending to be delegated to the Directors
and auditors. The companies in which these investors took
shares, were the large shipping, iron, coal and steel concerns.
There were comparatively few shareholders per company, the
largest being those quoted on the London or provincial stock
exchange lists. In the late sixties, the Panama, New Zealand
and Australian Royal Mail Company Limited had 700 shareholders
and was the largest in this group. Other large ones were
the Ebbw Vale Company and National Steamship Company with
around 500 shareholders each; Hopkins Gilkes & Co., Palmers
Shipbuilding Co., Bolckow Vaughan & Co., and John Brown &
Co. with around 300. At the other end of the scale the Park-
gate Iron Company and the Titanic Steel and Iron Company were
quoted with only 95 and 150 shareholders respectively. The
majority of the industrial companies did not either ask for,
or obtain a quotation, and these rarely had more than 200
shareholders apiece in the first ten years of their existence.
Large individual investments and a small number of shareholders

and little or no transference of shares,were the characteristics of investment in these home industrial companies.

Up to the 'eighties these three groups of investors
remained more or less distinct forces in the investment
market.   In 1877 Walter Newmarch with his London experience
considered that the "safe" investors who "considered 4-5% a
handsome return on their capital" represented about 80% of
the total number of investors.   More than this, the "safe"
type of investor was not only to be found now in towns, but
the "country rentier" was now appearing in the capital market.
In 1874 the "Bondholders Register" noted the appearance of
the "country bondholder, and with the relative turn away from
foreign investment in the "great depression", he became a
force in the market for home securities.

_____

1) 1877 Report, Qu. 349.
2) "Bondholder's Register", 1874, Vol.II, No.27, p.27.
   "Twenty years ago the country bondholder was a rarity.
   People's savings were carefully hoarded or deposited
   with the local banker....the man who lent his money
   to a foreign state was regarded as a fit candidate
   for a lunatic asylum.   But we have changed all that.
   The growth of Commerce, the spread of Railways and
   the dissemination of information by means of the
   Press have had their due influence...Were any statistics
   available we think our readers would be astonished at
   the enormous amounts of Foreign Securities which are
   held by provincial investors.   The country clergymen,
   the village practitioner, the retired tradesman, the
   ancient dame..now take counsel together or consult the
   local banker as to the most eligible security in the
   market".

The commercial classes had been badly hit by the crisis of 1866 which was most severe on the very companies which they had floated or in which they had invested. Until the 'eighties they tended to lie low, though some were attracted through organisations like Messrs. Chadwicks into the home industrial companies' boom in the early 'seventies. As a whole, however, the home industrial companies retained their "personal" investment character. In spite of more quotations on the local stock exchanges, the investments themselves were still of a permanent character.[1] And although Messrs. Chadwick's net had spread to 5,000 investors, the bulk of the capital was recruited for these home industrials from the vendors and the friends of the vendors. Robert Giffen in 1889 claimed that

> "the regular annual investment by individuals in their own businesses or properties..must always be the most important form of saving - far more important than the visible public investments".[2]

However the beginnings of issues of debentures and preference shares in these industries, which were appealing directly to "female and professional types of investors",[3] were appearing in the 'eighties and tended slowly to weigh down the balance

---

1) "Chadwicks Investment Circular", 1871, p.115.
2) quoted in F.E. Lavington, op.cit. p.227.
3) cf. Chadwick's appeal to ladies which we quoted above with the statement in the "Shareholders Guardian" in 1863, "that few women will read this paper" Dec.17, p.3.

against the wealthy "personal" investments.

While the actual number of shareholders in limited
liability companies and the classes from which they were
drawn provide some evidence as to the part which could be
played by investors in the control of the companies in which
(1)
they invested, the key to their actual practice lies in the
attitude of the investors towards shareholding. This can
be determined in some degree by asking two general questions.
Firstly what were the facilities for control laid down by
law? Secondly to what extent were these used and to what
extent were they insufficient?

The Acts of 1856 and 1862 were quite vague about the
question of control. To the Legislators, seeing industrial
organisation through the old partnership spectacles, the
problem hardly existed. Both laisser faire theory and past
practice had taught Robert Low that capitalists can look
after themselves. The law need only interfere in times of
difficulty. The Directors, it was assumed, would be elected
at the first meeting of the shareholders, and the Directors'
expert watchdogs, the auditors, were also to be controlled,
and paid, by the "owners" of the company. This was borne

---

1) e.g. the complaint could not be registered in the 'sixties
that the number of shareholders was too large to accommodate
in the largest hall in the country.

out by many of the early prospectuses.   It was not uncommon
to read "A Provisional Committee of Directors will act until
(1)
a Board is elected at the first Shareholders Meeting".   And
the auditors usually worked in pairs, "one of which is
appointed by the Directors, and one to be elected by the
(2)
Shareholders".   The impression gathered from this type of
prospectus, is one of a small number of shareholders with a
large degree of interest in and control over the proceedings
of the company.   There had been a slight change of tone
from the prospectuses and reports of the earlier chartered
companies.   For example, the prospectus of the British Iron
Company, 1824, referred to "the first meeting of the
Proprietors".   The P. & O. Steam Navigation Company adopted
the same nomenclature for its shareholders in the annual
reports.   The speculative cost book mines were similarly
(3)
straightforward in "Inviting adventurers to join them".
This more picturesque language had disappeared in the
'sixties and the sober word "shareholder" was applied to
investors all and sundry.   But the invitation to subscribe
still had the character of an invitation to join the company,
rather than an invitation to invest in the company.

---

1) e.g. Prospectus of North Eastern Iron and Wagon
   Company, 1865.
2) e.g. Prospectus of Alton Coal, Coke & Iron Company Ltd. 1873
3) e.g. Prospectus of the "Portland Iron Cost Book Company".

The accepted view was that legislation on company democracy was unnecessary, that with heavy investment and unpaid liability it would naturally come into being as it had done in the partnerships. But by 1867 according to the Committee on the Companies Acts of that year, there were already holes in the fabric of "natural democracy". By 1885, the whole issue of democracy was tending to be put on one side as Utopian, and attention was concentrated on the narrower and more immediate question of protection of the investor against "palpable roguery".

Apart from the financial swindles perpetrated in the boom of 1864-6 and revealed to the world by the crash of the latter year, the first signs of the rents in the "natural democracy" fabric were seen in the attendance at the shareholders meetings. Walter Newmarch who, from the start had viewed rather cynically the "untold blessings" that would be brought about by the Limited Liability system, said in 1867 "I know companies (in another place 'it very often happens') of one thousand or two thousand shareholders where meetings are attended by only 30 or 40 persons".[1] But we must allow here both for his cynicism and his almost exclusively London experience, where, as suggested above, resided the largest number of "safe" investors whose experience of companies and

1) 1867 Report Qu.983.

investment was always secondhand through a banker or solicitor,
and who naturally did not attend meetings.   In the industrial
companies however, where the greatest degree of control and
interest was expected, a slightly similar position was developing.   Not so much in those companies where the "shares were
held locally" but for example "in Palmers Iron and Shipping
Company (Sheffield) with 300 shareholders, where the shares
are held all over the country, the number who attended the
annual meeting was not more, I suppose, than 25".   Where the [1]
local capital market was sufficient, the interest and control
were present, but where the very reason for "turning limited",
was the insufficiency of the local market, then, dutifully
assisted by Chadwicks connections through the country, lack
of interest began to appear.   Chadwick had an answer to this
charge which will be stated later.

This development of lack of interest on the part of the
shareholders, when they are dispersed through the country or
when they spread their investments over several companies
rather than invested heavily in one, was again stated before
the 1877 Committee.   Bonamy Price, speaking of the move away
from the partnership tradition said, "I think persons are
becoming accustomed to take shares in various companies
rather than have a larger sum in one business".   And a [2]

---

1) Henry Pochin, 1867 Report, Qu.2342.
2) 1877 Report, Qu.1240.

company solicitor, John Morris, repeated the Newmarch obser-
vation on attendance at company meetings. "So long as a
company pays dividends and everything goes smoothly, one-
twentieth of the shareholders only attend the meetings and
you cannot get more of them to do so. Directly you get
into difficulties the proportion increases: you get a fifth
or a sixth; but by all the power in the world you could not
generally get half."(1)

Alongside this non-attendance at meeting and the spread
of the investors throughout the country had developed the
use of "proxy" voting. The railway companies were of course
past masters at this art, but the method had not, apparently,
been used to any extent in other joint stock companies before
the late sixties.(2) But in the 'seventies any book purporting
to deal with the details of company administration, had a
section on the use of proxies and often a fascimile form for
company directors to copy. The extent of their use and the
reactions of the shareholders to them are very difficult to
determine. But the following figures of an occasion of their
use in the Great Western Railway Company in 1864, gives some
indication of the reactions of the "safe" investor. 15,200

---

1) *ibid*. Qu.975.
2) It was stated in the 1867 Report Qu.1793 "proxies are
connected with new companies, not old ones. In the
East India Company and the Bank of England, a ballot
could be demanded."

proxies were sent out at a cost, printing, postage and stamps, of £380. Of these 5,000 were sent back signed, (implying support of the Board), 2,200 were sent back unsigned, and 8,000 remained in the hands of the shareholders.[1] The result was that with one-third only of the votes, the Directors had secured complete power for their policy.

While non-attendance at meetings and the use of proxies was becoming a matter for comment in a number of companies, it must not be assumed that it was very widespread. In the iron and steel companies where the capital was said to be two-thirds recruited from the vendors and friends of the vendors, the control by the shareholders was close, though probably more by personal contact than actually through the rather unwieldy shareholders meeting. In the cotton spinning companies in Oldham in the 'seventies and 'eighties there was also close supervision and control. Meetings were held quarterly and balance sheets were published in the local press.[2] "We in the trade know how to examine these balance sheets"[3] and the investors were usually those very people.

---

1) "Herepath's Journal" 1864, p.18.
2) cf. "The Accountant" 1887, p.74, "The information is published and freely criticised in the local press to an extent which is simply unknown elsewhere".
3) J.C.A. "Limited Liability and Cotton Spinning", 1886, p.8. the author goes on to suggest, however, that "outsiders" were at that date investing in "Cotton" and they were not in this knowledgeable position.

The position in 1886, was that "the directors are as a rule
well looked after, meetings are frequent: generally they
are held quarterly so that I do not think there is much to
complain of in that respect".[1]

The degree of control in the companies which was exercised by the shareholders depended, then, not on the rules or
lack of rules of conduct of the company laid down in the
Limited Liability Acts, but on the composition of the investors
in the company. This was felt by many to be inadequate, and
steps were suggested to change or supplement the law in this
respect.

To overcome the inability of shareholders to attend
meetings owing to their dispersion through the country, it
was suggested that shorthand notes of all that took place
should be sent round to them.[2] The cost of this, though large,
it was hoped would not stand in the way of this move towards
company democracy. Newmarch in 1877 was even suggesting a
compulsory balance sheet for all companies,[3] but this was a
little ahead of the times for even the "Shareholder's
Guardian", which, to a considerable extent, lived up to its
name, designated such a demand as "preposterous".[4]

---

1) 1886 R.C. on the Depression, Qu.4592.
2) 1867 Report, Qu.983 and 1877 Report, Qu.261.
3) ibid. Qu.286
4) "Shareholders Guardian" May 9th 1866, p.364.

To supplement the law, the organisation of "Shareholders Protection Associations" were a favourite suggestion. This type of body had been set up in some Railway companies and after some rather bad cases of swindling in the Limited Liability companies this idea seemed a real panacea. When the "Shareholders Guardian" proposed to set up a "Shareholders Protection Association" in 1864, a shareholder wrote in and said "the value and importance of your suggestion that shareholders should combine for mutual defence cannot be overestimated",[1] but after pushing and advertising the body for six months the editor had to announce reluctantly that one could not be formed owing to lack of consistent support from the investors. The scope of the association was too great, and the London shareholders were too much concerned with dividends and premiums.

Actual combination of shareholders proved difficult, but advice to them on how they should look after their own interests was easy, and this is continually found in the books and journals on the joint stock companies. Some suggestions were constructive. The "Shareholders Guardian" answered the question "What is to be done" with "Find honest auditors, pay them liberally, make them do their duty ...encourage them to sift boldly and to speak freely".[2] As shown above in a number

---

1) "Shareholders Guardian", March 1st 1864, p.136.
2) ibid. July 18th 1864, p.282.

of companies, the election of an auditor was directly and not
just officially within the power of the shareholders.   But
apart from the actual increase in the number of auditors and
accountants brought about by the 1862 Act,[1] their services
to the shareholders were doubtful.   "The Statist" which
tended to concentrate on the blacker side of company finance
wrote in 1887 "an honest accountant's certificate honestly
applied is one of the rarest features in an industrial
prospectus".[2]

Another regular form of advice was "watch your directors".
In 1863 it was pointed out that "under the circumstances the
Statute itself (1862) will afford very little security to
Members of a Company....this will (as heretofore) consist in
their ascertaining that the Directors and Officers managing
its affairs are honest and able men".[3]   The "Economist"
restated this in a more practical fashion.   "So long as the
directors stay in the company, its affairs if not prosperous
are at least honourable....go once every three months to the

1) cf. Beresford Worthington, "Professional Accountants" 1895,
   p.50, "This statute undoubtedly proved the best friend
   the profession ever had", and he goes on to point out the
   increase in the number of Accountants in London, Liverpool
   and Manchester between 1864-1890 was over twofold p.93.
2) "Statist" 1887, Vol.I, p.284.
3) James Bigg, "Collection of Consolidating Statutes of
   Trading Companies" 1863, Preface.

office and examine the register of shares".[1] This method
remained until the end of the century the favourite, and in
some ways the most effective, method of judging the soundness
of a company.[2] But with the very wide dispersion of shares
which occurred in new companies and the selling of shares in
the old ones, this method was no longer so effective. The
amount that Directors invested in relation to the total capital
of the company was, of necessity, becoming so insignificant,
that this touchstone alone would not suffice..

David Chadwick who played such a large part in the formation of home industrial companies likewise considered the
chief security for investors lay in their Directors. The
attendance at meetings, he considered, was not so important
as making sure in the promotion of the company that the vendors
retained a considerable interest in the concern.[3] What this
meant when seen through the eyes of the Directors was well
expressed by Thomas Vickers before the 1886 Committee on the
Depression in Trade and Industry. "It has been an advantage
to my company to be a limited liability company - because I
have always had as much power as a director of this company
as I had as a partner and the resources of the company are

1) "Economist" 1866, p.820.
2) cf. "The Investors Review" edited by A.J.Wilson, 1892-1900
   His analyses of Companies were always based on this method.
3) 1877 Report, Qu.1998. "The directors in our companies have
   always been among the largest shareholders", and Qu.2050,
   "we never allow a vendor, or only in a few cases, to
   take his hands off the property".

greater than those of the old partnership." [1]

This was the position in the industrial companies where the shareholders were usually wealthy men with some knowledge of the industry in which they had invested their money.   The Directors of these companies could certainly be trusted to conduct the firm to the best of their ability, for not only were they encouraged by   financial agents like Chadwick, to have a large interest in the company, but also the amount of directors qualification shares was large.   But the spirit of "unity is strength", and "co-operation" which had so dominated the discussions and hopes of the framers of the limited liability acts had completely disappeared in the straight-forward statement of Thomas Vickers, quoted above.

While this disparity between practice and theory applied in a number of cases, not all the supporters of Limited liability had in the first place accepted very seriously this concept of "co-operation leading to a better England".   As shown above a section of the theorists maintained that joint stock companies should only be formed where the enterprises they were to undertake could not be carried out through the resources of an ordinary partnership.   And if they did attempt to compete with private enterprise then the "company would go to the wall". [2]   With this idea dominating the

---

1) R.C. on Depression in Trade 1886, Qu.3440.
2) "The Bankers Magazine" 1860, p.411.

founders of a company it was not to be expected that they would encourage democracy inside the company. It was thought that such a principle would lead to divided counsels and immobility of decision as against the quick thinking single entrepreneur. Chadwick was only expressing the opinion of hundreds of Directors and founders of industrial limited liability companies when he asserted "The nearer you can approach to the management of a private concern the better, and in nearly all the great companies that we are associated with that has been part of our policy to recommend and the directors and shareholders have adopted it, giving great powers to a very well paid general manager." [1]

In these companies, although the shareholders did not in any sense exercise control, they had little complaint. With the less experienced investor and with the "safe" investor the lack of control was clearer and more serious. We have mentioned their in-attendance at meetings, and their lack of interest in the concern. This was paralleled by both useless and dishonest Directors.

The evidence that this type of Director existed is legion. In 1867 the epithet "guinea-pig director" was already in common use. [2] Numerous cases were being cited

1) 1877 Report, Qu.2007.
2) e.g. "Herepath's Journal" 1867, p.392, "a Note on Guinea-pigism".

where the Director's share qualification was given to him by
the promoter in order to use his name as an attraction for
investors.[1]   In 1877 the Vice Chancellor, Malins, regretfully
observed that "in this great town there are a great number of
military and naval men who have a great deal of time on their
hands and very little money and for the sake of the occupation
allow themselves to be led into these things".[2]   Pamphlet
literature played its due part in entertaining exposure of
this "company rascality".   "Sir William's Speculations or the
Seamy Side of Finance" is an amusing work where the hero (or
villain) Sir William Mavell finds "that a title is very
literally a handle by which to raise a new born Joint Stock
Company to life",[3]   though after the handle had been well used
the story ends, as all such stories should, with the arm of
the law proving too strong for Sir William and he is lucky
to retire safely, though hurriedly, to the South of France to
finish his days.

But the very colourful nature of the exposures of these
directors immediately shows that there is a tendency to
exaggerate.   Against the evidence given above, must be put the
fact that in almost all of the "converted" companies, which

1) 1867 Report, Qu.1063, and "Chadwicks Circular".
2) 1877 Report, Qu.2482.
3) Title as quoted in text, "by the Author of 'a Bubble of
   Finance'", 1880, p.12.

were not insignificant in the 'sixties and 'seventies, the
Directors were the old partners of the firms.   In many cases
the prospectus announced that they were to be in office for
the first five or seven years of the companies' existence.[1]
This may have been contrary to the principles of democracy
within the company, but it ruled out the possibility of a
Board of "Sir Williams".   Also Vice Chancellor Malins' statement, it should be noted, applies only to London.

The critics of the Directors of public companies made
some play with the "pluralist" tendencies that were appearing
as early as the sixties.   The Joint Stock Companies Directory
published annual lists of directors from 1865 onwards, and
analyses of these lists were made, revealing to a dutifully
shocked public that in 1868, for example, one man was a director
of 13 companies, 2 of 12, 3 of 10, 6 of 8 and 13 of 5 companies.[2]
But again these figures must not be taken on their face value
alone.   For example, Henry Pochin was director of five
companies in the North of England and at the same time he was
the largest shareholder in all five.[3]   No one doubted his
right to hold these positions.

Generally speaking up to the 'eighties, it can be stated
that as with the promoter, the "professional type" of Director

1) e.g. Bocklow Vaughan & Company Limited, 1864, & John
   Brown & Co.
2) W. Bartlett and H. Chapman, "A Handy Book for Investors",
   1869, p.170.
3) 1867 Report, Qu.2288-9.

was not yet generally known in the joint stock company. The
evidence points much more to Directors being recruited from
the old partnership class, the retired and successful business
man with money and ideas, and, which was more important
sociologically, younger men, friends of, or known to these
two classes. Leadership in industry became in some ways
more defined and also "there was opened a career in business
for men of talent earlier in life."[1]

To sum up the position of relations between the investor
and the company up to 1885, a distinction has to be made, as was
made above with the types of investor, between the different
types of company.

The first group were those companies with a thousand and
more shareholders. The group included the incorporated
companies, railways, docks, gas and water companies, telegraph
and some shipping companies. Added to this group by the
Companies Acts were the Joint Stock Banks. In these companies
in the words of the "Bankers Magazine", "the proprietors throw
up the reins and leave them in the hands of the directors".[2]
"Herepath's Journal" repeats the same fact later.

---

1) "The Accountant" 1888, p.384, report of paper read before
the British Association, Sept.1887 by Mr. Jamieson.
2) "Bankers Magazine" 1860, Vol.XX, p.411. The same article
complains that though they are called "proprietors" in
reality they are lending money to managing proprietors
upon the security of the trade and nothing else. The
shareholders never do a day's work, they are mere sleeping
partners.

"Theoretically speaking and in the eyes of the law Shareholders are all powerful – this is a legal fiction; practically it is the reverse".[1] "The Economist" completes
the observations twenty-five years after the "Bankers
Magazine" made its comment, in an article on "The Indifference
of Bank Shareholders". "The shareholders look mainly to
the dividend paid and care but little how it may have been
earned".[2] All three of the remarks it should be noted were
confined to shareholders in the big companies, that is mainly
the "safe" investors. By the 'eighties in these companies
the interest of the shareholders was being concentrated on
the rate of dividend and the marketability of the shares.
Direction and control was delegated to the Board of Directors,
who, though not "professional directors" in the sense of
little personal wealth but great financial acumen, were in
their turn, delegating this responsibility to paid managers.

The second group of companies were the home industrials.
Marketability and transferability of shares was difficult
and although by the 'eighties, shares in some of these
companies were being spread throughout the country, in most
of them the shareholders were few and wealthy. The control
exercised by the shareholders was mainly of a personal

1) "Herepath's Journal", 1867, p.363.
2) "The Economist", 1887, p.107.

character, and the security of the investor lay in his knowledge of the men whom he elected to the Board of Management,
and the financial and personal interest these latter had in
the concern.   Shareholders protection committees were rarely
considered in these companies.   And the development of non-
voting debenture and preference issues was only in its infancy
in the 'eighties.

Outside these two clearly defined types of company, it
is impossible to generalise as to the method of management.
For companies which were, in any degree, in competition with
private concerns, e.g. hotel companies, and amusements, it
was suggested that almost dictatorial powers should be assumed
by the Directors or the Managing Director.   In others e.g.
cemetery companies, where the greater part of the work was
routine, both the shareholders and the Directors could leave
the running to "an efficient manager, well paid".   Owing to
lack of detail, however, concerning the actual management and
running of these types of companies, it is necessary to fall
back on the general trends in the organisation of these
companies for any picture of the management.   The share
denominations were high and partly unpaid, the investments
tended to be local, and the number of shareholders was small
enough to allow of some direct control.   The general forces
for and means of control by shareholders were present.

The position of management and control of limited

liability companies up to the decade of the 'eighties was that
while the law had laid down few definite provisions for
democracy in the company, the number of investors per company,
the type of investors and directors, and the size of the
company, except in a minority of cases, raised no obstacles
to such a "democracy" taking place.   The next twenty-five
years of company development saw little change in the law
towards legalising democracy, but a big change in company
practice making "democracy" in the most important business
units an impossibility.

In the period 1885-1914 the investors were drawn roughly
from the same groups as outlined above in the first twenty-
five years of limited company development, but both the total
number increased and the lines between the different groups
became blurred.   We will deal briefly with the position of
the three types of investors in this latter period, bearing
in mind that the distinction between the groups is in some
cases a little artificial.

The concept of the rentier investor became clearly established in this period.   The investor, that is, who lived
entirely on the income from his or her investments, the capital
for which he or she had either saved personally or had
inherited.   Supplementing this group in the "safe" investment

class was the retired member of the middle class whose income
in his last years depended either directly, or indirectly
through annuities, on dividends from investments.   A third
type, having the same outlook in the investment market as
the above, was the professional man, and the higher salaried
classes.   These groups had increased rapidly with the
increase in the administrative services, and with the greater
complexity of the business unit on both the productive and
distributive sides.   (1)   These groups looked to investment to
supplement both their incomes and their social prestige.   In
the background in this period both providing part of the
demand for the growth of these three classes, and providing
part of the means for their existence was the development of
imperialism.

The commercial and "native trading" classes remained a
force in the investment market, but no longer a unified force.
Some had been absorbed into the positions of "overseers" in
the large amalgamated companies.   (2)   Others, who had regarded
with mild surprise joint stock comings and goings of the
previous twenty-five years, were now themselves drawn into
the joint stock net.   Self confidence in one's own business
and in the doctrine of "sticking to one's last",   (3)   now gave

1) For general figures of the rise of this class of A.L.
   Bowley, "Wages & Income in the United Kingdom since
   1860", pp.92-94.
2) "The Journal of the Institute of Bankers", Vol.X, p.424,1889.
3) cf. "The Statist" 1886, p.670.

place to confidence in the Company Limited leading both to
the formation of private limited companies and to investment
by small business men in large public companies rather than
re-investment of profits in their own concern.[1]

The wealthy industrial and commercial classes remained
the most important, as a homogeneous group, section of investors in home industrial and commercial company market. They
tended "to put a substantial portion of their capital into
industrial undertakings in which they take an active part
and which..they consider their own".[2] But in each company,
while they remained homogeneous they were tending to be out-
numbered and out-invested by other groups taking pre-ordinary
issues.

While the groups of investors in the market increased
mainly in size, and to some extent there was a relative
increase in the "safe" types of investor compared with the
other two, there was an important development in the attitude
of these groups towards investment. It was this change of
attitude that had the greatest effects on.the question of
control and management of the company. In brief the development was a change from shareholding to investment; a change
from taking shares through interest in the company,to investing
here and there in order to secure a regular income. Naturally

---

1) 1896 Report, Qu.1894, the representative of a small
traders' association agrees that "many of them are
shareholders".
2) L. Joseph, op.cit. p.8.

this development was most marked in the first two groups of
investors suggested above.   And it is with them that we will
deal in detail.

We have mentioned above the lack of interest shown in
the conduct of the very large incorporated and joint stock
companies by their shareholders.   In this latter period this
lack of interest and the concept of investing purely for
dividends was further intensified by on the one hand an
increase in the number of shareholders per company and on the
other by the withdrawal, to a certain extent, of the more
wealthy investors.   The developments in railway companies,
which were always the first haven of the "safe" investor,
throw some light on the tendencies in the larger limited
liability companies.   The number of investors in the railway
companies in the United Kingdom had risen to between 700,000
and 800,000 in 1902.   This did not mean that there were this
number of separate investors, multiple holdings in several
railways was a common feature, but it is certain that there
had been an absolute increase in the actual numbers of
individual investors.   The withdrawal of the wealthier
investor was shown in the discussion that took place in the
'eighties around "paying interest out of capital".   There

---

1) From "Return showing the holdings of Debenture
   Preference and Ordinary Stock of Railways of the
   United Kingdom", 1902, XC.

was very great pressure from railway companies to have this
permitted,[1] and one of the chief reasons put forward for
allowing the change was the change in the type of railway
investor.

> "The simple explanation of the growth of railways
> without the aid of interest during construction
> is that the shares have been, as a rule, held by
> wealthy men.   But innumerable small capitalists
> are now troubled to find an outlet for their
> money and they find it extremely inconvenient to
> invest without getting any return whilst works
> taking years are being got ready."[2]

By way of proving the effects of "interest during construction" the "Statist" showed that the Hull & Barnsley
Railway Company which secured these powers had average share-
holdings of £350 whereas the average in the other companies
was c.£1500.[3]

Influencing this stratum of investors and the slightly
more adventurous section just above them in this direction
of impersonal investment and lack of interest in the company,
was the tremendous propaganda for "Scientific Investment"
which started in the 'eighties.   The essence of scientific
investment was the careful watching of the dividends paid,

---

1) The figures given in R.W.Perks, "Is it desirable to alter
   the Law which prohibits Railway Companies from paying
   interest out of capital?" 1883, show that in 1881, one
   Company applied for permission to do this, 1882 - 10, and
   in 1883 - 46.
2) "The Accountant" 1885, p.4. and cf. "Statist" 1885, Vol.I,
   p.515: "now sought to reach the less wealthy classes by
   throwing out the bait of interest to be paid during
   construction".
3) "The Statist" 1885, p.686.

and the share quotations on the Stock Exchange, of a number
of companies at home and abroad, and then the distribution
of investments evenly over, say, thirty of these companies
in ten different countries.   "Do not carry all your eggs
in one basket" was probably written on the hearts of these
investors when they died.   The touchstone of investment had
now become the quotation on the Exchange, and the principle
was "spread your investments and invest and re-invest".
Neither the purposes of the company, the   character of the
Directors nor the democracy of the shareholders meeting were
important considerations.   The fall in share denominations
and the need to spread risk in the "great depression" made
this propaganda both appealing and successful.

An outburst in the "City Quarterly" in an article "A
Stockbroker Looks at his Public" illustrated the apparent
falsity of this type of investment, and also the development
away from direct investment and control.   The writer was
discussing the number of these small investors who came to
his office to enquire officiously about their investments.
"..and is Miss Cotswold, whom you know, a whit the wiser?
You know she is not.   She comes up here about once a week
to talk about her Turks.   What business has she to depend
upon the Turkish Government for her income?" (1)   (my italics,J.B.J)

---

1) "The City Quarterley Magazine", Vol.I, 1885, p.47.

It is not difficult to substitute for "Turks" any home
railway, bank, insurance or brewery share.

In addition to this advice to spread investments rather
than to concentrate on one or two and see to their management, these books also advocated pre-ordinary investment.
We have dealt above with the tremendous growth of these stocks
and shares in the period 1885-1914.   Here we have to consider
the effects of this on the relations between the investor and
the company.   It must be noted first that although these
issues were most popular with the "safe" investor, their
influence was not confined purely to the large companies which
already by the 'eighties had ceased to be "democracies" in
any real sense.   Pre-ordinary issues also became part and
parcel of the finance of industrial companies new and old.
With these voteless issues providing up to 60% of the capital
in some of the industrial companies in 1914,[1] the concept of
carrying on trade with other people's money was becoming
generally accepted.   But viewing it from the angle of
security, this development was even welcomed in some quarters
as leading to closer control over the conduct of the business
by the equity shareholders for it was their interests that
would suffer most in the event of bad management.[2]   When these
equity shares were held mainly in a few hands, which was the

---

[1] See Appendix E for full figures.
[2] cf. "The Economist" 1875, p.245 - "the smaller the variable
capital (i.e. ordinary) in proportion to the business done,
the more likely there will be careful management".

case in a number of the "converted" industrial companies,
this statement holds good.   But with the dispersion of
ordinary shares among thousands, even this security dis-
appears.   It is true of course that the debenture holders
from their very position as creditors must have had some
influence on the policy of the company, but when the debenture holders were individual investors, the means of expression of this group became less and less direct as the actual
use of debentures increased.[1]

In the 'seventies when debentures were being first
generally introduced into industrial companies, the holders
of this stock often met separately to nominate trustees of
their interests.[2]   This was accepted as being one of the
reasons why investors could take debentures without any fear
of dishonesty and loose management by the company.[3]   But in
the 'nineties and in the twentieth century, the investors in
debenture bonds were confronted on the prospectus with the
names of the trustees, and they had little opportunity, even
if they had so wished, to change them.   Moreover the practice in the 'seventies of having individuals as trustees had

1) There was appearing a reverse tendency in 1914.   The big
   insurance companies by holding blocks of debentures were
   exerting considerable indirect influence on the direction
   of the company.
2) e.g. cases in "Investments", 1887, March 29th.
3) This view was expressed in "Chadwicks Circular" 1874, p.228.

given place to that of having banks or insurance companies.
While the amount of control that could be effectively asserted
by debenture holders through trustees must not be exaggerated,
it was clear that the mechanism of this control had by the
twentieth century passed into the hands of those who were
intimately linked with the management, rather than neutral as
heretofore.(1)

It was this development of pre-ordinary issues that had
the most influence in divorcing ownership and control in the
home industrials.   The ordinary shareholders in these
companies, though being drawn from a larger circle than before,
were still of necessity deeply interested in the company.
They had few facilities for "spreading" their investments,
because the necessary pre-requisite, the Stock Exchange quotation, did not often exist.   The number of actual ordinary
shareholders in these companies remained small.   The editor
of the Financial Review of Reviews was surprised in 1909 at
the number of industrial concerns with less than a thousand
shareholders.   "An average of 500 per company would be a
liberal estimate".(2)   And the selection of companies which he
was considering numbered 5,000 of the most important.   The

---

1) cf. 1897 Report, Qu.948 referring to this question of
   trustees "..you might say the directors were themselves
   the trustees".
2) "The Financial Review of Reviews", 1909, Dec. p.18.

industrials among the 40,000 not considered probably had
even smaller numbers of shareholders.

The craze for converting private firms into "private"
joint stock companies had a similar effect.   It tended both
to a small number of ordinary shareholders and the control
of the company in the hands of those who conducted the business. [1]   It can be suggested that in a number of these companies
the vendors took debentures and attempted to sell the ordinary
shares on the market, thus leading to common position in
larger companies of the shareholders dispersed without any
interest in the concern, but against this it should be pointed
out that the companies that were formed on this basis were
usually very unstable from their commencement, and ended up
in the Bankruptcy Court before they had exerted any positive
influence on the industrial life of the country.

The position so far as ordinary shares are concerned
remained very similar in most of these industrial companies
to the position outlined for the years 1856-1885, but the
widespread use of pre-ordinary voteless stock had considerably altered the position from the point of view of the
company as a whole.   We have shown above how these pre-ordinary

---

1) cf. H.W. Jordan, "Private Companies", 1915, p.15: "if the
Articles of Association of the new Company are judiciously
framed the Vendor need not surrender any of his control
over the business".

issues tended to be quoted and directly offered to the class
of investors who had no local contact with the company and
who took no interest in the running of the business.

The "meagre provisions" for democracy and control in
limited companies which had been laid down by the 1862 Act
had been to some degree sufficient when the investors were
mainly ordinary shareholders.   But when up to 60% of the
capital of companies was being raised by pre-ordinary voteless
stocks and shares "rule of thumb" democracy was no longer
adequate.   "The Economist" had characterised railway debenture holders in 1872 as "those who contributed all the real
money to the concern..but were partners with no powers of
management".   (1)   By 1914 not only railways but all companies
were issuing debentures, and the debenture holders had been
joined in their anomolous position by preference shareholders.
And it must be stressed that home industrial companies, which
from the point of view of the high percentage of ordinary
shares held by the Directors, and the small number of shareholders per company, gave the appearance of unity of ownership and control, had played no small part in the issue of
pre-ordinary stock.

Corresponding to this increasing lack of interest in the
running of the company manifested by the large numbers of

1) "The Economist" 1872, p.513.

investors who were under the influence of the "scientific
investment" prophets, and the tendency to remove investors
from the position of any right to control by the issue of
pre-ordinary stocks and shares, there were changes in the
roles and composition of the Board of Directors of these
companies.

With the coming of the professional promoter, and the
rentier investor, there appeared also the professional
director.   "Professional Directors are another class of
men created by the application of the Act". [1]   The "Director-
ship of Companies was made something of a business in itself". [2]
An illustration of how true these statements were was given
by an experiment in "Answers" in 1891.   An advertisement was
inserted for a Director with the additional statement that
his qualification shares would be found by the promoter.   No
less than 141 replies were received in a week.   The applicants
were not merely people out for a sudden rise to fame, but
included 1 Earl and 1 Viscount, 4 Barons, 7 Baronets, 13
Honourables and 14 Army Captains, amongst others. [3]   New

1) "Phillips Investors Annual", 1887, p.35.
2) Peek "Prospectus Makers and the Public", 1890. He showed
   that 971 of the Directors whose names were in the 1889
   Directory of Directors (10,837 altogether) were connected
   with four or more companies. This number of Directorates
   per person was regarded as the beginning of the
   "professional" ranks.
3) From "The Accountant", 1891, p.333.

recruits to the field were being found everywhere.   Judge
Emden expressed the position well in 1900 when he wrote "the
tempting facilities offered by this modern machinery now
attract classes that in the past had not tested the flexibility of their consciences in the subject of accounts and
balance sheets".
(1)

The growth of combination in industry at the end of the
nineteenth century and in the twentieth brought a new purpose
to the holding of Directorships.   Apart from the necessity
of having a number of names that would attract investors,
ornamental and interlocking directorates also proved a way of
maintaining the right relationships between companies, and a
means of deciding on a common line of policy between different
companies in an industry.   Any difficulties that might lie
in the way of such a move towards interlocking directorates
such as qualification shares and the confidence of the shareholders could be and was easily overcome by presenting
Directors with the shares necessary and by use of the "proxy"

---

1) "The 19th Century and After", Dec.1900, p.960..   That
   these are not only "coloured" views of the rise of professional directors is seen from Mr. Edgar Speyer's note
   before the 1905 Committee.   "Having had 20 years'
   experience of business life in the City...I am more than
   ever impressed with, i) the growth of pluralist or
   "guinea-pig" directors particularly among men of public
   life: ii) the number of ornamental directors sought after
   in many cases obviously as decoys on the front page of
   the prospectus." 1906 Report, p.30.

vote.

Within the board of directors itself there were appearing
further divisions.   Those with names which attracted the
investor, called various names from "guinea-pigs" to "ornamental"
were usually not at all concerned with the management of the
concern.   They only wanted the Directors fee.   A second group
on the board were mainly there owing to their connections with
other companies or traders through which orders might come.

> "I have been in consultation with two managers of
> companies (shipping and insurance) and both of
> them told me distinctly that the class of men
> they wanted for directors were men who would
> bring business to the company; and it was quite
> well understood in a tacit way that their share
> in the administration of the company would be a
> silent share".(1)

And behind these there was, according to a number of contemporaries, a man or group of men who were the main drive of
the company.   E. Manson went as far as stating "every company
is in a sense a one man company, that is to say is controlled
by a ruling spirit.   Directors are mostly dummies and shareholders mere dividend drawers.   Unity of management and
control is from a commercial point of view a most desirable
thing."
(2)

While pointing out again that these remarks should not

---

1) 1896 Report, Qu.1695.
2) "Law Quarterly Review", 1895, No.XLII, p.186.

be generalised to apply to all and every Board of Directors
throughout the country.   In most of the private companies
the Directors, even if they did "judiciously frame the Articles"
in order to get control, rather than let the company be run
by the shareholders, did understand the company of which they
were Directors.   Likewise in the industrial companies the
ideas of London society and paintings by Whistler were only
slowly attracting the Directors away from a close personal
interest in the firm.   (1)   However it is interesting to note at
the same time that in this period when discussing "guinea-
pigs" the assertion that they exist in the City, has been
widened to "in the City of London at least".

The general tendencies that we have noted so far in the
relations between the investor and the company and the management of the company are fourfold.   First the investor with
the introduction of smaller denominations of shares and the
propaganda for scientific investment became less interested
in the company as such and more interested in investment and
dividends.   Secondly the use of pre-ordinary stock had the
result in all types of companies of creating a large amount

---

1) A well known example of the attraction of London society
for "captains of industry", was the case of Frederick
Leyland, the shipping magnate.   Once he had made his
fortune he left shipping and concentrated on obtaining
the best that London could provide, from paintings by
Whistler to the largest houses.

of capital which was used and controlled in industry and
business by others than its legal owners.   Thirdly, the outcome of the weakening of local investment and the greater
complexity of management, there appeared divisions within the
Boards of Directors, the role of some directors was to attract
investors, others to attract trade, and there was a general
tendency to leave a greater and greater part of the direction
to the technical staff.   Fourthly, the background of these
three developments, there was an increase in the number of
investors and the number of limited liability companies.   The
sum total of these changes was a far cry from the spirit of
the 1860's, when it was said that due to Joint Stock and
Limited liability "the many have changed places with the few
as the rulers and directors of affairs", [1] and "as in the
working men's co-operative societies .... so in the gigantic
undertakings in the metropolis, whose capital is told in
millions, the same feeling is manifested". [2]   But spurred on
partly by cases of fraud and partly by ethical and idealistic
hopes, legislators, moralists and pamphleteers in the years
1890-1910 tried to cajole and force company evolution back
on the straight path of co-operation in every sense of the word.

---

1) "Shareholders Guardian", July 12, 1865, p.557.
2) R.S.E. Farries, "Joint Stock Companies", 1865, Introduction.

Apart from the campaign against false prospectuses which
we have noted above and which led for a period to a tightening
up of their issue, this campaign was launched around four
points.   Firstly, against the practice of raising capital by
debentures: secondly, on the shareholders rights to control:
thirdly, against ornamental directors: and fourthly, a demand
for increased publicity of the company's accounts.

In the campaign against debentures, apart from the gradual
realisation by most writers that "the debenture holders supply
the capital but they have no control", the chief methods of
attack were ethical.   From Edward Carpenter to John Ruskin,
the social philosophers were agreed that debenture interest
was near enough to usury to be distasteful.   W.C. Sillar,
secretary of the Anti-Usury association had as early as the
late 'sixties and 'seventies published four pamphlets against
interest on debentures.   And in 1880 the "Contemporary Review"
continued the discussion by publishing an article on "Usury
and a Rejoinder" by John Ruskin and the Bishop of Manchester
respectively.   Five years later R.G. Sillar read a paper at
St. John's, Cambridge, on the question and in it he brought
out clearly the basis of the attack on debentures.   If usury
were not allowed and "there was a return to justice...over-
trading could not exist.   The capitalist having to take an

interest _in_ business instead of usury _from_ would be compelled
to deal with honest men". (1)   The more socialistic philosophers
attacked the question more in terms of an address to investors
..."do you realise you are living in idleness on other people's
sweat". (2)   The Journal considered this attack of sufficient
importance to merit a long defence by H.S. Foxwell in 1886.
He answers that it is efficiency of the business unit that
counts in the long run, and goes as far even at that date to
assert there is no difference between the debenture holder
and the shareholder.

> "It is urged that the change (i.e. abolish interest)
> would increase the direct responsibility in trade
> which at present is shifted by the owner of capital
> on to the shoulders of the employees.   But respon-
> sibility cannot be diffused: to make it effective
> it must be concentrated.   The notion of government
> by the many is as transparent a fiction in industry
> as in politics...for all practical purposes because
> of large scale industry responsibility is as
> effectually delegated by the ordinary shareholder
> in a company as by the debenture holder or the
> depositor in a bank." (3)

However with the Fabian Socialists supporting Local
Government Loans the attack on moral grounds against debentures rather faded into second place before the campaign
against them by the commercial classes based on the injustices

---

1) This was published as a pamphlet in the same year, "Usury",
   R.G. Sillar, p.15.
2) Caroline Haddon, "Where Does Your Interest Come From?
   A Word to Lady Investors", 1886, p.3.
3) "Journal of the Institute of Bankers", 1886, p.74.

(1)
done by them to creditors.

The attempts to reform the shareholders meeting into something effectual were similarly without result, though the campaign was not so concentrated and interesting. Already by 1885 many of the advocates of "more power to the shareholder" had lost hope. For example Skinner in the introduction to his year book in 1879 had written "the shareholders may do much to protect themselves", in 1884 was writing "shareholders as a body are scarcely capable of effective action". The attack was more a series of half-hearted suggestions to shareholders which everyone knew would not be adopted, than anything definite in the shape of a change of law. It was agreed that shareholders meetings were a farce due to proxies. "In effect the chief use of the proxy is to shield maladministration, to baulk enquiry, to thwart reform and its legitimate use is relatively so trifling that it would be better done away with altogether". (2) And "no abuse is more common in the management of companies than the proxy one". (3) But nothing was done. And for a suggestion to get a better

---

1) e.g. the Associated Chambers of Commerce had at least one resolution along these lines at their annual meetings 1890-1900.
2) Walker and Watson, op.cit. p.148.
3) "Investors Review" 1895, p.165.

attendance at shareholders meetings the "Dictionary of
Political Economy" had to go back to the suggestion that
"compulsory reserve liability" might do the trick.[1] If this
had not succeeded the next logical step would be back into
the old partnership form of unlimited liability. The dis-
illusionment had gone thus far. With this general inability
to induce the shareholders to take a greater part in the
control of the affairs of the company, the attempts to reform
joint stock practice in this direction come to an end. After
this the main efforts were concentrated on lessening fraud,
and thereby increasing the investors security. · The control
of companies by the shareholders was given up as a lost cause.

The Directors had always received their due attention,
and naturally those wishing to reform the company system were
very concerned with them. The leading idea was that they
should have a substantial interest in the concern they were
directing. In 1888 a new Companies bill was drawn up which
laid down that Directors should have between them one-fifth
of the total capital of the company.[2] This Bill did not get as
far as the House, but the lines of attack were clear. We
noted above the general advice given in journals to investors
to ascertain the holdings of their directors as this was

---

1) "The Dictionary of Political Economy", 1892-6, p.370.
2) "The Economist", 1888, p.738.

considered as an indication of their sincerity in the undertaking. But by the twentieth century this was not so effective. Directors complained that it was not at all easy to
obtain ordinary shares in some of the well established undertakings, they were never put on the market, and their value
(1)
was difficult to determine. This factor, and the very size
of the undertakings, was making it steadily less and less
possible for the Directors to hold a really substantial
portion of the equity shares. After the failure of this
bill, and an abortive attempt to less the numbers of fraudulent
(2)
directors through the Winding-Up Act of 1890, there were
further discussions on the position of directors in the House
of Lords Committees in the 'nineties. A Bill was before the
House of Lords committee which would make the Directors liable
for false balance sheets and prospectuses. This was very
strongly opposed by the promoting interests. Their arguments
ran along the lines, firstly that the Director's role was not
that of manager or accountant, he was merely there to be
consulted, secondly that if the Bill were passed the "honest"

1) 1896 Report, Qu.873.
2) Under this Act the Official Receiver had power to examine
   and prosecute directors for fraud. But in 1894 the House
   of Lords decided that the receiver had to give evidence
   of fraud before being granted a court order for investigation. With the result that in 1894 - 210 persons
   publicly examined, 1895-176, 1896-54 and 1897-26. "Chamber
   of Commerce Journal", 1899, p.32.

directors would decline the risk of directing a company and
dishonest men with nothing to lose would take their places.
These arguments were successful and nothing drastic was done
about Directors in the 1900 Act.   This attempt and failure
effectively to prevent fraud by means of making the Directors
take a greater part and a greater interest in the company was
paralleled by an attempt, with slightly greater success, to
ensure increased publicity for the accounts of the company for
the benefit of both shareholder and creditor.

In 1867 William Newmarch had declared "A limited liability
company trades on publicity.   The whole essence of limited
liability is publicity".[1]   But beyond the addition of the word
"limited" both the creditors and the shareholders were left to
find their own methods of obtaining the publicity they wanted.
In the 'nineties the matter was coming to a head as a result
of pressure from both these sections.   Registration of all
mortgages and charges and the publication of a balance sheet
were the two measures most in favour.   Partly because of the
formation of the "private" limited company and partly through
the already dictatorial attitude assumed by many Boards of[2]

---

1) 1867 Report, Qu.1093.
2) "Many Boards of Directors evidently consider that so long
    as dividends are paid, the shareholders have no claim to
    learn how they have been earned or what provisions have
    been made as to the future", "Investors Review" 1893, p.99.

Directors, the struggle for a public Balance Sheet was fierce
and confused. The Associated Chambers of Commerce at its
Annual conference in 1898 after years of preliminary discussions found themselves so completely divided on the subject
of balance sheets that it was decided better to make no
mention of the subject at all at the conference. [1] The com-
promise suggestion that was regularly put forward, that it
should be left to the discretion of the company whether a
balance sheet should be issued or no, was useless. It was
pointed out in 1893 that in the previous few years fourteen
brewery companies were formed asking the public to subscribe
in preference and debenture issues a sum amounting to
£17,727,000. And not a single one of these companies intended
to issue a balance sheet, [2] which decision they defended and
insured by the statement that the public had not been asked
to subscribe for ordinary shares, all these being held in
private hands.

In the companies where the ordinary shares were held by
the public, the directors often frightened the shareholders
in agreeing to stay in darkness with the argument that the
publication of any light on the subject of profits might
lead to competition and labour troubles. F.B. Palmer before

1) Chamber of Commerce Journal, report of annual conference
   of Associated Chambers of Commerce, 1898.
2) A.J. Wilson, "Hints to Small Investors", 1893, p.41.

the 1898 Committee said:

> "I repeatedly have before me companies whose great
> difficulty is the excessive profits they are
> making and the great danger this would be if
> people got to know this, the labour danger and
> the danger of competition....again and again I
> have had companies that have been obliged to
> reconstruct in order to capitalise the great
> mass of profits latent in the business in order
> to meet labour difficulties and otherwise." (1)

From the aspect of the individual company whose aim was to
make profits, this attitude, although it had given up the
ideal of shareholders democracy, was perfectly logical.   But
viewed from the wider angle of society it would have made
Cobden turn in his grave.   For he had supported limited liability because he thought it would remove the blot of accumulation of capital in a few hands, and because he thought "it
would tend to bridge over the gulf which now divided different
classes and to diminish that spirit of alienation between
employers and employed that they all deplored."
(2)

The result of the prolonged enquiries and discussion on
this subject was that eventually all public companies had to
issue balance sheets and the rights of the debenture preference
holders to receive these alongside the ordinary shareholders
were also recognised. (3)   But in practice the whole question was

1) 1898 Report, Qu.681.
2) Speech in debate in House of Commons, 1854, quoted in
   Journal of the Institute of Bankers, 1886, p.499.
3) 1906 Report, para.82 - passed into Law in 1907 Act.

in reality only removed one stage further on, for now the
accuracy and adequacy of the balance sheets became the bone
of contention.

By 1914 the methods of control and direction of the
business unit in this country had changed radically.   The
partnership form prevalent in the fifties and sixties had
given place to the limited liability company in almost every
sphere.   The sources of the capital for industry had also
been increased.   The number of investors in limited companies
(excluding incorporated companies, railways etc.) had risen
from 50,000 in 1860 [1] (an over-estimate) to between 250,000
and 500,000 [2] (an under-estimate) in the first decade of the
twentieth century.   In each unit the individual suppliers
of capital had risen from the partnership groups of three,
four, to ten, to be numbered in hundreds and in some cases
as many as 30,000. [3]

---

1) Given in "Limited Liability Companies Journal" 1862, No.1,p.3
2) 250,000 was the figure given in "The Financial Review of
   Reviews", 1906, Vol.I, p.79.   500,000 was given in an
   article by Leo Chiozza Money quoted by Jesse Quail in "The
   Contemporary Review" April 1907.   Both these figures are
   confined to an estimate of the number in "public" companies
   only.   The difference between them is due to the inclusion
   of railways in Money's estimate.   Jesse Quail attacks
   Money's figures strongly as being an under-estimate, but
   the issue of Capitalism vs. Socialism entered in the
   argument to prevent a disinterested calculation.   Although
   even if the observer were unbiased an accurate figure at
   this date was an impossibility due to the dispersion of
   holdings through several companies.   J.H. Clapham op.cit.
   Vol.III, p.298 estimated about 1,000,000 separate
   investors in 1914.
3) Mentioned as the largest (excluding railways) in H.Lowenfeld
   "Investment an Exact Science" 1909, p.199.

While the post war period shows an even greater change
in the figures both of the capital raised through joint stock
and the number of investors. For example, it is estimated
that 13,000,000 people subscribed to War Loans,[1] and a percentage of these found their way into the capital market after
the war with the vogue of very low share denominations. And
in the number of shareholders in individual public companies,
30,000 was now insignificant. The usual figure ranged between
30,000 and 125,000.[2] These two decades, 1918-1938 would
naturally show a much greater change in the methods of control
and the attitude of investors towards the company from the
1860's than does the earlier date of 1914, but the basis of
the changes that took place were already laid solidly by
1914. This we have attempted to show above. It remains to
sum up the form and character that these changes took, and
the conclusions that can be drawn.

First in the formation and practice of the company. In
the 'sixties and 'seventies Directors, auditors, and trustees
for the debenture holders were still to a certain extent
provisional and dependent on the wishes of the shareholders.

1) "Accountants Journal", 1923-4, p.186.
2) "Bulletin of the Federation of British Industries",
     July 1934, p.182.

By 1914 dummies signed the deed and the company to the
prospective investor "springs into life like Minerva, fully
armed"[1]. The whole character and tempo of company formation
had been transformed and speeded up.

Secondly the investing classes were supplemented by new
groups of safe investors, and the whole attitude towards
investment changed from the ideas of partnership to those of
small investments, well spread, returning a regular income.
Smaller share denominations and greater contact between
companies and investors throughout the country by means of
stock exchanges, stockbrokers and branch banks assisted this
change. Shareholders meetings lost their constructive features
entirely and became either a "farce"[2] or an opportunity for
rivals or busybodies to air their views[3]. Corresponding to
this lack of interest or "culpable negligence", "the English
shareholder possessed the very type of director which he
deserved"[4]. The function of these directors too had changed.
Instead of being the elected agents of the shareholders, they,
or their names on the prospectus, became the decoys for the
investors to take shares. The actual management was removed

1) D. Finnie, "Capital Underwriting", 1934, p.129.
2) Walker and Watson, op.cit. p.148.
3) 1897 Report, Qu.1267: "it is always the discontented
   ones who come to the meetings".
4) "Financial Review of Reviews", Sept.1908, pp.17-18.

one stage further on to paid officers or individual directors.

The pace at which these changes took place naturally evoked attempts to delay them and keep some form of the "co-operative joint stock" ideal.   But whereas in the 'sixties and 'seventies the remedies proposed were for greater collective action by the shareholders, for example, circularising all the names of the shareholders, and forming protection associations, in the twentieth century the idea of control had gone and suggestions and remedies were concerned solely with security.   It was hoped that less "coloured" prospectuses, publication of balance sheets, and spreading of investments would lead to this.[1]

The collective result of these changes was twofold; first in regard to the formation of 'the company.   The opinion of the investor of the merits or demerits of a particular undertaking were no longer important.   It was thought impossible and unnecessary for them to form any opinion on

---

1) This is for example the burden of Mr. Harold Brown's memorandum before the 1895 Departmental Committee of the Board of Trade on the Companies Acts.   "The true remedy is to make investors to understand the perils of investment and that they should not invest unless they know the directors and should divide their investments" p.74.   As he was the representative of the London Chamber of Commerce he did not agree with the publication of balance sheets.

(1)
the matter. The formation depended more on the connections of the vendor or promoter with underwriting syndicates
and groups of stockbrokers and "key" investors. This was
less so in the industrial companies formed outside the
influence of the City of London, but even in these companies
the success of the company depended on the opinion of agents
and not on the investors.

Secondly there were changes with regard to the actual
running of the company once formed. In the partnership
form, the interests of those who provided the capital and
those who directed the concern were to a large degree identical, as they were often the same people. In the limited
company on the other hand, by 1914, the interest which the
directors had in the company in terms of the amount of money
invested grew of necessity smaller compared with the amount
subscribed by the ordinary investor. This applied to both
the public industrial as well as the public trading and
commercial companies. The effect was that the company
tended to develop a momentum of its own. Even when its

---

1) "I think it is clear that the theory that intending
   shareholders really inquire into the merits of the
   proposed company or the transaction upon which its
   formation is proposed and forms a really reliable
   opinion upon it, is more or less a fallacy."
   ibid. p.73.

profits were nil owing to the lack of effective control being exercised by the owners of the capital the money could go on existing.

> "So long as a business is conducted by those who own all the capital, it will only be extended as the prospect of greater profit offers an inducement to do so. But if the capital is supplied by the many and the management confided to a few, it may become in the interest of the few to carry it on although the many derive little or no profit from its operations". (1)

This was the prophecy of the Journal of the Institute of Bankers in 1886. The report of the Inspector General on Bankruptcy of that year showed that this was already the case in some companies.

> "Companies have been promoted...and carried on by managers and directors whose interests have not always or necessarily been identical with those of the shareholders. A divorce has been established between the supply of capital on the one hand and the responsibility which naturally attaches to the ownership of capital on the other".(2)

The developments in company finance and in the relations between the investor and the company in the thirty years between 1885 and 1915 did a lot to encourage, and the remedies effected did little to hinder, the spread of these tendencies to most of the companies operating in the various fields of English industrial and commercial life.

---

1) "Journal of the Institute of Bankers", Vol.VII, 1886, p.511.
2) Reported in the above Journal, Vol.VIII, 1887, p.483.

CHAPTER X.

CONCLUSION

The chief trend in business organisation in Great Britain between 1856 and 1914 was the development of the limited liability joint stock system which took the place of the partnership as the usual form by which the entrepreneur raised capital and by which the business was directed. The significant fact about the rise of the company system in Great Britain is that it was necessary, not to carry through the "Industrial Revolution" as was the case in most European countries and in America, but to carry through the "widening and deepening" of the capitalist system, once the capitalist method had been accepted, and a major part of the "revolution" achieved.

The "delayed" introduction and use of the system in Great Britain was due in the main to the size of the accumulated sources of capital at the direct disposal of entrepreneurs, and the power of private accumulation and re-accumulation to keep pace with the demand for fixed capital investment. The "more round about methods of production" necessitating greater amounts of fixed capital, and the growth and spread of accumulations of capital in non-entrepreneurial hands broke down this self sufficiency and led to a demand for greater capital than could be supplied by individuals

and a demand for new avenues of investment. The limited
liability company proved the effective method of satisfying both these demands.

But the company limited was not a static organisation.
In order to secure centralised direction of the enterprise
and at the same time to obtain a steady flow of capital
into industry given a changing investment class, the system
of limited liability itself underwent changes. Further,
while the right of limited liability had been granted in
the 'fifties and 'sixties mainly in order to assist large
enterprises, new advantages of this "right" were discovered.
The small trader found it gave him security. So apart
from the internal changes in the company system there were
changes in its scope.

The "unlooked for developments" in company law that
had taken place between the introduction of the right to
limited liability by the 1856 and 1862 Acts and 1914 fall
under two headings. Firstly, in the large companies,
share denominations fell, new types of share and stock
issues were used extensively to attract capital, the promotion of the company was passing out of the hands of the
"entrepreneur" into those of the professional promoter
and syndicates of underwriters, and the management was
passing from the technical "proprietors" of the company

into the hands of Boards of Directors who owned of necessity
a very small percentage of the total capital of the company.
The attitudes and habits of the investors in these companies
were changing at the same time.   Firstly, from being
"adventurers joining in the company", they began to spread
their investments over several different companies in order
to maintain security of income and capital.   Secondly from
personal investigation of the company in which they took
shares, they began to rely on the opinions of stockbrokers
and the stock exchange, and in some cases left the actual
investment to trust companies.

The second major change in the character of the limited
system was that the scope of the company moved from solely
large concerns, which owing to the need for greater fixed
capital than could be supplied by individuals or banks had
to appeal to the public, to small concerns which required not
so much additional capital as additional security.   It was
found in practice that some of this security was afforded
by the limited liability system.

These changes of character and scope were almost all
completely foreign to the ideas of the framers of the Acts
in the middle of the nineteenth century.   For example, the
attraction of both preference and debenture stocks was their
fixed rate of interest.   Yet one of the chief arguments put
forward in the discussions on limited liability was that

investors wanted to lend not at a fixed rate, which they could do by ordinary loans, but at a fluctuating rate with some security of capital. Again Robert Low in moving the adoption of the 1856 Limited Liability Act had specially stated that he was opposed to "one man companies",[1] but by 1914 the development of small "private" companies was so extensive that it could be claimed that the limited company system "had in part reverted to and in part absorbed partner-ship".[2]

These developments in the limited system appear quite logical and natural when studied in detail, but the sum total of the changes had altered completely the relation of the limited company to society as a whole. For example the laisser faire answer of Newmarch in the 'seventies "that no member of the public is bound to deal with the limited company" had some relation to reality and therefore could be accepted. But the same answer could not be made in 1914 with any purpose. Again the ability of Directors to control the capital of thousands of shareholders with little or no check and guidance could not adequately be answered by the statement "men can make any contracts they wish".

McCulloch had brought in the question of the effect on society as a whole in the discussions in the 'fifties, but

1) "Speech of Rt. Hon. Robert Low", op.cit. p.6.
2) "The Accountant's Journal", 1927-8, p.546.

he had been laughed out of court by the "individualists".
By the twentieth century other doctrines based on laisser
faire reasoning had undergone important modifications.
Doctrines on the role of the state, the right of Free Trade
etc.   Should not the laisser faire limited liability doctrine also have been reconsidered?

But in fact no general revaluation was made.   The
enquiries and legislation from 1890 onwards attempted to
lessen the amount of obvious abuse that was taking place
in the company system and to bring the out-of-date law more
into accordance with commercial practice, but both the
remedies suggested and those adopted were only tinkering
with the problem and dotting the i's and crossing the t's
of accepted practice.

The reasons for this absence of revaluation lay partly
in both the diverse practice of the limited system and the
diverse views expressed on its effects.   In practice, the
limited company assisted both the rise of combinations and
amalgamations by making centralisation of capital possible,
and the small trader in his efforts against monopoly by
reducing his risks, and increasing his ability to obtain
capital.   Again, while leading to the control of the capital
of many in the hands of few, the limited system helped the
small investor to obtain a security of capital and a rate of
interest which would not have been possible in a partnership

system.

The views on its effects similarly varied. Viscount
Goschen was still maintaining in the twentieth century that
the ideals of the originators of the system, namely, that
it would lead to "co-operation" and a dispersion of wealth,
were being fulfilled. In a paper read before the British
Association in 1887, G.Auldjo Jamieson had referred to "the
levelling of eminences"[1] brought about by the limited system
and Goschen attempted to prove this with figures of the
increase in the number of investors, and the decrease in the
average amount invested.[2] This may have been so, but the
implication that there was, as a result, "the co-operative
employment of capital" was not accepted by other contemporaries. H.S. Foxwell could point out as early as 1888
that

> "The slow progress of co-operative production and
> the gradual extinction of the small employer,
> force us to accept the conclusion of Professor
> Walker that 'Whatever may be true in politics,
> the industry of the world is not tending towards
> democracy, but in the opposite direction'." [3]

1) Reported in "The Accountant" 1888, p.384.
2) G.J. Goschen, "Essays and Addresses", 1905, p.223 ff.
   The paper was written in 1887, but the note added in 1903
   strikes the same note. "The general result may be taken
   as unquestionable. The number of shareholders has grown
   even in a much larger ratio than the colossal growth in
   the aggregate capital.....the humble shareholder claims
   his part." p.256.
3) From a paper read before the British Association on
   monopoly in 1888. Quoted in "Papers on Current Finance"
   1919, p.267.

The limited liability company did not seem to Foxwell to give to capitalism even a "bastard democratic form". [1] For a general summary of the effects of the limited joint stock form in leading not to co-operation but to a divorce between ownership and control, this statement by J.A. Hobson is the best contemporary effort.

> "Indeed the whole tendency of the modern evolution of the art and instruments of investment is, by widening the distance between the ownership and the economic operation of capital, and by increasing the elaboration of capitalistic processes, to remove the legal owners of ships steam engines factory plant merchandise and other joint stock property from the possibility of exercising any direct personal control over the property." [2]

The "more round about methods of production" and the "more round about methods of investment" through stockbrokers the stock exchange and trusts rather than direct to the entrepreneur, may have combined to increase the number of investors, but, at the same time, the ability and power of the "humble shareholder to claim his part" were by these very developments considerably weakened.

The organisation of industrial and business units as

---

1) "Studies in Capital and Investment", edited by G.D.H. Cole, Chapter on "the Evolution of Joint Stock Enterprise" by Cole. It is interesting to note on this question of "bastard democracy" that the German Nazi party passed a law in 1937 "which practically eliminates the authority of the shareholders meetings". "The Economist" Feb.6th 1937, p.299.
2) J.A. Hobson, "An Economic Interpretation of Investment" 1910, p.1.

limited liability companies in Great Britain in the period
1856 - 1914 enabled "full exploitation of economic change"
to take place and with a greater degree of independence of
the banks at a faster rate than would have been possible
under the continuance of the common law partnership system.
A study of the changes within the system consequent on the
need to reach out to ever widening circles for capital and
the need to keep a centralised direction of the company,
reveals the ease and flexibility of the working of the
company system in this period.   The new techniques and
methods evolved by the company system arose out of the
necessities of the company rather than from the direction
and guidance of the law.

But by the twentieth century entirely new problems
were confronting the development of business organisation,
problems in their essence arising from the "social nature
of production" on the one hand and individualistic control
on the other.

In some of these problems the role played by the limited
system was not that of instigator but that of accessory and
accomplice.   For example, the limited system did not give
rise to combination and monopoly, but it assisted considerably their development.   Others were the direct outcome of
the spread of the company system and the methods of investment

and control.   For example, the problem of the divorce of
ownership and control, which although not a major feature
of the company system in 1914, was appearing quite clearly
as the natural outcome of the limited system.   Or again,
there was the problem of increased rigidity brought about
by the necessary use of fixed interest stocks by the company
in order to attract investors and to concentrate control.

These and other problems brought about by the "deepening
and widening" of capitalism were neither effectively discussed nor solved in the pre-war period, and in the post-war
decades while the problems have been both recognised and
intensified, the solution appears no nearer.   The individualists are still searching for an effective touchstone
of the right of individuals.   Can they make any contract
they wish, as Low claimed in the nineteenth century, or are
there certain rights which the State cannot allow, and if
so what governs their limitation?   The "Collectivists"
and "Socialists" on the other hand who see the solution in
State control of business units are confronted with the
problem of convincing individual entrepreneurs to give up
their present profitable rights and privileges.

A P P E N D I C E S

Appendix   A

Percenatge of the paid up capital of new companies

going to vendors in each of the years 1885 - 1914

Figures from the returns relating to Joint Stock Companies

Year.	Total capital considered as paid up. £ 000's.	Capital paid up by the public. £ 000's.	Amount considered as paid on Vendors shares. £ 000's.	Percentage of total capital going to Vendors.
1885	24,116	15,840	8,276	34
1886	39,660	21,416	18,244	46
1887	49,635	27,092	22,543	46
1888	77,066	39,735	37,331	48
1889	80,607	52,101	38,506	42
1890	81,231	37.701	43,530	53
1891	51,262	17,435	33,530	67
1892	45,365	16,724	28,641	64
1893	41,410	13,355	27,855	68
1894	50,486	17,387	32,899	66
1895	103,012	37,915	65,097	64
1896	145,681	61,743	83,938	58
1897	133,726	50,283	83,443	62
1898	137,055	51,160	85,895	62
1899	117,712	42,244	75,468	64
1900	103,125	34,854	68,271	66
1901	59,999	21,247	38,752	65
1902	43,600	13,846	29,760	69
1903	49,534	13,259	36,275	74
1904	30,696	8,146	22,760	75
1905	38,877	21,237	17,640	46
1906	43,264	15,191	28,073	65
1907	42,322	15,866	26,456	63
1908	32,554	11,471	21,083	65
1909	20,372	7,251	13,121	65
1910	22,148	9,232	12,916	58
1911	17,603	7,076	10,527	60
1912	21,153	9,425	11,728	55
1913	22,821	9,455	13,366	60
1914	23,383	9,318	14,065	61

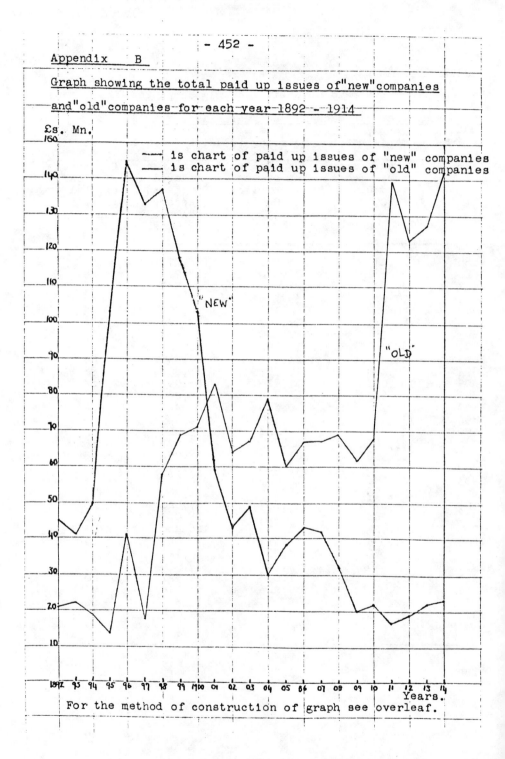

Appendix   B

Graph showing the total paid up issues of "new" companies
and "old" companies for each year 1892 - 1914

£s. Mn.

------ is chart of paid up issues of "new" companies
——— is chart of paid up issues of "old" companies

"NEW"

"OLD"

Years.

For the method of construction of graph see overleaf.

Appendix B. (continued)

Method of Construction of Graph.

The term "new" companies refers to
companies being formed and registered in the particular
year in question.

The term "old" companies refers to
companies already existing in the particular year in
question.

The figures for the paid up issues
of "new" companies each year is the total of the amounts
subscribed by the public and the amounts considered as
paid up on Vendors' and other shares. Source : The
Annual Returns of Joint Stock Companies.

The figures for the paid up issues of
"old" companies each year has been calculated as follows :

> The total amount of additions of paid-up
> capital of all companies in existence in
> any one year,(i.e. "new" and "old") -
> minus ∤ the amount paid-up on new companies
> in that year - plus - the amounts involved,
> share capital only,in liquidations,compulsory
> and voluntary,in that year.

For example,in the year 1900, The total additions to
the share capital of all companies was £103 mn.
The amounts paid up on new companies was £103 mn.
The amounts involved in liquidations were £71 mn.
Therefore the paid up issues of "old" companies
equals, £71 mn.

Sources : the Annual Return of Joint Stock Uompanies,
          the Annual Winding Up Reports.

APPENDIX C.

Share denomination in period 1856 - 1865.

Tables compiled from "Limited Liability
Joint Stock Companies List", 1864 - 6.

I. Companies formed 1856-1865 inclusive and believed still
to be in existence at the latter date.
3720 companies given with share denomination.

Denomination of Share	Number of Companies	% of Total
a. Up to £5	597	16.06
b. £5	868	23.3
c. Above £5 and up to and including £10	1134	30.5
d. Above £10 and under £100	813	21.87
e. £100 to £5,000 inclusive	308	8.27

II. Companies formed 1856-1863 inclusive and believed still
to be in existence in 1865.
2040 companies given with share denomination

a.	420	20.6
b.	568	27.85
c.	568	27.85
d.	308	15.1
e.	176	8.6

III. Companies formed 1864–1865 inclusive and believed still
to be in existence in 1865.
1680 companies given with share denomination

a.	177	10.5
b.	300	17.8
c.	566	33.7
d.	505	30.1
e.	132	7.9

APPENDIX D.

Table showing % paid up capital to issued
capital in 1885 and 1915 of Companies
given in Burdett's Official Intelligence.

(Table compiled from figures given in the
Tables in A. Essex Crosby unpublished
thesis, "Joint Stock Companies 1880-1935")

I. General.

The average % of paid up capital for all the companies
given in Burdett's Official Intelligence for these years
is as follows:

			% of issued capital paid up
1885	1,585	Companies	60%
1895	2,581	"	67%
1915	5,337	"	88%

II. Particular.

Type of Company.	Year	Number of Companies	Percentage of issued capital paid up
Commercial & Industrial	1885	507	78%
	1915	1,922	97.8%
Iron Coal & Steel	1885	102	77%
	1915	342	98%

Type of Company	Year	Number of Companies	Percentage of issued capital paid up
Shipping	1885	52	82%
	1915	103	98%
Financial Land & Investment	1885	226	61%
	1915	518	90.4%
Banking	1885	144	24.6%
	1915	80	26.2%
Insurance	1885	87	21.8%
	1915	102	32.3%

Appendix E

Tables showing the relative uses of ordinary,

preference and debenture issues by the companies

listed in Burdett's Official Intelligence, 1885-1915.

(These tables are compiled from figures given by A.Essex-
Crosby, op cit.)

I. Figures for all Companies given in Burdett.(except
home railways etc.)

Year	Number of Companies	Total Capital share and loan £,000's.	Percentage of the total capital raised by each method.		
			Ordinary.	Prefer-ence .	Debenture.
1885	1,585	419,240	69,6	9.7	20.7.
1895	2,581	953,662	55.1	15.9	29.0
1915	5,337	2,433,398	50.1.	21.2	28.7

II. Figures for Industrial Companies given in Burdett
(those under the headings of "Commercial and Industrial",
"Shipping", and "Iron, Coal and Steel".)

1885	661	114,558	74.4	8.8	16.8
1895	1,060	247,712	60.6	17.5	21.9
1915	2,367	898,456	47.6	29.7	22.7

Appendix E. (continued)

ILL.Figures for the companies in different industries and
Trades given in Burdett.

Year	Number of Companies	Total Capital Share and Loan £,000's	Percentage of total capital raised by each method. Ordinary.	Prefe- rence.	Debenture.
Brewery Companies.					
1885		not given separately			
1895	189	94,686	36.4.	29.0	34.6
1915	348	193,940	30.8	26.3	42.9
Commercial and Industrial Companies					
1885	507	65,299	73.5	9.7	16.8
1895	893	191,232	58.1	18.4	23.5
1915	1,922	652,632	45.8	31.9	22.4
Financial,Land and Investment Companies					
1885	226	72,149	46.2	10.3	43.5
1895	409	199,633	41.0	18.9	40.1
1915	518	202,561	54.7	15.9	29.4
Electric Supply Companies					
1885		not given separately			
1895	31	7,201	59.1	21.2	19.7
1915	96	40,594	38.7	21.8	39.5
Coal,Iron and Steel Companies					
1885	102	36,962	74.0	8.0	17.0
1895	113	42,466	66.2	16.3	17.5
1915	342	179,419	54.0	24.4	21.6

Appendix E (continued)

III. Continued.

Shipping Companies

1885	52	12,297	80.8	3.8	15.4
1895	54	14,014	78.1	6.6	15.3
1915	103	66,405	46.2	25.4	28.4

BIBLIOGRAPHY

A   SELECTED   BIBLIOGRAPHY.

I.   Books and Pamphlets.

The object of this bibliography is not to provide an
exhaustive list of either the books quoted or the
books read on the subject of this thesis but rather
to indicate the nature and scope of the contemporary
works existing on the subject.   Only those books
and pamphlets with direct bearing on the problems of
the development of the limited liability company and
of investment have been included.   Some of the post-
War volumes dealing with wider problems of industry
and the limited company which have been used have been
mentioned in footnotes.

Andrew, Samuel. "50 Years of the Cotton Trade. Address before the
    Economic Section of the British Association", 1887.

Aubrey, W. H. S. "Stock Exchange Investments", 1896.

Ayres, Henry. "Banks and Banking under Limited and Unlimited
    Liability", 1863.

Ayres, Henry. "The Financial Position of Railways", 1868.

Bagehot, W. "Lombard Street", 1873.

Baker, G. Bartrick. "Sound Investments for Small Savings",
    1889.

Bartlett, E. J. "How to Invest Capital", Second edition, 1875.

Bartlett, E. J. "The Investor's Directory", 1876.

Bartlett, William, & Chapman, Henry. "A Handy Book for
    Investors", 1869.

"Beaton's Guide Book to the Stock Exchange", 1870.

"Beaton's Guide to Investing Money - with Safety and Profit",
    1870.

Begbie, M.B. "Partnership en Commandite", 1852.

Bell, Lothian. "Principles of the Manufacture of Iron and Steel", 1884.

Bell, Lothian. "The Iron Trade", 1886.

Bigg, James. "Collection of Consolidating Statutes on Trading Companies," 1863.

Boult, Swinton. "Trade Partnerships", 1855.

Bourne, H. R. Fox. "English Merchants", 1866.

Bowie, A. G. "Romance of the Savings Banks", 1898.

Bray, C. "The Income of the United Kingdom and its Mode of Distribution", 1857.

Brooks, C.P. "Cotton Manufacturing", 1889.

"The Bubbles of Finance", by A City Man. 1865.

Buxton, Charles. "The Cream of the Pro's and Con's of Partnership Law", 1854.

"Capital and Investment (General Securities Corporation Ltd)", 1909.

Carter, J. R. "Stock Exchange Securities 1877 and 1887 compared", 1888.

Chapman, S. J. "The Cotton Industry and Trade", 1905.

'Civis'. "The Railway Question", 1856.

"Counsel to Ladies and Easy-Going Men on their Business Investments", 1892.

Cox, Edward W. "The New Law and Practice of Joint Stock Companies" - second edition, 1855; fifth edition, 1862.

Cracroft, B. "Consols Chart", 1874.

"Credit and its Bearing on the Crisis of 1866", 1866.

Crump, A. "A new Departure in the Domain of Political Economy", 1878.

Crump, A. "Theory of Speculation", 1874.

"Description of Consetts Iron Works," 1893.

"Dictionary of Political Economy", 1892-1896, edited by
    I. Palgrave.

Digby, K. E. "The Sale and Transfer of Shares in Companies",
    1868.

"Duncan on Investment and Speculation", 1894.

"The Electric Trust", 1903.

Ellis, A. L. "Rationale of Market Fluctuations", 1876.

Ellis, A. L. "Trustees Guide to Investments", 1887.

Ellis, Guy. "Appreciation of Gold and its Effects on
    Investments", 1895.

Ellison, T. "The Cotton Trade of Great Britain", 1886.

Emden, A. "The Shareholders Legal Guide", 1884.

Evans, C. Worthington. "Notes on the Companies Act, 1900",
    1900.

Evans, C. Worthington. "Notes on the Companies Act 1907",
    1907.

Evans, D. Morier. "Facts Failures and Frauds", 1859.

Evans, D. Morier. "Speculative Notes and Notes on Speculation",
    1864.

Fane, R. G. C. "Limited Liability", n.d.

Farries, R. S. E. "Joint Stock Companies" - first edition,
    1865; third edition, 1874.

"A Few Remarks founded upon the Periodical Reports furnished
    by the Directors of the P. & O. since 1860", by A
    Shareholder, 1867.

Field, E. W. "Observations of a Solicitor on the Right of
    the Public to form Limited Liability Partnerships", 1854.

"Financial Reform Association, 1848-1898", 1898.

Fitz-Wygram, Loftus. "Limited Liability made Practical, the Reduction of Capital of Companies and the Sub-Division of Shares", 1867.

Ffooks, Woodforde. "Law of Partnership an Obstacle to Social Progress", 1854.

Foxwell, H. S. "Papers on Current Finance", 1919.

Fry, Henry. "Epochs in Atlantic Steam Navigation", 1895.

Gabbott, E. R. "How to Invest Money", second edition, 1905.

Garcke, E. "Progress of Electrical Enterprise", 1907.

Gibbons, David. "The Limited Liability Act", 1855.

Gilbart, J. W. "The London Bankers, an Analysis", 1845.

Goschen, G. J. "Essays and Addresses (with notes)", 1905.

Graham, A. "The Impolicy of Limitation of the Responsibility of Partnership in Manufactures and Commerce", 1838.

"Great Industries of Britain", 3 vols., 1877-1880.

Greg, W. R. "Political Problems", 1870.

Greg, W. R. "Rocks Ahead", 1873.

"Gregory's Hints to Speculators", 1895.

Griffiths, Samuel. "Guide to the Iron Trade of Great Britain", 1873.

"Guide to the Unprotected in Matters Relating to their Property and Income", by A Banker's Daughter, 1863.

Haddon, Caroline. "Where does your Money come from, A Word to Lady Investors", 1886.

Harrison, W. G. "Joint Stock Companies Acts", 1856.

Hawes, William. "Unlimited and Limited Liability", 1854.

Healey, C. Chadwick. "A Treatise on the Law and Practice Relating to the Articles of Association of Joint Stock Companies", 1875.

Healey, C. Chadwick. "Treatise on Joint Stock Companies", 1886.

"History of the Cunard Steamship Company", 1886.

Hobart, Lord. "Remarks on the Law of Partnership Liability", 1853.

Hobson, J. A. "An Economic Interpretation of Investment", 1910.

"The Hooley Book", 1904.

Hooper, W. E. "The Stock Exchange in 1900, A Souvenir", 1900.

"How to Swindle the Public", 1888.

Howell, John. "Partnership-Law Legislation and Limited Liability", 1869.

Hurrell, H., and Hyde, C. "Joint Stock Companies Practical Guide", third edition, 1889.

Hutton, James. "Appointment of Public Accountants to Audit the Accounts of all Joint Stock Companies", 1861.

"Investment vs. Speculation", 1907.

"The Investor's Guardian Guide to Investment", 1873.

Jaycee. "Public Companies from the Cradle to the Grave", 1883.

J. C. A. "Limited Liability and Cotton Spinning", 1886.

Jeans, J. S. "England's Supremacy", 1885.

Jeans, J. S. "The Iron Trade", 1906.

Jeans, J. S. "Pioneers of the Cleveland Iron Trade", 1875.

Jeans, J. S. "Notes on Northern Industries", 1878.

Jeans, J. S. "Railway Problems", 1887.

"Joint Stock Company Fraud", 1888.

Jordan, H. W. "Private Companies", 1915.

Joseph, L. "Industrial Finance", 1911.

Kellet, T. W. "The Limited Liability Act and the Depression of Trade", 1885.

Kennedy, John. "History of Steam Navigation", 1903.

Laing, John. "The Theory of Business", 1867.

Lavington, F. E. "The English Capital Market", 1921.

"The Law of Limited Liability and its Application to Joint Stock Banking Advocated", 1863.

Lawson, W. R. "British Railways", 1913.

Levi, Leone. "History of British Commerce", 1878.

"Liabilities of Shareholders and the 'Rights of Creditors' under the Limited Liability Act of 1822", 1867.

Lindsay, W. S. "History of British Shipping", 4 vols., 1876.

Lindsay, W. S. & Cobden, R. "Remarks on the Law of Partnership and Limited Liability", 1856.

Lowe, Robert. "Speech of the Rt. Hon. Robert Lowe on the Amendment of the Law of Partnership and Joint Stock Companies, February 1st, 1856", 1856.

Lowenfelt, Henry. "Investment and Exact Science", 1909.

McCulloch, J. R. "Considerations on Partnership with Limited Liability", 1856.

A Manchester Man (Potter, Edmund). "Practical Opinions against Limited Liability", 1855.

A Manchester Man (Potter, Edmund). "A Reply to the Rt. Hon. E. P. Bouverie, M.P.", 1855.

Manson, E. "Debentures of Trading Companies", 1910.

"Mathieson's Vade Mecum for Investors", 1883.

Morgan, H. L. "Personal Liabilities of Directors of Joint Stock Companies", fourth edition, 1859.

Moss, Edwin. "Remarks on an Act of Parliament for the Formation of Companies with Limited Liability", 1856.

Nash, B. D. "Investment Banking in England", 1924.

Nash, R. L. "Money Market Events", 1869.

Nash, R. L. " A Short Enquiry into the Profitable Nature of our Investments", 1880.

Neale, E. V. "The Distinction between Joint-Stockism and Co-operation", n.d.

Norman, G. W. "Papers on Various Subjects", 1869.

Packer, Axford. "How the Public are Plundered by Promoters of Companies, Foreign States, Syndicates and Money Lenders", 1878.

Parsons, A. "The Limited Liability Act and its Legal Interpretation", 1855.

"Partnership en Commandite", 1848.

"Partnership with Limited Liability", reprinted with additions from "The Westminster Review", 1854.

Peek, Sir H. W., "Prospectus Makers and the Public", 1890.

Perks, R. W. "Is it Desirable to alter the Law which Prohibits Railway Companies from paying Interest out of Capital?" 1883.

Phillips, Edmund. "Bank of England Charter, Currency, Limited Liability and Free Trade", 1856.

Platt, James. "Essays", 1863.

Platt, James. "Business", 1882.

Playford, Francis. "Practical Hints on Investing Money", 1856.

Playford, W. M. "Hints to Investors", 1882.

"Profitable Investment in Stocks and Shares", (Westminster
    Stock Exchange), 1903.

Pulbrook, A. "Responsibilities of Directors and the Working
    of Companies under the Acts, 1862-1900", 1901.

Relton, W. "Saving and Growing Money", 1887.

Rolleston, Sir John. "The Elements of Safe Investment", 1916.

Schultze-Gaevernitz, G. von. "Cotton Trade in England", 1895.

Scratchley, Arthur. "Average Investment Trusts", 1875.

Scratchley, Arthur. "Industrial Investment and Emigration",
    1851.

Seyd, Richard. "Record of Failures and Liquidations in
    Financial Wholesale and Manufacturing Branches, 1865-
    1876", 1877.

Seyd, Richard. "Record of Failures and Liquidations in
    Financial Wholesale and Manufacturing Branches, 1865-
    1885", 1885.

Sillar, R. G. "Usury", 1885.

"Sir Williams' Speculations, or the Seamy Side of Finance",
    by the author of "A Bubble of Finance", 1880.

Smith, James W. "A Handy Book of the New Laws of Joint
    Stock Companies", 1863.

"The Successful Investor" (General Securities Corporation,
    Ltd.), 1905.

Sweet, George. "Limited Liability", 1855.

Sweet, George. "The Limited Liability Act, 1855", 1855.

Tangye, Richard. "One and All, the Growth of a Great
    Industry", 1889.

Temple, J. A. "Hints upon Finance", 1880.

- 470 -

Turner, C. W. "Treatise on the Conversion of a Business into a Private Limited Company", 1907.

Urlin, R. D. "Hints on Business", 1884.

Van Oss, S. F. "Stock Exchange Values, 1885-1895", 1895.

Walker, J. D. & Watson, -. "Investors and Shareholders Guide", 1894.

Wall, R. E. "Hints to Intending Investors", 1891.

Ward, R. A. "Notes on Joint Stock Companies", 1865.

Ward, R. A. "A Treatise on Investments", 1852.

Warner, Edward. "The Impolicy of the Partnership Law", 1854.

Wheeler, J. F. "The Stock Exchange", 1913.

Wheeler, J. F. "Partnerships and Companies", 1912.

Whitehead, John. "Guaranteed Investments; their Merits as Investments considered", 1858.

Wieser, C. W. von. "Die Finanzielle Aufbau der Englischen Industrie", Jena, 1919.

Williamson, J. "The Clyde Passenger Steamer", 1904.

Wilson, A. J. "Practical Hints to Small Investors", 1893.

Wilson, A. J. "Practical Hints to Investors", 1897.

Wordsworth, C. "Law of Joint Stock Companies", 1865.

Worthington, Beresford. "Professional Accountants", 1895.

Wright, G. H. "Chronicles of the Birmingham Commercial Society and Chamber of Commerce, 1783-1913", 1913.

Yeats, J. "Manual of Commerce", 1872.

II. Periodicals, Journals, Year Books, and Directories.

Where journals have been used for isolated articles only the reference is to be found in the footnotes.

"The Accountant", 1874-1910.

"The Bankers Almanak and Directory", 1860-1885.

"The Bankers Magazine", 1856-1900.

"Bentley's Quarterly Report to Saving Classes", 1861.

"The Bondholder's Register", 1873-1874.

"Bowyers Investment Review", Bristol, 1865-1870; issued by George Bowyer, stock and share broker.

"Burdett's Official Intelligence", 1882-1914.

"Capital and Investment", London, 1873.

"Chadwick's Investment Circular", 1870-1875, London.

"The Chamber of Commerce Journal", 1881-1910.

"The City Quarterly Magazine", 1885-1887, London.

"The Commercial Review", 1912-1914.

"Companion to the British Almanak", London, 1860-1885.

"The Company", 1890-1891; organ of The Shareholders' Defence League.

"The Co-operative Wholesale Society Annual", 1880-1900.

"Cotton", 1876-1877; journal of the cotton trade.

"The Cotton Spinner and Manufacturers Directory", John Worrall, Oldham, 1884.

"The Critic Black Book", 1901-1904; edited by Henry Hess.

"Directory of Directors", 1885-1914.

"The Economist", 1856-1914.

"Fairplay", 1890-1914.

"The Financial Guardian", Manchester, 1889.

"The Financial Reformer", 1865-1906.

"The Financial Register", 1857,; edited by H. Ayres.

"The Financial Register and Stock Exchange Manual", London,
    1873-1878.

"The Financial Review of Reviews", 1906-1914.

"Four Shilling Year Book", 1908-1912; issued by "The
    Financial Review of Reviews.

"Hansard", 1854 et seq.

"Herepath's Railway and Commercial Journal", 1856-1900.

"Horncastle's Manual for Investors", 1890-1900.

"Insurance Guide and Handbook", 1857; edited by C. Walford.

"Investments", Liverpool, 1885-1887.

"The Investors' Blue Book", 1903-1905.

"The Investor's Monthly Manual", 1865-1910.

"The Investor's Review", 1892-1900.

"The Investors and Stock Exchange Magazine", 1863.

"Joint Stock Companies Directory", Charles Barker & Sons,
    1865-1869.

"Joint Stock Companies Journal", 1856, London.

"Joint Stock Manual", 1873-1874; edited by S. Hayman and
    published by the "Mercantile Review",

"The Joint Stock Monthly Record, Reporter and Share Register",
    London, 1866-1867.

"Journal of the Institute of Bankers", 1879-1880 - 1914.

"Journal of the Royal Statistical Society", 1860-1900.

"Journal of the Shareholders Corporation", London, 1880.

"Limited Liability Companies Journal and Universal Share
      List", London, 1860-1864.

"The Limited Liability Joint Stock Companies List, Almanak,
      Register and Directory", 1864-1868, Layton.

"The Limited Liability Review", London, 1874.

"The Manchester Chamber of Commerce Monthly Record", 1890-1900

"The Money Bag", monthly journal, 1858.

"Phillips Investor's Annual", 1887.

"Public Appeals for Capital", 1890, 1891; issued by
      Mathieson & Sons.

"The Railway Banking, Mining and Insurance Almanak", 1866-1870.

"The Shareholders Circular and Guardian", 1863-1866.

"The Statist", 1878-1900.

"The Stock and Share Review", 1883-1884.

"The Stock Exchange Review", London, 1870.

"The Stock Exchange Year Book and Directory", Skinner,
      1875-1900.

lII. Unpublished Theses and MSS.

Ayres, G. L. "Fluctuations in New Capital Issues on the
      London Money Market, 1899-1913" - M.Sc. (Econ.) thesis,
      1934, London.

Cairncross, A. K. "Home and Foreign Investment in Great
      Britain", - Ph.D. thesis, 1936, Cambridge.

Essex-Crosby, A. "Joint Stock Companies, 1890-1930" -
      M.Com. thesis, 1937, London.

Rix, M. "An Economic Analysis of Existing Legislation
      concerning the Limited Liability Company" - M.Sc. (Econ.)
      thesis, 1936, London.

Company files, Somerset House.

Prospectuses of Public Companies in the Share and Loan
      Department, London Stock Exchange, 1820-1890.

IV. Parliamentary Reports and Papers.

1. Report of Select Committee on Joint Stock Companies,
   VII (1844)

2. Report of Select Committee on Investments for the
   Savings of the Middle and Working Classes,
   XIX (1850)

3. First Report,Royal Mercantile Law Committee,XXVII (1854)

4. Return of all Applications for Charters with Limited
   Liability,under I Vict.c.73., LXV (1854)

5. Report of Privy Council relating to Railways,LI (1857-8)

6. Parliamentary Return giving Share Capital of Railway
   and Canal Companies for Year 1857, LI (1857-8)

7. Report of Select Committee on the Companies Acts,X (1867)

8. Report of Select Committee on Trade Partnerships,1872.

9. Report of Select Committee on the Companies' Acts of
   1862 and 1867, VIII (1877)

10. Report of the Royal Commission on the London Stock
    Exchange, XIX (1878)

11. Royal Commission on the Depression of Trade and
    Industry, (1886)

12, Report of the Departmental Committee appointed by
    the Board of Trade to enquire what Amendments are
    necessary in Acts relating to Joint Stock Companies
    under the Acts of 1862 to 1890, LXXXVIII (1895)

13. Report from the Select Committee of the House of Lords
    to report on Companies Bills, LX (1896)

14.   ..   ..   ..   X (1897)

15.   ..   ..   ..   IX (1898)

16. Return showing the holding of Debenture, Preference
    and Ordinary Stock of Railways of United Kingdom
    and number of shareholders, XC (1902)

17. Report of the Company Law Amendment Committee,
    XCVII (1906)

18. Annual Returns relating to Joint Stock Companies 1866 ff.

19. Annual Reports of Board of Trade under Companies
    Winding Up Act 1893 ff.

DISSERTATIONS IN EUROPEAN ECONOMIC HISTORY
An Arno Press Collection

Atkin, John Michael. **British Overseas Investment, 1918-1931** (Doctoral Dissertation, University of London, 1968). 1977

Brosselin, Arlette. **Les Forêts De La Côte D'Or Au XIXème Siècle, et L'Utilisation De Leurs Produits** (Doctoral Thesis, Université de Dijon, 1973). 1977

Brumont, Francis. **La Bureba A L'Époque De Philippe II** (Doctoral Dissertation, Université de Toulouse, 1974). 1977

Cohen, Jon S. **Finance and Industrialization in Italy, 1894-1914** (Doctoral Dissertation, University of California, Berkeley, 1966). 1977

Dagneau, Jacques. **Les Agences Régionales Du Crédit Lyonnais, Années 1870-1914** (Doctoral Thesis, Université de Paris-VIII, 1975). 1977

Dennis, Kenneth G. **'Competition' in the History of Economic Thought** (Doctoral Dissertation, Oxford University, 1975). 1977

Desert, Gabriel. **Une Société Rurale Au XIXe Siècle:** Les Paysans Du Calvados, 1815-1895 (Doctoral Dissertation, Université de Paris, Sorbonne, 1971). 1977

Fierain, Jacques. **Les Raffineries De Sucre Des Ports En France:** XIXe -- début du XXe siècles (Doctoral Dissertation, Université de Nantes, 1974). 1977

Goreux, Louis-Marie. **Agricultural Productivity and Economic Development in France, 1852-1950** (Doctoral Dissertation, University of Chicago, 1955). With the Revised French Version. 1977

Guignet, Philippe. **Mines, Manufactures et Ouvriers Du Valenciennois Au XVIIIe Siècle** (Doctoral Dissertation, Université de Lille III, 1976). Two vols. in one. 1977

Haines, Michael R. **Economic-Demographic Interrelations in Developing Agricultural Regions:** A Case Study of Prussian Upper Silesia, 1840-1914 (Doctoral Dissertation, University of Pennsylvania, 1971). 1977

Hohorst, Gerd. **Wirtschaftswachstum Und Bevölkerungsentwicklung In Preussen 1816 Bis 1914** (Doctoral Dissertation, University of Münster, 1977). 1977

Huertas, Thomas Francis. **Economic Growth and Economic Policy in a Multinational Setting:** The Habsburg Monarchy, 1841-1865 (Doctoral Dissertation, University of Chicago, 1977). 1977

Jankowski, Manfred. **Public Policy in Industrial Growth:** The Case of the Early Ruhr Mining Region, 1766-1865 (Doctoral Dissertation, University of Wisconsin, 1969). 1977

Jefferys, James B. **Business Organisation in Great Britain, 1856-1914** (Doctoral Dissertation, University of London, 1938). 1977

Kirchhain, Günter. **Das Wachstum Der Deutschen Baumwollindustrie Im 19. Jahrhundert** (Doctoral Dissertation, University of Münster, 1973). 1977

Von Laer, Hermann. **Industrialisierung Und Qualität Der Arbeit Eine Bildungsökonomische Untersuchung Für Das 19. Jahrhundert** (Doctoral Dissertation, University of Münster, 1975). 1977

Lee, W. R. **Population Growth, Economic Development and Social Change in Bavaria, 1750-1850** (Revised Doctoral Dissertation, University of Oxford, 1972). 1977

LeVeen, E. Phillip. **British Slave Trade Suppression Policies, 1821-1865** (Doctoral Dissertation, University of Chicago, 1972). 1977

Metzer, Jacob. **Some Economic Aspects of Railroad Development in Tsarist Russia** (Doctoral Dissertation, University of Chicago, 1972). 1977

Moe, Thorvald. **Demographic Developments and Economic Growth in Norway, 1740-1940** (Doctoral Dissertation, Stanford University, 1970). 1977

Mueller, Reinhold C. **The Procuratori di San Marco and the Venetian Credit Market:** A Study of the Development of Credit and Banking in the Trecento (Doctoral Dissertation, Johns Hopkins University, 1969). 1977

Neuburger, Hugh. **German Banks and German Economic Growth from Unification to World War I** (Doctoral Dissertation, University of Chicago, 1974). 1977

Newell, William Henry. **Population Change and Agricultural Developments in Nineteenth Century France** (Doctoral Dissertation, University of Pennsylvania, 1971). 1977

Saly, Pierre. **La Politique Des Grands Travaux En France, 1929-1939** (Doctoral Dissertation, Université de Paris VIII, Vincennes, 1975). 1977

Shrimpton, Colin. **The Landed Society and the Farming Community of Essex in the Late Eighteenth and Early Nineteenth Centuries** (Doctoral Dissertation, Cambridge University, 1965). 1977

Tortella[-Casares], Gabriel. **Banking, Railroads, and Industry in Spain, 1829-1874** (Doctoral Dissertation, University of Wisconsin, 1972). 1977

Viallon, Jean-Baptiste. **La Croissance Agricole En France Et En Bourgogne De 1850 A Nos Jours** (Doctoral Dissertation, Université de Dijon, 1976). 1977

Villiers, Patrick. **Le Commerce Colonial Atlantique Et La Guerre D'Indépendance Des États Unis D'Amérique, 1778-1783** (Doctoral Dissertation, Université de Paris I, Pantheon-Sorbonne, 1975). 1977

Walters, R. H. **The Economic and Business History of the South Wales Steam Coal Industry, 1840-1914** (Doctoral Dissertation, Oxford University, 1975). 1977